SURVIVING THE FLIER

SURVIVING THE
FLIER

BASED ON THE TRUE STORY

*Based on the memories and **unpublished memoirs** of the last survivor, Alvin Jacobson, the gripping story of the only WWII submariners to escape their sunken sub, elude the enemy, and return home.*

R. J. Hughes

PHOENIX FLAIR PRESS

Surviving the Flier
By R.J. Hughes

http://www.survivingtheflier.com
http://www.ussflierproject.com

Printed in the United States of America

ISBN: 978-0-9846124-0-6

Published by Phoenix Flair Press
Muncie, IN

Cover design by R.J. Hughes
Maps created by R.J. Hughes

Dedicated to all those
"On Eternal Patrol"

Particularly those who
rest with the *USS FLIER*
beneath the Balabac Strait.

Acknowledgements

When this project started more than five years ago, I had no idea how large and complex this would be and how many people would become a part of this. I need to thank so many people, especially:

God, who has been the author of my life, and He is the one I need to thank first and foremost. He has been there for me through thick and thin and given me more than I ever would ask, even when it wasn't what I was asking for!.

My wonderful husband Justin, who is nearly as much an author of this piece as I am! Yes dear, this is the point at which a writer says 'I couldn't have done this without you," but guess what? That doesn't mean it's not true! You're my best friend and my support. Thank you for helping interview, work the website, edit the manuscript, and put up with me during this whole project..

My mom and dad, siblings and in-laws who all stayed interested in this project, helping me talk through points, critiquing the manuscript and making this a better story. We've always been there for each other, and I hope, always will be. I'm so blessed to have you.

To Jo Ann Cosgrove of Taylor University, who located and acquired a large number of obscure books for my research through the InterLibrary Loan Program. I often wondered if she cringed when she saw my bizarre requests or considered it a challenge.

To the crew of the *USS Redfin SS-272*, particularly Jack March, Larry Coleman and Charles "Red" Schwertfeger for sharing the history of their boat and their stories and for supporting this project sharing their time, expertise, photos, and documents

To Charles Hinman of the *USS Bowfin* Museum, who helped me with details about the *Flier* and her men through his websites "On Eternal Patrol" and "*USS Flier*", numerous e-mails and phone calls.

To my team of editors and friends who read this manuscript at various points in its development to help me develop it. Thank you Heather Kittleman, Wendy Skorupa, and Elizabeth Dillivan, among others who are mentioned elsewhere here.

To Lt.Aerik LaFavre, Associate Professor of Naval Science at the `University of Michigan's NROTC for doing research for me about U of M's NROTC during WWII.

To Heather Pannozzo and Liz Butler for all your assistance in the past year in so many ways.

To the staff of the National Archives and Records Administration, for locating and mailing various records of this story to my home, especially Amy Schmidt of the Modern Military Records for finding the reports of the Coastwatchers after several other requests had turned up empty.

To the family of Lt. James Liddell, USNR, who opened their home and library to me in my search for *Flier* information and sources. It was a great insight into another point of view of this story, and an amazing visit.

To Alvin Jacobson Jr. and his family, especially Mary, Nelson and Steve. They opened their lives to me so I could see and write this story with as much accuracy as possible. They put up with a lot of interviews, e-mails, phone calls and questions as well as provided tons of information about their father and the men he served with. My one regret is Al isn't here to see this project for himself.

To all those whom I didn't mention by name and those who requested anonymity, who, many times when I needed it most, gave me encouragement, help, or found information for me…thank you.

Last, but certainly not least, I want to thank the men of the *USS Flier*. In a way, I'm sorry this book is written, because they paid the ultimate price and gave their lives so I and my family can live in freedom decades later. Thank you for being willing to do so, and for your sacrifice. May you never, ever be forgotten.

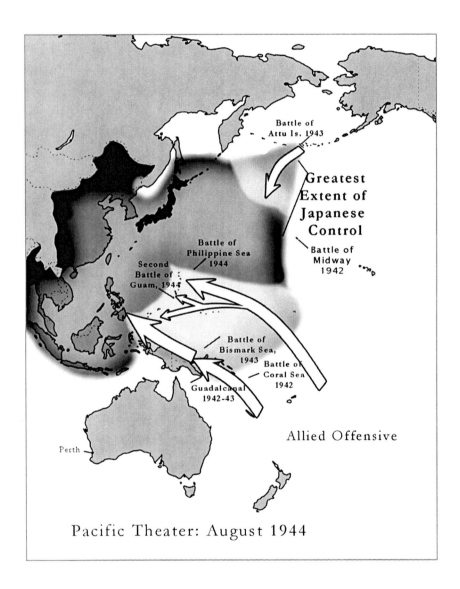

Pacific Theater: August 1944

TABLE OF CONTENTS

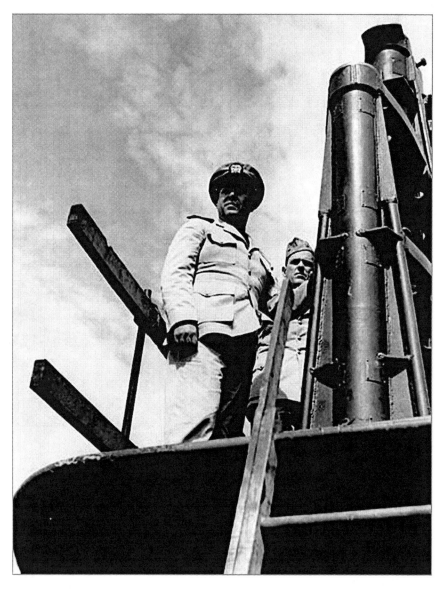

Lieutenant Commander John Daniel Crowley, overseeing the construction of his new boat, USS Flier. Taken before her launch, in October ,1943. Official US Navy photo.

-PROLOGUE-

CARIBBEAN: DECEMBER, 1943

"She's bringing her guns to bear!" Signalman Rose shouted.

"Damn!" Captain Crowley swore. The merchantman bearing down on them was flying Old Glory, but seemed unable to see or unwilling to believe the recognition signals Rose was frantically sending their way. His boat, less than six months old and in perfect condition, faced her first battle, not with an enemy, but a mistaken friend.

The Captain's eyes scoured the horizon. The Caribbean here was too shallow to risk an underwater escape: if that merchantman had deck guns, she was guaranteed to carry racks of depth charges. The only solution was a surface run, but that would only prolong the fight, and if that merchantman called in reinforcements...

It had only been two months since this boat's sister sub, *USS Dorado*, had been sunk by a friendly plane. He had no intentions of following suit.

There! A small summer squall was building just astern to the portside. If it lasted long enough to reach, they could run there and dive, hiding from the merchantman's Sonar under the drumming of the rain striking the water's surface.

"Full speed!" The Captain yelled, calling out the coordinates. "Hang on, boys!" He called up to the lookouts perched on the small deck overhead.

The sub's engines roared, and she nimbly turned and fled before her attacker, her sharp nose cutting through the waves so cleanly seawater washed high over the deck, spraying the deck crew liberally. Captain Crowley was grateful they were in warm waters. His last command had been in the Alaska's Bearing Sea, where hypothermia was a constant threat.

SPLOOSH! A fountain of water sprayed up off the bow and a corresponding *BOOM* followed as the merchantman fired her warning shot. "Give her everything you've got!" Captain roared down the bridge to the Conning Tower. "We can refuel at Panama!"

His sub poured on more speed, the seas behind her churned to froth.

"She's aiming to kill sir!" One of the lookouts shouted.

"Evasive maneuvers!" The Captain ordered while hanging on as his boat suddenly lurched starboard. The merchantman's next shot went wide, but she was undoubtedly re-adjusting her aim. By the time she got off her next shot, the sub zigged again, evading the hit.

"Hold on baby," Crowley muttered through his clenched teeth. "Just a few more minutes..."

A heavy shell went screaming past, narrowly missing them. Crowley ducked instinctively, even as it splashed off their starboard side, followed by the boom of the massive guns. Captain heard shouting above, and saw his lookouts and signalman clinging to whatever piece of frame was handy each time the sub careened madly, but still doing their jobs. The bridge lookouts where hauling themselves back into position as fast as they could, hanging on to the bridge wall for support. 'They may be inexperienced, but they'll do fine,' Crowley thought with pride.

Now if only they could survive the next few minutes.

The waves became choppier as they approached the storm. It seemed to have grown since Crowley first spotted it. His boat started buck wildly, throwing her nose higher and higher before sliding down the face of the wave

"The merchantman is losing ground!" A lookout called down to him.

"Thank God," he muttered. "Mister Adams!" he called down to the Conning Tower as heavy raindrops began to slam against the metal skin of the bridge, "start taking soundings, I want a deep hole to hide in as soon as we can!"

"Taking soundings, aye sir," the officer said, from deep within the command center of the sub.

They hit the main part of the storm, the skies blackened, and rain fell so thick that he could barely see the bow. The crew topside was soaked to the skin in seconds, and waves swept high over the deck and threatening to wash them away. He gripped the bridge wall in front on him even harder.

Curtains of rain stung the Captain's exposed face and hands, but swiftly shrouded the submarine. Lightning lashed across the sky. It missed them, but now it was only be a matter of time before Mother Nature finished what the merchantman was trying.

"She's coming in!" Someone yelled over the thunderous din of the storm. Larger and more vulnerable to the storm, the merchantman was losing ground, despite her best efforts. Soon, she would lose sight of her quarry.

"Sir!" Adams called up, "we have sounding of six–zero–zero feet,"

The Captain lunged across the slick deck, grasping the dive alarm as he yelled, "Take her down!"

"*AOUUUGAH! AOUUUGAH!*"

The lookouts dropped to the deck in seconds and jumped down the hatch, as the hiss of escaping air from the ballast tanks forced the deck to plunge with heart stopping swiftness. Crowley counted them when they vanished into the interior of his boat, "One, two, three, four, five, six..."

Boom. He heard the muffled last shot of their attacker, firing blindly in the thick grey rain, and smiled. It wasn't what he'd hoped for this boat's first battle, but they'd won.

The waves were roaring just feet away as the Captain jumped down after the last crewman, pulling and dogging the hatch after him. Seconds later, they all heard the gurgle and slap of the water covering the bridge. Fifty feet down, and the sub still felt some surge and push of the storm above. One hundred feet down, and all was quiet around them.

"Sonar, report," Crowley said.

"I can't hear anything above the din of the storm overhead," the sonarman responded, pressing the phones to his head, listening intently.

"If we can't hear anything with our new equipment, they sure can't with whatever outdated crud they have." Captain said, shaking the water out of his eyes and hair, and grabbing the towel that the boat's steward handed him. "Thanks, Findley. All and all, not too bad, considering we've only had thirty days training and are still working all the kinks out."

"Very true sir," Adams said, "despite this just being a so-called simple run to Pearl, it's been quite eventful, even before we hit the Canal. The men acquitted themselves very well down here, I must say."

"As they did up top," Captain replied. "I am very proud of this crew, and excited for our future!" The last bit he said loud enough for the Conning Tower and Control Room below to hear. It brought a rousing cheer from the new crewmen, and Captain grinned. He had a good feeling about this new boat.

It was just as well that he couldn't hear the conversation going on in the Crew's Quarters, just feet away. Several of the men, unassigned to battle stations during the encounter, had retreated to their bunks as practiced, to stay out of the way. It was eerie, lying in the red light of battle, able to do little other than pray that it was not your final day, and it had shaken some of the men badly.

"I thought we were in the safety zone," one of the new enlisted men said. "I thought all friendly planes and vessels around are notified to our position and told to avoid the area for miles around us?"

USS Flier, taken in April 1944 off the coast of California, after a refit. Official US Navy Photo

"We are and they were, or better have been," said an older hand. "I don't like it; it's not a good omen."

"Don't be ridiculous," the Engineering officer, Liddell, said, as he emerged from his inspection of the now-cooling engines. "It's a crowded sea, these things happen. I was on the *Snapper* right after Pearl Harbor, and we were attacked by one of our patrol bombers who thought we were a Japanese sub. She's still fighting. *Harder* and *Scorpion* were also attacked just outside the Canal like this and they are doing VERY well. It's not an omen, it's just a mistake."

"Yes sir," chorused several of the hands. They were wise enough to not mention the *Dorado*. Moments later, Liddell, called to another duty, left.

"I don't care," one of the Motor Macs muttered after he left. "It isn't a good omen. She feels jinxed to me, and I don't like it. You didn't hear it from me, but I say *Flier* is unlucky. I'm going to get off of her as soon as I'm allowed. She's not going to make it."

-1-

FREMANTLE: AUGUST 2, 1944

"Sign here". The Petty Officer said, handing me the clipboard and receipt.

"Are we all set, sir?" Pope called from down below.

I glanced down the Main Hatch and said, "Get me James."

Two seconds later, the face of our chief cook, James Westmoreland, appeared at the end of the tube. "Sir?"

"Did we get everything? The last load of coffee? The right stuff?"

"Last load of Hills Bros. arrived two hours ago; we're all set for stores. I stuck the *Redfin* with that mistaken load of Navy coffee."

I glanced up at our sister sub moored to our starboard-side. "Poor Bastards," I grinned.

"No kidding, sir" he shouted back. "Once we get our potatoes, we're done."

"Very good," I looked back at Pope. "Make it quick." I ordered.

"Aye sir," he replied.

The inch-thick steel plate was hoisted into place, sealing the hatch shut from the inside as the bolts were driven home. No one would use that hatch again until we were safely back in port, however long that would be.

They pounded twice on the plate when they finished, the sound ringing up to me in a strange metallic echo. "All set," I said, signing the receipt. The Petty Officer signaled his men, and they quickly slit the dusty bags open and dumped the potatoes down in a thunderous roll until the eight-foot shaft was filled to the brim. I slammed the heavy steel door down on top, and cranked the wheel until it locked. The Petty Officer and his crew quickly gathered up their burlap bags

Taken in Fremantle, between July 5 and August 1, 1944, this photos shows Captain Herber "Tex" McLean, Commander of Submarine Squadron Sixteen, aboard the Flier, likely awarding Flier's captain and crew with the awards they won during her first patrol. Official US Navy Photo

and headed across the submarine nest to their ship, the submarine tender *USS Orion.*

"Ensign Jacobson!" someone yelled at me. I looked up to see a young enlisted man waving from the lookout platforms. "Where do I stow these, sir?" He asked pointing to *Flier's* broom and flags flying from our periscopes.

"Give them to Mr. Turner, he's our steward. He'll show you where they go."

"Yes sir!" He said, scrambling up the periscope and radar apparatus. This kid was one of our new hands, and excited to finally serve on a submarine. His name was Elton, and he looked like he couldn't have graduated from high school yet.

Moments later, Elton vanished down the bridge hatch, broom, flag and brag rags tucked under his arm[1]. *Flier* was now black and anonymous, with no mark, designation, number, or name on her. She could be easily mistaken for a British or Dutch boat by the casual observer, and once in the open ocean, telling friend from foe would be nearly impossible from a distance.

Mooring lines splashed in the water and thudded onto the deck of the *Redfin* as crewmen started to cast off. Restrained now by just two lines rather than her usual six or seven, *Flier* pulled heavily against those, as if eager to get underway.

I climbed up to the bridge to take the first watch as we navigated out of the harbor. It was incredible to think that, less than a year ago,

---

[1] The "Broom" was a naval tradition that started in the British Navy in the seventeenth-century and was revived by the submarine force in WWII. It indicated a "clean sweep" patrol, or a patrol that the sub sank every target she engaged or fulfilled their special mission. The "Brag Rags" were miniature flags made to appear like small versions of the national flags of the ships that were sunk. Each flag represented one "kill." Since submarine patrols were top secret at the time, and their crews forbidden from talking about their patrols, this was one of the few sanctioned ways the crews could compare notes and brag about their accomplishments.

I was a struggling engineering student at the University of Michigan, listening to Cmdr. Scott tell us about the submarine force and his adventures on his submarine *S-43* during my ROTC classes. He inspired me to request the Submarine Force, along with a dozen others, but only two of us passed the testing and interviews. Now here I was, a commissioned Ensign, starting out on my second patrol, and my first as a fully qualified submariner.

"Morning Ed," I called to my mentor and friend, Lieutenant John "Ed" Casey, as he climbed to the bridge from the Conning Tower below, his ever-present cup of coffee in his hand.

"Morning Jake," he said, lifting the mug in greeting. "Thanks for the coffee."

"You know, personally, I don't taste a difference, but whatever makes the crew happy."

"Good boy. You'd taste the difference after a couple of months out on sea, I guarantee it. I think Navy coffee can chew a hole through the mugs *and* the intestines."

"Yeesh. I've had coffee in my day, but James seems to try and make it into acidic slurry on purpose. What does he do? Double the recommended amount?"

He grinned. "I hope he triples it. Gotta have something to keep me awake during the day, especially if Captain keeps doing those night training runs like that one last night." He took a loud slurp and sighed contentedly "This is good stuff."

"Whatever you say, Ed. How's the family? Heard much from Betty Ann?"

"Letter upon letter, almost as many as I wrote her during our last patrol. Want to see the latest photo?" He was already digging his wallet out of his back pocket. "There we are. That's my Betty Ann and little Ricky. She said he's growing by leaps and bounds, and giggling all the time." He handed me the photo of a young, pretty girl, proudly standing behind a baby boy, who was hanging on to her fingers as he walked across the lawn, both smiling at the camera. Despite the fact that the photo had to be new, the corners were already bent and frayed, showing how often he must have looked at it since mail call nearly four weeks ago.

"Gee, you're not a proud father, by any rate, are you?"

"No, not at all." He smiled, taking back the picture and touching the surface tenderly as though he could touch his family. "He's grown so much since I saw him last. I was there the day he was born, same month *Flier* was commissioned, so I got to spend the first few weeks with him. Then I got to see him again last spring, when he was giggling and starting to scoot across the floor. When we get back, I'll have to find him something for his first birthday and ship it home. With luck, it might even get there in time."

"If we come back here, you'll find some great stuff. I sent a lamb's wool rug and three boomerangs to my parents. Didn't realize I'd need to get them all inspected and authorized in duplicate to send them home though!"

"Be glad that's all you had to do. Maybe I'll find him a stuffed koala or a boomerang."

"Send him a kangaroo."

"Somehow, I doubt the Navy would authorize that," he laughed. "I would also like my wife to still be speaking to me when I get home."

"Spoilsport."

He laughed, tucked the photo back into his wallet, and said, "How about you? How's that large family of yours?"

"Pretty well. Mom said Charles is still doing well on the *Boise*. I think they're in that mess in the Marianas right now, but you know how censored the mail is these days, it's only a guess. My sisters Edna Mary and Marilyn are getting ready for their next year of college, and Muriel is looking forward to her junior year in high school. My brother David graduated from High School this past May and enlisted in the Army Air Force, and might be leaving soon for either Europe or the Pacific."

"You two scare him off of the Navy?" Ed joked.

"Believe it or not, David gets severely seasick. He loves to sail, but if he's in Lake Michigan or anything larger, he's feeding the fish over the side. So I guess he decided to head as far from the ocean as possible. I didn't realize he was thinking vertically.

"At the moment though, my parents and sisters are all living at the cabin on Spring Lake enjoying the summer, swimming and sailing, and gardening, I just wish I was there with them."

"Well, maybe next year."

"We can all hope."

We stood side by side for a moment, looking over the harbor, until Ed said, "Heard about the *S-28*²?"

"Old news," I shrugged. "She sank on a training run with all hands near Oahu, didn't she? Her loss was announced just as we came to port last month."

"Mmm-hmm." He paused, and then said, "Did you know that she was Captain Crowley's command before *Flier*?"

"Huh… That would explain a few—"

"Good morning, gentlemen," our XO³ Lieutenant Jim Liddell, said, as he climbed up through the Bridge Hatch. We quickly stood at attention, and just as quickly Jim said, "At ease. Are your units ready for departure?"

"Yes sir," we chorused.

"Good," He turned to look over the fore bridge, and I could

---

² *USS S-28* was an older submarine launched in 1922. After several war patrols near Alaska, she was re-assigned in 1944 as a training vessel based out of Pearl Harbor. After sinking with all hands on July 4, 1944, it was determined that she sank in waters too deep to be raised, and was left a war grave. She has never been found.

³ XO: Executive Officer, second in command.

almost hear him mentally checking off the various duties that should be done by now on deck: torpedo skids closed and latched, all storage containers closed and latched, bow light folded to deck and secured, the starry Jack still flying at the bow, with crewman waiting to stow her as soon as we cast off...

Yeoman[4] Walter Dorricott climbed out of the Bridge Hatch at Jim and Ed's feet, holding *Flier's* immense Sailing List[5], as well as his ever present clipboard.

"Good Morning sirs!" Yeoman Dorricott saluted when he scrambled to his feet.

"Everyone accounted for?" Jim asked, as we saluted back.

"Yes sir," Dorricott was grinning widely, smiling at some private joke. Lord knew what it was, and it would likely be dangerous to ask. "As you probably heard, Donald See, fireman first class, reported for duty in the place of Jim Alls, who needs to stay ashore. We also had two last minute additions to the crew, a new Ensign under instruction, Phil Mayer, and a torpedoman named Lucius Wall. That brings our total of new hands to thirteen. "

"I heard Mayer is fresh out of Sub School, so he'll be studying for his quals then," Liddell said.

"Yes sir, along with twenty of the enlisted this tour."

"All right then. All those who went back to the States accounted for?"

---

[4] Yeoman: A Ship's secretary and recorder. He took care of all paperwork. *Flier* carried two Yeomen, Dorricott and Earl Dressell.
[5] The Sailing List is a list of the name, rank, and serial number of every person on board a submarine any time it leaves the dock for any reason. In addition to those names were the names and contact information of next of kin for every person, as well as last wills and testaments. As gruesome as it sounds, these lists were necessary in case the worst happened, and once the list was passed off, no one could come aboard for the sub's run, no matter how short or insignificant it seemed. Any time a civilian rode a submarine, their name and last will were also included.

"Yes sir. Georgie Laderbush was the last one back and is stowed and ready to go."

"It was his mother's health that called him home, was it not?" Liddell asked.

"Yes sir, all the way back to Maine, and I gather from Georgie that she is still alive, which reminds me," Dorricott glanced around, leaned in to us, and lowered his voice as we reflexively leaned in to hear him. "Kit Pourciau just received news of his mother's passing in the last mail call. I gave him time to write a letter home before leaving, since it was too late to arrange for a hardship leave. I have informed COB and asked him to keep an eye on Kit, but if you notice that he's not his usual self…"

"Thank you Dorricott," Liddell sighed, raking his hands through his hair. "Now, this issue with the chief…" Liddell raised an eyebrow in our direction.

"I saw him with my own two eyes a moment ago," Dorricott said, his smile returning.

"Everything's taken care of sir," I jumped in. I had bailed Chief Pope out of the local jail after he confused a bathroom and the middle of a busy street. "There will be no charges for the uh…incident…this time."

"Thank God." Liddell muttered. He looked at the short list of names quickly, almost muttering to himself. "I notice Baumgart has decided to stay for the patrol despite the incident an."

"Yes sir," Ed said, "though scuttlebutt is he's planning to ask for a transfer and fight the charges when we return from patrol. He feels a few beers shouldn't have busted him down in grade, especially when others were just as drunk but not demoted. But he's a professional on patrol, we're lucky to have him."

"Don't I know it. He'll have to take up his discipline problem with the captain, and I wish him good luck, he'll need it." He eyed Dorricott again, sighed, and said, "All right, what is it? Grin any wider and your face will split in half."

"Sorry sir, I just got a telegram this morning, it has some good news."

"Oh?"

"My Barbara had a baby boy sir, I have a son! Medric Thomas Dorricott!"

"Well congratulations, Dorricott!" We all clapped him on the back and shook his hand while he grinned even wider.

"I can't wait to see the photos in her next letter when we return," he said, "I wish I could go home to see him, but…"

"I know son, we all want to go home. I know several men who have children they've only met through letters and photos. Still, you never know, but congratulations, all the same." Jim said, swinging down to the deck beneath us, Dorricott at his heels.

Almost on cue, an Admiral from COMSUBSOWESPAC [6], followed by two Marines, and our CO, Lieutenant Commander John D. Crowley, strode out of one of the immense doors in *Orion's* hull. They quickly stepped down the steep iron stairs to the deck of the *Hake*, then crossed to the *Redfin*. Sailors from both subs and the *Orion* snapped to attention as they passed.

Crowley stepped smartly across the gangplank to where Liddell and Dorricott stood at attention. Dorricott gravely handed Captain Crowley the Sailing List. Captain turned around, stepped back across to the *Redfin,* saluted, and handed it to the Admiral. The Admiral accepted the list, said something to Crowley briefly, and then saluted back, the Marines mirroring the action. Captain crossed back to *Flier,* and the *Redfin* sailors hauled the gangway away almost as soon as his foot cleared it. Captain Crowley gave the order to fire up the engines, and a minute later, *Flier's* engines coughed, then roared to life,

---

[6] COMSUBSOWESPAC: Short for <u>Com</u>mander of <u>Sub</u>marines in the <u>So</u>uth <u>West</u> Pacific

spewing black, greasy clouds of diesel smoke across her stern. As the Captain, Jim, and Dorricott hauled themselves up to the bridge Captain gave the order to cast off. Jim plunged into the Conning Tower, as the final two lines were hurled to *Redfin's* deck, and *Flier's* great bronze props churned the brackish water to foam. The close gap between the subs began to widen as she delicately maneuvered away from our tender while the few of us on the deck waved our farewells.

At the mouth of the harbor, we passed *USS Harder*, the current and soon to be defeated (if we had anything to say about it) leader of the submarine forces. She appeared to be returning from a night training run, her flag and fourteen brag rags flying boldly from her periscope, and her crew out on the deck, enjoying the sun. Captain waved to her Captain, Sam Dealey, who waved right back.

"I see scuttlebutt is right, as usual, sir," I said to Captain.

"Yup. Dealey gets to take her out for one more patrol before stepping down." He replied.

"Chances of scuttling her record?"

"If *Flier* performs as well as her last patrol, *Harder* will soon be eating our wake on the scoreboards."

"I like the sound of that, sir."

When we were finally free of the harbor and all of the protective mine fields and anti-sub nets, *Flier's* props bit deep and she flew through the waves, forcing a fierce wind and fine salt spray against my face that made me shiver despite my coat. We had a full complement of officers and lookouts on deck standing watch. Though we were more than four days from enemy territory, it was not safe to be complacent in these waters.

My morning shift went quickly and uneventfully. Allied planes circled overhead, watching for anyone who was outside the Bombing Restriction Lane. I slipped comfortably back into my watch routine: with the binoculars, sweep the horizon from starboard to port, then the sky from port to starboard, then the sea from starboard to port, then look around with my eyes for a whole picture, all while subtly adjusting in balance for the drifts and drafts of a ship gliding on top of the waves.

We pulled into Exmouth Gulf the evening of our second day at sea for a standard refueling, and stayed the night.

The following morning, I took my first cup of coffee out onto the bridge for some fresh air and sunlight, two things which would become scarce in the coming weeks. Though early, the city and harbor hummed with workers intent on their duties, doing everything they could to ship us back and forth as quickly as possible. There were few Australian accents, since most of the Aussies who had joined the military were in the European and African Theater, but I heard British, American and Dutch accents from various quarters.

As I enjoyed these few quiet moments, I wondered where we were being sent this time. On our first real patrol, *Flier* had left Pearl Harbor, patrolled near Formosa, through the Philippines and ended in Fremantle. At the moment, Captain was the only person on board who knew what we where we were assigned to go and like all submarine commanders, he was forbidden from telling anyone anything about the mission until we were out of reach of land for the remainder of patrol. No one would knowingly or willingly put their sub brothers in danger, but the Navy took the simple precaution of limiting the number of people who knew where we were going while bars, pubs, and girls were still available.

Captain climbed out into the cool morning air and moments later, the engines thrummed under the decks. "Morning Jacobson," he greeted me, his coffee cup steaming in the cool winter air, like my own. "Morning sir," I stood at attention, while still holding my cup. "As you were, Jacobson," he told me with a half-smile. I resumed my station looking over the half-wall that shielded the bridge. "Permission to hold target practice this morning Sir?" I asked.

"That target Ed told me about last week?" He asked, sipping the coffee.

"Yes sir, we passed it on our way in I believe."

He took another sip, then said, "Yes we did. Very well, I'll sail her there for you. We should be there by 1100 hours."

"Thank you Sir."

"Dismissed, Jacobson."

I dropped through the bridge hatch and the cool, salt smell of the harbor vanished instantly under the combined stench of diesel oil, sweat, and cigarette smoke. The new scents of fresh paint and floor wax would fade too soon under the old cooking and body odor smells yet to develop and ripen into a healthy "sub air" mix.

From the crowded Conning Tower, I dropped down again to the Control Room, packed with bronze, steel, and copper instruments and pipes. I stepped through the hatch and found Pope, who was our Chief Gunner's Mate, finishing his morning chow. I caught his eye, and pointed forward to Officer's Country. He nodded and tossed his tin tray into the sink, then followed me to the Wardroom, where I found Ed, our Chief Gunnery Officer, finishing his morning meal.

The three of us went across the two-foot wide hall to the "privacy" of Ed's cramped cabin for a hurried whispered consultation about the morning's exercise.

"Captain said he'll sail us up to that target for gunnery practice."

"ETA?" Ed said, sipping his coffee.

"1100 hours."

"Good. I think I'm favoring a surprise practice this morning, how about you two?" Ed said.

"I like the idea sir," Pope said. "It's the only time we'll have a safe environment to have a surprise practice. Keep the men on their toes."

"It's sort of expected though," I replied.

"Expected is different from 'definitely going to' sir," Pope pointed out, "and no one on the gunnery crews knows WHEN we'll get there, so they'll be able to practice dropping everything, grabbing their gear and getting on deck."

"Sounds good to me," Ed said. "Aren't you due to be on watch when we get there, Jacobson?" He asked me.

"Yes sir," I said. I always called him sir in front of the enlisted men.

"That'll help. I'm supposed to be in Conning Tower, so it'll be easy to announce the gunnery practice when you sight the target. Pope?"

"Technically off duty sir, but I'll be all right."

"Sounds like a plan then. Dismissed."

Pope ducked out of the room, while Ed marked something in a book on his deck. Many more photos of his wife, son, in-laws and extended family were taped to it and the wall next to it.

"Do you have enough photos yet, Ed?" I teased.

"Not nearly, Jake." He grinned. "You'd better get to work."

"Yes sir," I said. "First order of business: BREAKFAST!"

James and our second cook, Clyde, were in fine form this morning. Breakfast featured fresh eggs, (fried and scrambled) sausage, toast, biscuits and gravy, doughnuts, and coffee in the Wardroom. Then, with another cup of coffee to ward off the morning wind, I scrambled back up the ladder to the Bridge, where *Flier* was pulling out of Exmouth' s harbor.

A few hours later, the call came from the lookout rings, "Target in sight sir."

I trained my binoculars on the landscape and saw it: the long, low silhouette in the water.

"Attention all hands! Target Approaching! Man the guns!" Ed's voice crackled over the ship's radio as the General Quarters Alarm sounded. In moments, Ed and Pope leapt out of the bridge hatch, and about ten seconds later, the gunnery crews, some still pulling on their flak jackets and holding their helmets to their heads, flooded out and ran to their various stations.

One team, under Pope, leapt to the deck below, ran aft, uncapped and released the muzzle of the large four-inch .50 caliber gun from its support frame.

My team rushed to the 40-mm aft bridge gun. Two men, the pointer and trainer, leapt to the seats on either side of the gun and cranked her hard to starboard, while a loader jumped to the deck below and cranked open the ammo locker and began handing the rounds to the loader on the deck.

Tunk–tunk–tunk–tunk. Ed's team on the 20 mm machine gun on the fore bridge started their assault on the target. "Move it men!" I called, ramming cotton wads in my ears.

The fourth round slammed into place in the feed, and *Flier* shuddered under the *"Boom!"* of the 40–mm.

The water around the target mushroomed in the air as the bullet struck near. Small explosions blossomed all around it as the 20–mm honed in.

"BOOM!" Flier lurched as the 4–in roared beneath me. Soon the water around the target surged and foamed under the assault.

Flier flew past her target, then heeled around hard starboard and shot from the other side. It was nearly impossible to see the target with the water for yards around frothing and exploding.

"Cease Fire!" Ed boomed, and the frantic energy ground to a halt. We couldn't waste all our ammo on an exercise.

"Excellent work!" He shouted over the wind, "restore the equipment and reload the lockers. That'll be all."

In minutes the spent drums and shells had been hurled into the sea and the exterior ammo lockers had been stocked full again from the main ammo locker deep in *Flier's* belly. Then the crew vanished through the bridge hatch into the sub, and the sea was quiet with only the six of us on the deck maintaining the watch once more. I concentrated on the silhouette, now easier to see, despite the glittering waves. According to the gunnery officers in Perth, that old wreck had the dubious distinction of being the most shot-at ship in the world.[7] Every passing battle ship, submarine or airplane would target it. It was hardly more than a rusted-out tube now, full of holes.

Flier's engines roared again and she turned her nose north and west. Australia faded from a crisp red-brown rocky shore to a bluish shadow then vanished in the afternoon haze. She had been a great and gracious hostess, and already, the crew was vociferously wishing to return to Fremantle after patrol.

I knew in my gut that I would see Fremantle again. I just didn't know that when I did, I would be scarred, severely sunburned, and under a top-secret gag order.

---

[7] This "target ship" was likely the SS MILDURA and what's left of her is still visible near Exmouth. She grounded on a reef by a typhoon in 1907 and was used as a target by warships and planes during WWI, WWII and decades afterwards.

2

GATEWAY TO WAR

Hours after Australia had vanished beyond our stern, Captain ordered an officer's meeting in the wardroom, leaving COB[8] in charge. Breakfast had long since been cleared away, though the coffee pot was full, and fresh doughnuts beckoned from the sideboard. We helped ourselves and took our seats, waiting for Captain.

He entered carrying new charts rolled tightly under his arm, placed them at his seat at the head of the table. He drew the green curtain doors of the room closed, and Ed did the same with the other doorway. Then Captain grabbed the ship's com. "Attention All Hands! Our Patrol Area is the South China Sea."

Through the curtains, I heard the excited conversation of the men, as they digested this small bit of information, while Captain turned to us, his face all business. Though he spoke low to limit people hearing the meeting as they passed by, we all knew everything he said would be common knowledge among the entire crew shortly, and probably before we adjourned. On a submarine, secrets didn't stay that way for long.

"Our orders are straightforward. We're to proceed through Lombok Strait, then to Makassar Strait and Sibutu Passage, then, unless told different, we're to take Balabac Strait via the Natsubata Channel. For the next five weeks, we're assigned Patrol areas 201 and 202 in the South China Sea, beginning with 201. We'll switch patrol areas every Sunday.

---

[8] COB, or "Chief of the Boat" is a senior enlisted man aboard. He advises the CO and XO about the crew and disciplinary matters as well as is in charge of day-to-day operations. While not strictly in the chain of command, the COB and his opinions carry a lot of weight with both enlisted men and officers. According to Al Jacobson, *Flier's* COB was Edgar W. Hudson.

"If all goes well, after sundown on September 11, we'll head home, via Mindoro Strait, Sibutu Passage, Makassar, Lombok, and yes, home to Fremantle and Perth by the end of September." That brought a quiet cheer from us, and moments later, a much louder one from the forward torpedo room. Captain smiled, shook his head, and continued. "As usual, we're engaging in unrestricted submarine warfare with the enemy, so keep your eyes open for any and all convoys as well as those fools traveling alone." He leaned forward slightly, causing us to huddle in closely, as he dropped his voice to a mere whisper. "As a Special Assignment, if we can, we are to watch for and sink four supply submarines that are likely operating out of Saigon supplying enemy outposts in the Philippines. HQ has given us a wide hunting ground and is keeping our area free of Allied submarines, so keep your eyes peeled for any signs of any other submarines."

For three days, *Flier* plowed northward without seeing a soul. Captain Crowley tested us with emergency dives and surfaces, forcing *Flier* to go from surfaced to submerged in less than forty-five seconds. This tested the nerves of those of us on watch outside, since the first dive warning we usually received was the loud "hiss" of air escaping the ballast tanks as she began her dive, while we scrambled for the bridge hatch.

Between duty shifts there was always the great food and entertainment to be found on board. During the daytime hours and between training runs, Captain would allow those crewmembers who wouldn't be allowed on deck after crossing Lombok to come outside for tanning, fresh air, and exercise. After dark, entertainment could be found inside. The Navy gave us our own library, record player with record collection, and a movie theater complete with projector, screen and reels. Most of us had also brought books, stationary for writing letters to family, and decks of cards for the inevitable poker games. Some had managed to bring special things onboard. Leon

Patrol
Area

Philippine
Sea

Sulu Sea

Balabac
Strait

Celebes
Sea

Makassar
Strait

Java Sea

Lombok
Strait

Indian
Ocean

Exmouth
Gulf

Flier's Planned
Second Patrol:
2 August –
approx. 22 Sept.
1944

——Flier's Planned
Route to
Partol Area
·······Flier's Planned
Route Back to
Fremantle

Fremantle

Holbrook had talked his sister out of her hand-cranked phonograph and records last time he was home, and they added more variety to our indoor entertainments.

A few days out of Exmouth, the crew started to mesh together as a team. It helped that most of us had already served together on the last patrol, and many had earned their certification, but we had to work together as one unit if we were going to continue to be successful.

This deep in the war, the cross section of the crew was amazing. Several had been on the battleships and destroyers during Pearl Harbor. I knew Don Tremaine had been on *USS Maryland* and Jarrold Taylor on the *Pennsylvania*. Some were regular Navy, but others, and me, were Reservists that had been activated. Some had been Skimmers[9] before entering Sub Service, others had tried to join as soon as they were free to volunteer out of boot camp. At 40 years old, the oldest among us was Ken Gwinn, the Torpedo Chief. Almost a fifth of us were under twenty years old, and the youngest was Dick Lambert, a new torpedoman, due to celebrate his seventeenth birthday late this month. We came from all over the country: I heard southern drawls, the unique accent of New England, the familiar cadence of the Midwest. Several men came from New York City, another group from Chicago, and at least four had been born abroad. Some had never seen the ocean before joining the Navy, while others were Navy Brats, and still others, like me, were just obsessed with the water.

One night before we entered Lombok I entered the galley bleary-eyed to get a cup of coffee before my night shift. The Mess Hall had been taken over by the men and the stainless-steel walls were now blanketed with posters, photos, news articles, anything and everything that took our minds off of the danger we were heading

---

[9] Skimmers: a term for surface sailors.

into. The carefully prepared and posted menu was now all but covered by a Betty Grable poster, though no one minded, least of all the cooking staff. Rita Hayworth's smile gleamed from over the water fountain, while postcards from Hawaii, New York, San Francisco, Paris, Perth, and other exotic locales were pasted in between photos and posters of cars, girls from home, and other "lucky" items. The Andrews Sisters finished up their rendition of "Boogie Woogie Bugle Boy" before the record hissed softly on the last groove. Our baker, Melvin, and steward, Turner, were taking the freshly-baked bread out of the oven. I closed my eyes and breathed deeply, suddenly remembering my home in Grand Haven, and my mom and sisters baking bread and rolls for dinner.

"Whoa! You'd better open your eyes when you go waltzing through here, sir!" Clyde Banks's voice called. The trapdoor to the cool room was open at my feet, and our second chef, along with Elton, looked up at me from the chilly bottom.

"Whoops! Sorry about that, Clyde."

"No problem sir, I just didn't want you joining us, it's rather tight quarters as is."

"You sure? I think I see a spare inch just to your left there," I said with a grin.

"Very funny, sir."

Since the food stores had barely been touched this soon into patrol, Clyde and Elton were trying to stand on the same square foot of space, which was already on top of a bunch of packages of frozen something-or-other. "Actually sir, I was about to send the non-qual[10] to find you," he said, jerking his thumb back to Elton. "Those pork shoulders seem a bit older than we thought they were when we got them."

---

[10] Non-Qual: A submariner who is not yet qualified. After submarine school, a submariner is not qualified until he completes his exams on the job. Each non-qual has a year to finish his qualifications, though many do so much sooner.

"Making a change in tomorrow's menu then, I take it?"

'Yes sir. The whole chickens seem to be holding their own, so I think I'll swap the scheduled roast chicken for some pulled pork. James already agreed with me, so if it's all right with you, I'll make it official."

"Whatever you want, I know better than to mess with you, since you have the power to serve us all gruel for breakfast, lunch and dinner if you want!" I laughed.

"And don't you forget it, sir!" he smiled.

"You know, the crew would probably hang ME by the toes for upsetting you!" I laughed, "I can hear Lt. Casey now, 'We don't have the best cooks in the Navy just to let some wet-behind-the-ears commissary officer[11] offend them three days out!'"

"You learn quick, sir," he said, hoisting himself up onto the floor. "I'll keep that toe-hanging in mind though, it might come in useful."

"All right, all right, I'd better stop now before I give you any more ideas. Menu change is fine by me, need me to inform Doc?"

"If you would, sir," he bent down to grab Elton's forearm to haul him up.

I searched Doc[12] out and quickly informed him. At this point in the patrol, changes in the menu were not a problem, but later, we had to keep track of nutrients and the vitamin supplements that may be needed.

---

[11] Commissary Officer: One of the junior officer positions, he requisitions, receives, stores, and accounts for all ship's stores. In addition, he is involved in the meal planning and oversight of the cooking staff, including coordinating with the sub's Pharmacist's Mate so he can provide proper supplements.

[12] Pharmacist's Mate or "Doc": the only medical person on a submarine. Even today, sub work is too risky to allow a highly-trained and valuable person like a doctor or nurse to patrol, so a Pharmacist's Mate is assigned. While his job was technically to oversee the crew's health, provide first aid, and inform the Captain if someone's condition warranted a transfer to a larger vessel, many Pharmacist's Mates during WWII also performed surgeries including minor amputations and appendectomies. *Flier's* "Doc" was Peter Gaideczka.

Returning through the Mess Hall, I caught an interesting conversation between Pope and Earl Baumgart. They appeared to be nursing their coffee, among other things.

"All I'm saying," Baumgart was quietly insisting, "Is she may have slid into the water smooth as cream, but ever since, she's been plagued with problems."

"She's still here, ain't she?" Pope retorted. "She's like a kid sister, quick to get into trouble and just as quick to weasel out of it with barley a scratch."

"Is that what you call Midway? A 'scratch?'"

"She got out, got fixed, and went on to a spectacular patrol, what more do you want?"

"Wait, what happened at Midway?" Elton said, sweat-faced, slamming and latching the cool room trapdoor.

"Tell you what kid," Pope said, "put on some Glenn Miller and I'll tell you."

Elton jumped on one of the Mess Room tables and shuffled through the shelf full of records. Clyde, finished with his inventory paperwork, winked at me as he passed, pulling his well-worn deck of cards from his pants pocket and said "I have the last bit of my salary burning a hole in my pocket. Who's up for a game of poker?" He slid onto a bench at another table.

"I'm in" Baumgart slid into place across from Clyde.

"Me too," Pope strolled over, mug in hand, "especially if Lady Luck will not desert me." He affectionately patted Betty Grable's bottom on her poster. "Sir? Are you in?"

"No thanks." I said, waving my cup. "I'm more of a cribbage man."

Trumpets blaring out "American Patrol" erupted from the record player. "Hey, can I play?" Elton grinned, turning around.

"Sorry kid. You know the rules. No playtime until you're fully qualified. Hey, Turner, you play, don't cha?" Pope said.

"Sure do." He grinned. A quick glance at Melvin confirmed his duties at bread making were complete. "And I have some dishes the kid can do, unless you still need him." He looked at Clyde.

"He's all yours."

Elton rolled his eyes. "Dishes?" he asked in disbelief.

"I've got some oil filters to clean if you'd prefer..." Baumgart offered with a grin.

"No, no, dishes will be fine. At least I can hear the story."

"Sure thing kid," Pope turned to Clyde, "Deal 'em." I tucked myself in to the table next door. I'd heard bits and pieces during the last patrol when I was a rookie, but this was the first I'd heard the whole tale

Clyde flicked the cards around the table with a practiced grace as Pope lit his cigarette and took a long draw on it.. "Now where was I?" he mused, "Ah yes, Midway.

"Well, first of all, Midway is a tricky base to get into even on a calm day. It's this ring of reefs surrounding three spits of sand, and the harbor and channel have to be regularly dredged to keep them deep enough for ships and subs. Whenever you come to Midway, they send a pilot who's familiar with the waters to the sub to help guide you in.

"Of course, the day *Flier* attempted it, was in the midst of one of the worst winter storms that season. It was one of those storms that howled for days on end. The moment we hit the shallower waters around Midway, the waves started to break over the deck and into the induction valves, flooding the engines. We had to shut down the diesels and push forward on battery power alone. Half the time, the waves and rain were so bad you couldn't see the islands at all."

Pope glanced down at his hand, told Clyde, "I'll take three," and tucked these in his hand with barely a glace before resuming.

"Midway radioed us to stand by for the pilot, but by the time he came out on the tug, it was far too dangerous to transfer the man aboard, so the tug signaled us to follow her wake into the channel. Captain slowed down a bit to let the tug get well ahead of us, then entered the channel. Just after we passed the entrance buoys, this massive wave comes out of nowhere, picks up *Flier* and shoves her starboard. Captain ordered us hard to port to correct Mother Nature, but another wave grabbed us, picked us up and dropped us on the reef, neat as you please. Shook us so badly, it knocked Baumgart here out of bed, didn't it?"

"I wasn't the only one," he grunted looking at his cards, and throwing a few quarters in the pot. "Dishes and food went flying and no one knew what was going on."

"To make matters worse," Pope grinned, warming to his story and the rapidly growing audience drifting in from the Crew Quarters, "some screwdriver got thrown into main terminal, and the short-circuit started a fire that spewed thick, oily smoke up and down the sub. Seawater was flooding in the engine rooms and the Forward Torpedo Room, everything was chaos.

"Meantime, Captain was throwing *Flier's* rudder back and forth and trying desperately to either back her back off the reef, or throw her over the reef, and to time her power runs with the waves that engulfed her, but every wave just threw her higher and higher."

"Full house," Turner grinned.

"What the—!" Pope laughed.

"Apparently, you'd better be a storyteller or a card player." Turner smirked, "cause you sure as hell can't do both at once!"

"Nah, you were just lucky that time. I'll get you next round." Pope said gathering and shuffling the cards. "I'm watching you."

"You're also just jabbering without finishing the story."

"Yeah, yeah. So, in the meantime, the anchor detail had gone to the foredeck to try to drop anchor to prevent *Flier* from climbing higher up the reef, and this huge wave swept two guys, Jimmy and Gerber, overboard and Dag got slammed into conning tower, laying open his side with a deep cut, didn't you Dag?"

A crowd of men now surrounded the table, and Dag was in the back. "Sure did," he said, pulling up his shirt to reveal the deep, jagged, red line that trailed down his side. "Don't forget this one," he said, pointing at the scar running from his lower lip to his chin, "and my winning SMILE!" He grinned, revealing a mouthful of missing teeth. "Couldn't shut my mouth and damn near broke my jaw. Took the dentist at Pearl forever to fix me up."

"Yeah, yeah, go on about yourself, why don't cha?" Pope grinned before resuming his story with his spell-bound audience. "*Flier* kept getting battered, she twisted back and forth, and I thought she might start spinning like a top next. Cap ordered the ballast tanks and two fuel tanks dumped, hoping that would lighten us enough that the next big wave combined with our churning props would push us off, but the storm wouldn't cooperate. The shafts got banged to hell and began leaking water. We were running all trim and bilge pumps and a bucket brigade besides to keep ahead of the flooding in the stern.

"Up on deck, Banchero spotted Gerber in the water, and threw him a life ring, then the crazy fool threw himself in the drink when the ring didn't fly far enough. Both of them were swept out of sight into the lagoon, and we hoped they would be okay. But Jimmy…well, we didn't see Jimmy after the wave took him, we couldn't even throw him a life ring." Pope's voice dropped from the jovial storyteller in a moment to soft regret. The game screeched to a halt for a few seconds. Some of Pope's spellbound audience bowed their heads in a moment of silence, a couple crossed themselves. After a moment, Pope seemed to shake himself back to reality and continue.

"Suddenly, there was this beam of light shining through the rain, and the silhouette of a massive ship. It was the newest sub rescue ship at Midway, *Macaw*. Word passed down to us that she was coming, and we set up a cheer. We were saved! Ten minutes later, they send us a three word message: '*We are aground.*'" The room groaned. "Sure enough," Pope resumed, "there she was, just next to us, with all of her men scrambling all over the deck trying to pry her free too."

Baumgart won that hand, dealt another, but the story continued with hardly an interruption, and the Mess Room now packed with avid listeners. "For days the storm continued, sometimes calmer, sometimes furious, but never quiet enough to pull either *Flier* or *Macaw* free.

"Six days later, on a Saturday, the storm finally cleared and we could see the *Macaw's* sister ship, *Florikan*, standing by outside the reef—"

"WITH the *Jack* AND the *Gudgeon*[13], who were trying to get into Midway, but we were blocking the way." Baumgart interrupted.

"Well, more the *Macaw* than us, her stern was the one hanging in the channel."

"Still humiliating," Baumgart grunted, with several of the old hands agreeing. "Especially when the *Kingfish* managed to get in during the storm around Macaw and us blocking the channel."

"Okay, granted, it wasn't our finest hour, especially when we found out *Florikan* been specifically sent from Pearl to fetch us and had been sitting out there for three days, waiting for the storm to let up.

"By this time, there was only a skeleton crew on both vessels. During the few lulls, nearly a third of our crew had been evacuated to the *Macaw* via the most rickety looking boatswain's seat[14] you've ever

---

[13] *Jack* and *Gudgeon* were fellow submarines. *Jack* would show up again in *Flier's* history, and survive WWII. *Gudgeon* would be lost with all hands four months after the Midway incident.

[14] Boatswains Chair: a chair or swing suspended by a cable between two points, or two vessels used to transport goods or people.

seen, and from there, most had been evacuated to the main island at Midway, where they found Gerber and Banchero already in the hospital, Gerber nursing a broken arm."

He paused for a moment to consider his cards, and a new hand piped up, "What happened to the other one, Kohl?"

"Cahl, James Francis Peder Cahl," Baumgart replied solemnly. "He was found washed up on the beach, but it was too late. He was buried at sea with full honors at Midway Island, while we were still stranded on the reef."

"Jimmy's belongings that were in his pockets and such were sent to *Flier* over the boatswain's seat, and Captain had to write Cahl's new wife the news." Pope said quietly, tossing his hand back at Baumgart. We all sat in respectful silence once again for a few moments until Pope resumed. "*Flier* was banged to hell. Steering was gone, our rudder bent beyond use. The prop shafts leaked everywhere. Though grounded, the sea around her was deep enough that most waves washed over the deck and some of the big ones broke over the bridge. The engines were clogged with crushed coral sand, and every wave brought a shriek of protest from *Flier*. We didn't know if she would float once we pulled her off.

"We had been wearing our lifebelts for those six days, and Captain and the Exec were at each other's throats—"

"Liddell?" Elton asked, incredulously.

"No, no, Liddell was our Engineering Officer at that time. No, our Exec for that patrol was a guy named Adams. He and the Captain got along like cats and dogs. We weren't the first ship, or submarine, to ground at Midway, but Captain's command was on the line. When *Scorpion* had grounded there for five hours last year, both her captain and exec were removed from command. But the way Adams acted, you'd think we were sunbathing naked on the deck rather than doing everything we could to get free. Captain was already under the gun, trying to do what was right for the remainder of what he probably thought was his last command, and Adams constantly angling for God knows what, didn't help.

"It eventually took the tug that tried to guide us into Midway, plus the *Florikan*, AND a floating crane to pry us free of the reef, and then we checked her bow to stern. Surprisingly, despite the fact that she couldn't steer, couldn't dive, and couldn't start her engines, the one thing she could do was float. So, we loaded everyone up for the return tow. Got to Pearl a few days later."[15]

"Without incident?" I grinned. "Not the way I heard it, Pope."

"No, no," chorused a bunch of the old hands. I had not been on the Midway patrol, but I had heard this part of the story again and again, usually from someone trying to explain the phenomenon that was Pope to a new hand.

"Way I heard it, *Florikan* and *Flier* ran into another winter storm a few days later, and the tow cable snapped. And SOMEONE volunteered to reattach it himself." I said slyly.

"Fished the crazy idiot out of the water," Dag grinned. "He tried to ride *Flier* like a bucking bronco in the waves, clinging to the deck as she threw him under water then high in the air, then over the side! It's a good thing you had that lifeline around your waist!"

"I got her reattached though, didn't I?"

"With A LOT of help!"

"Jinxed," Baumgart muttered under his breath.

"Oh get off it," Pope rolled his eyes, "she got through that just fine, and went on to have a spectacular first patrol. Moreover, we got rid of Adams and promoted Liddell, kept the Captain, had the latest

---

[15] The *Macaw* wasn't so lucky. Despite numerous attempts, she could not be pried off the reef. Salvage crews boarded, assigned to take every item of value and then blow her free of the reef, but during another winter storm on 12-13 February 1944, the sea pushed *Macaw* into deep water, and she sank, taking five hands with her, including commanding officer Lt Cdr. Paul. W. Burton. She partially blocked the channel, and was demolished using explosives. Her wreck has been surveyed and can be dived today at Midway.

technology installed, and to top it all off, we never would have been in the position to stalk those three convoys if we had gone on our original patrol." Several of the men nodded their heads and chorused, "That's right.'"

"You know what they say about serving three patrols on the same sub," Jarrold Taylor broke in, "It's not good luck!"

"Please! This is her second—"Pope said.

"Third! If you count Midway," Taylor cut in.

"Trouble stalks her wherever she goes." Baumgart growled, several other men nodding in agreement. "First Panama, then Midway…"

"Good!" Pope snorted, throwing down his cards. "A submarine who can't find trouble or who trouble can't find can't earn any record or any glory. Look at the *Harder*! Rumor has it, Jap destroyers made a special target of her and she turned right around and made dinner of four of them, a fleet record!" The argument was growing, expanding into several of the listeners, who were echoing, "That's right!" "She'll be a top scorer yet!"

"Hey, are we playing poker or not?" Clyde broke in. "I signed up for a poker game, not an insane debate!"

As the only officer in the room, I decided to head this off before it got any worse, "All right, gentlemen, that's enough, just—"

"I don't care what anyone says." Baumgart stood up at the table, towering over Pope. "I've been around submarines for years and on this boat ever since she touched water, and I'm telling you, she's ji—"

"You had better not finish that sentence Mr. Baumgart," Captain's voice rang out. He stepped through the bulkhead, coffee in hand, eyes blazing, with Jim right behind him. The men and I flattened ourselves against the walls, opening a direct path from the Captain to Baumgart. Captain continued in a softer, but authoritative voice, "unless you were *not* going to say something against my boat."

Baumgart backed down. "She…she's a joy to work on sir."

"Glad to hear it. From this point forward," he announced to the crew in general, "I will not tolerate any more talk about *Flier's* luck, at least so-called bad luck, from anyone. She's as lucky as any other boat in the fleet and she takes the same chances. Is that understood by all?" We were silent, and all nodded our heads. "All right Mister Liddell," he turned to his XO, "what's the movie feature this evening?"

Jim held up the film canister he was carrying in his hand and announced "Destination Tokyo, starring Cary Grant. Let's go!"

The poker game was cleared away, the sheet hung, and the projector quickly assembled. The men wanted to move past the confrontation. Baumgart slipped out, probably back to the engine room. I didn't feel like a movie, so I grabbed another cup of coffee before retiring to my cabin to re-read letters from my family.

I woke shortly before dawn of August 7th for my morning shift and splashed my face and hands with water. After a week, I was looking forward to my first shower tomorrow, when *Flier* suddenly bucked and exploded. My face smashed against the stainless steel mirror over my sink and cursing under my breath, I thundered down the hallway in my stocking feet and shorts with a fire crew on my heels. The fire alarm was blaring, and the red lights rigged on. I darted out of the firemen's way when I reached the control room. "What happened?" I hollered at no one in particular, as the firemen continued to dash towards the stern.

"Engine Explosion, number four, sir," one of the helmsmen yelled, fighting with his planeswheel. "They're trying to put it out now."

Captain Crowley, still in his pajamas, skidded into the room. He had heard "explosion". "How bad?"

"Don't know yet, sir." Liddell slid down the ladder from the Conning Tower. "Firemen are putting it out now, no reports yet of status or injuries."

The Control Room phone rang and Liddell picked up. "Yes?" he listened. "Thank God. Can it be repaired...How long before we know...Ok keep me posted." He hung up and turned to the Captain and me. "Fire's under control, and thankfully, no serious injuries. The number four engine is down, but Teddy Baehr is back there and thinks he can fix it, given some time."

"How much time?" Captain asked

"No idea, sir."

We were only twelve hours from Lombok.

"If he can't fix it we'll have to make for Darwin or Fremantle for repairs. We can't continue with only three functioning engines this early in the patrol." Captain said resignedly.

"Yes, sir," Jim replied.

Crowley's eyes were bloodshot and tired and he sighed as he raked his hands though his hair and glanced at his watch. "I think I'm going to change and come on duty. Keep me posted of any developments until then." He turned and went back to Officer's Country. I doubted he would be able to get back to sleep anyway. The adrenaline coursing through my veins meant I wouldn't need coffee to wake up for this shift...and possibly the next three.

Flier soldiered northward. On her three remaining engines, she could still make close to full speed, but the loss of one-quarter of her power could pose a serious problem in a tight spot. One of my roommates, Ensign Herbert "Teddy" Baehr, as Assistant Engineering Officer, was back in the engine room with the Motor Macs, leaving me to plot the passage through Lombok myself. Number Four spitted, screamed and growled several times over the day, while I tried to ignore the possibility that we would have a second scuttled patrol. Captain might have ordered the jinx talk deep-sixed, but if we limped back to Fremantle already with an exploded engine, the talk would be impossible to stop or ignore.

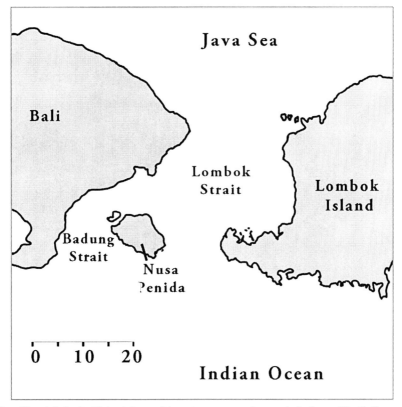

Map of Lombok Strait. Today, it is one of the main passageways between the Indian and Pacific Ocean.

I turned to my maps to distract me. In addition to Commissary Officer, I was Assistant Gunnery Officer, Assistant Torpedo Officer, and Assistant Navigator, Assistant Anything-they-could-come-up-with Officer. At least I was never bored.

Lombok was one of the main passages from the Indian Ocean to the South Pacific. Ten miles wide at the narrowest, and nearly forty miles long, it was flanked by the island of Bali on the west and Lombok on the east. For a submarine, it was a difficult strait to cross. With every tide, the fast, strong, currents, changed direction, and despite being one of the deepest routes into the Pacific, those currents made Lombok too dangerous to safely transverse submerged. The slopes of Lombok Island and Bali bristled with anti-ship guns, and the strait itself was patrolled by at least two patrol vessels. They were usually rickety wooden vessels with a couple of depth charges, but the real danger was their radio which could light up the shore guns in minutes. The best bet was to cross at night, when we'd be nearly invisible to the store guns, and try to elude the patrol vessels.

This time of year brought another problem, however. Phosphorescent algae were blooming, and if we moved too fast in the water, it might light up our bow and stern wakes like landing lights. Unable to submerge, unable to run, parading through Lombok was a bit like casually strolling out of prison through the front gate, at night, while carrying a small flashlight, and hoping that the guards won't notice.

We had already planned to arrive at Lombok at dusk, when we would be difficult to see, and then cross during slack tide of oh-dark-thirty. The wait time would allow us to watch and count the patrol boats and track their movements.

When I reported back on duty at the map table that evening, I saw that Jim had given some details and alterations to the chart and also some notes about charting the rest of the upcoming journey. 'Of course,' I thought to myself as I picked up my tools, 'all this work will depend on...'

"He did it! Hip, Hip, HORAAAY!!" The cheer erupted out of the engine room, along with the triumphant roar of Number Four. I looked down the hall leading aft to the Engine Rooms, and saw Teddy, on the crest of a human wave of cheering, back-slapping men, congratulating him on his apparently brilliant repair. After the ruckus died down a bit, Crowley and Liddell followed him back to the Engine Room to evaluate the repair. Ultimately, it was up to the Captain to decide if the repair and engine would be reliable enough to continue on for the patrol, or if we needed to turn around. After several long minutes when the entire crew seemed to be focused at the evaluation taking place in the Engine Room, another, louder cheer erupted. Captain apparently decided that the repair was good enough, and moments later, he appeared in the Control Room and ordered *Flier* full speed to Lombok.

To allow Teddy to rest after his near triple shift, I took the midnight duty as the Junior Officer of the Deck or JOOD. The cool night wind struck me like a blow as I stepped onto the bridge, and lifted the ever-present sheen of sweat off my skin, and soon, I was shivering beneath my coat. The moon, a large waning gibbous, hung low over the eastern horizon, illuminating the eastern shores of Bali, though the strait itself was still shrouded in shadow. If we were quick enough, we would be through the strait before the moon lit the water.

Captain climbed to the Bridge shortly after. "Status?"
"Radar has spotted one patrol boat," Jim, the Officer of the Deck, said, "about 6500 yards ahead of us in the mouth of the strait, as usual. We can't see the other one yet. The current has slowed, but slack tide[16] is still a half-hour away according to our calculations. There are no sightings of the algae yet."

"Very good," Captain said, "The gunnery crew is standing by. All ahead, standard speed." A gun battle in Lombok was suicidal, and we all knew it, but the possibility was very real. I took my position on the aft bridge, watching our wake for signs of a following enemy.

Flier slid through the waves, entering the main channel. With sixteen feet of draft beneath us, we had to delicately maneuver through the shallow places near the shore. The plan was to stick as closely as possible to Lombok's shadowed side and hide in that for the entire transit.

---

[16] Slack Tide: In places where the tides impact the currents, slack tide is the time at the height of high or low tides where the current rushing one directions slows, stops, then reverses as the other tide takes effect.

"3000 yards…" I heard Radar in the Conning Tower report on the distance to the patrol boat. The shores and water around was eerily quiet.

"2000 yards…"

Still quiet, with no sign of either patrol boat.

"1000 yards…"

The sea around us suddenly flared brilliant green. "Reduce speed to one-third!" Crowley ordered, and *Flier's* props slowed, causing *Flier's* nose to dip and create another splash of glowing algae. The new speed still caused some algae glow, but it was much dimmer, and hopefully, difficult to see from the island.

"Status of the chaser?" Captain asked Radar.

"She's 800 yards and closing, but shows no signs of having seen us. She should pass about 500 yards in front of us, and turn." I heard from below.

All we could do was sit dark and silent in the shadow, hiding in plain sight hoping the chaser wouldn't see us. I combed the shores of Lombok with my binoculars, but saw no sign of alarm from the jungle save the occasional scream of some animal or bird.

The low humming I had become gradually aware of evolved into the thrumming of a ship's motor ahead to port.

"I see her sir," I heard one forward lookout quietly call.

"All stop," Captain said in a softer tone speaking directly into the conning tower hatch, and soon *Flier* drifted slowly to a crawl.

I turned briefly to look over the port bow and saw not the chaser, but the brightly glowing green lines of her bow and stern wakes. She approached at a good clip, in a straight line, never deviating, or showing that she had seen anything.

As she reached the shores of Lombok, I could make out her details. She was a typical chaser for this region: a wooden fishing vessel pressed into hasty service with little arms or armament, except a gun or two and a couple of depth charges. If it wasn't for her radio, it would be easier to sink her than tiptoe around her.

She sped past us and a couple hundred yards ahead, turned, and began the pass back across the strait. Thankfully, she turned away from us, and re-crossed our bow even further away than before. As the sounds of her engines died away, and we breathed a collective sigh of relief.

When Radar reported that chaser was halfway across the strait, *Flier* pushed forward again. With the algae scattered in patches throughout the strait, we had to move carefully, and more slowly than we would have liked. At times, she seemed to crawl along. Hours ticked by. The moon was high when overhead when Radar reported another hit

"Second target acquired, 5000 yards ahead at three–two–seven relative and heading west." She was ahead of us and slightly to our portside then.

"ETA to crossing her path?" Captain quietly asked down the hatch.

"Approximately 34 minutes."

"Projected course of chaser at that point?"

After a slight pause, "She should be approximately a half-mile from Bali's shore, and turning."

"Wonderful," I heard the smile in Captain's voice. "Maintain course and speed."

Flier nosed through the waves, the algae a faint line at her bow and stern. Since the chaser was far enough away, we slowly maneuvered into deeper water further from shore, hoping the algae's dim glow would be harder to see from further away. Radar watched the chaser as she charged for Bali, but she never deviated from course, nor saw us as we crept across her path.

Well ahead of both chasers now, all we had to do was keep

hidden long enough to get out of range of the guns.

The mountains of Lombok and Bali flanked the exit of the strait. The famous volcanic mountains of Bali gleamed silver and black in the moonlight, rippling down to the water's edge. Some of the guys in Fremantle had said that the women of Bali are as beautiful as their island. If that was the case, I thought, they must be breathtaking indeed.

Soon, the sea opened up before us. 'A clean getaway,' I thought with relief.

By three a.m., with Lombok and Bali rapidly fading against the horizon, *Flier* roared ahead, her nose rising out of the water from the racing speed. The gunnery crew stood down, and life resumed its familiar pattern.

3

CHANGE OF PLANS

The next six days were uneventful. We crossed the Java Sea, passed through Makassar Strait to the Celebes Sea, then Sibutu Passage to the Sulu Sea and headed for Bancoran Island before rounding its north shore and turning into the heading for the entrance of Balabac Strait. We always traveled above water at night, and dove as soon as we spotted the first aerial patrol of the morning. The only ships of any kind we saw were native fishing vessels which we left alone. Sonar heard nothing except the sea life swimming and eating around us.

"I thought we'd see more action," I heard Elton and a few of the younger hands complain to Ken Gwinn, our Chief Torpedo man, during an afternoon when he was showing them the finer points of torpedo maintenance.

"Be grateful," he replied, "Trust me, we'll see action before you know it, and maybe then you might not be so eager."

The qualifying boards began for the new and unqualified hands. Despite the intensive training at submarine school, there was no substitute for working an active submarine, and the new guys were constantly underfoot. I would be working my station in the Control Room and turn around to find a non-qual intently inspecting the air bank gages, sketching electrical systems, or hovering over my shoulder watching me navigate. It was a little nerve wracking, but I had been in that position last patrol, and cut them a break.

Flier approached Natsubata Channel, the safest route through Balabac Straits, on Sunday, August 13. I was plotting our course on the Control Room map table when our chief radio man, Walter Klock, dashed out of the Radio Room and flew up the ladder to the Conning Tower. Moments later, he thudded to the floor, Captain hard on his heels. He pushed past Klock to the radio room where Klock's assistant, Bernard Fite, was standing at attention in the hallway. Captain bolted into the Radio Room, and bolted the door shut behind him. That could only mean one thing: an Ultra.[17]

Several minutes later, Captain emerged from the room, and went up to Officer's Country. Ten minutes later, I was called into the meeting along with Teddy Baehr, since we were going to be sharing navigational duties with Jim that night. Jim was pouring over a chart of Balabac when I arrived, along with a set of bearings, and was marking a path through the strait.

"The *Puffer's* on the west coast of Palawan and attacked a large south-bound convoy this morning." Captain started with no preamble once all four of us were in the room, "GHQ wants us to try and hit it, and estimates it'll be here," Captain pointed to a position outside the strait, "twenty-five miles off the west coast of Balabac by 0230 hours tomorrow morning. In order to do that, we're going to have to run full speed on the surface through Balabac, instead of picking our way through slowly.

"Balabac is believed to be mined, so GHQ sent us the track the *Crevalle* took when she went through here a few weeks ago. That's what Liddell's marking out now. Due to the limitations of enemy mines, we want to keep *Flier* in the deep water of Natsubata Channel, more than one hundred fathoms[18] if possible. Anything less than fifty might be dangerous."

Jim, finished marking the *Crevalle's* track, said, "Are we being

---

[17] Ultra: The most top-secret classification of message transmission in the US Navy during WWII. It was so top secret, only the commanding officer of each vessel was permitted to receive, decrypt, and destroy the message, and they had to sign a confidentially contract that bound them to secrecy for decades. It was jokingly called the "burn before you read" code level. WWII Ultras led to wild goose chases more often than not, but did help track down and destroy significant numbers of ships.

[18] Fathom: A fathom is 2 yards or 6 feet of depth.

ordered to follow *Crevalle's* track?

"No, it was specifically noted to be informative, nothing else."

"This looks similar to what we had already planned. I'm seeing a couple of things here: One, the *Crevalle* must have been coming from the north. If we were to deviate to follow the track precisely, it would take us too long to reach our rendezvous in time. They also track very close to Natsubata and Roughton Reefs, far too close for my comfort.

"They didn't tell us WHEN the *Crevalle* went through here, did they?"

"No."

"So we don't know when or what time of day she went through here. If she went through at a strong spring high tide, that might have bought her a few more feet of clearance or weaker currents," he was talking more to himself at the moment, but Teddy and I listened closely. "We're just past the last quarter moon, so we'll have weaker neap tides rather than a spring tide. And at the rate we're going, we'll get there..." he did some rapid calculations, "between the low and high tide, such as they will be, and that will be when whatever currents we'll may face will be the strongest."

He looked up at the three of us. "Captain, I'm sure you'll agree that the dangerous point is here: the bottleneck between the Roughton and Natsubata Reefs to the north and Comiran Island to the south. The waters around both are quite shallow and easily minable. Between them lies Natsubata Channel, which is known to have deep water, though our charts don't record how deep in some places. *Crevalle,* as you can see, passed very close to Roughton."

There were hardly any marked soundings[19] on the chart, and what few that did exist seemed to show the fingers of the reefs

---

[19] Sounding: The depth of the ocean at a particular spot. Taking a sounding means using Sonar to measure the depth beneath a vessel.

extending for miles into the channel.

"Continuous soundings are in order then," Captain said. "What was the course you had planned on?"

"Through the known center of Natsubata, about eight hundred yards south of *Crevalle*. It should be the deepest water.

"Additionally, if we were to happen across any patrol or local vessels, this give us more room to maneuver, especially considering there are reported strong currents throughout this area, which will likely change direction while we transit tonight.

"It looks like we can intersect the *Crevalle's* track here, just past that bottleneck, without loss of time or safety."

"What's the weather like this evening?" Captain asked us.

"Cloudy sir, possible storms coming in from the west." I said. "We probably won't be able to take bearings on the stars, but the mountains of Balabac and Palawan should be visible enough to be seen for that purpose."

"As well as Comiran, when we pass it," Captain said. "There are known Japanese bases on the eastern coast of Balabac that we'll have to pass within five miles of."

"There are also rumors of a light or lighthouse on either Balabac or Comiran sir, possibly both," Teddy interjected.

"We'll have to keep an eye out and see if that's true then. All right, we'll be running dark tonight. That close to the enemy, I don't want so much as a cigarette butt on deck to light the way to us. I'm also going to post the full complement of lookouts on deck and the bridge, and battle stations in the Conning Tower. As we get closer, I may put more lookouts on deck.

"As soon as we sight Comiran Island by Radar or lookout, we'll begin continuous soundings, and we'll take bearings by Radar every five minutes to stay true to course."

"Yes sir," we chorused.

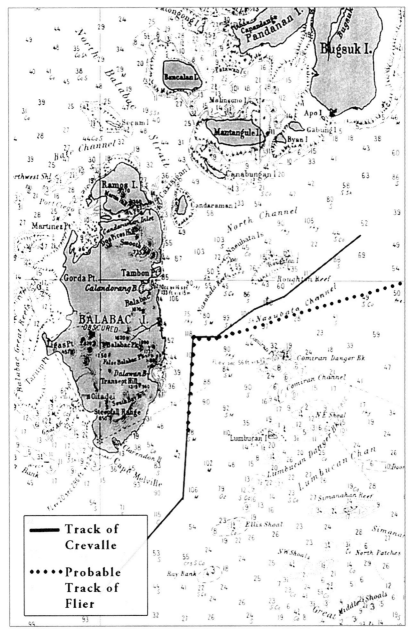

Based on testimony at the investigation into the loss of USS Flier, this is the track Crevalle took on 8 May, 1944, heading east through Balabac Strait. The track of the Flier is conjectured based on testimony from the Flier's navigator, Lt. Liddell.

"Does anyone have anything else to contribute for passage tonight?" Captain asked.

No one did.

"Very well. Hopefully, the fates are smiling on us all. Dismissed."

The afternoon wore on as *Flier* flew south-west. The lookouts on deck were rotated every four hours to keep them alert. No one else was in the area, not even a small fishing boat. That was a good thing, since some of the fishing boats were known to carry radios and report ship locations to one side or the other, but the complete lack of seagoing population as we got closer to the archipelago made me nervous for some reason.

Dinner came, Turner serving us some of James's fabulous stew with Clyde's and Melvin's fresh bread and biscuits. News of the convoy we were ordered to destroy had already filtered among the crew, and the growing anticipation became almost palpable.

That night, Teddy and I were assigned to rotate every four hours between the Map Table in the Control room and JOOD on the bridge outside. Teddy, sopping up the last bits of stew with a biscuit, "volunteered" to take the first shift on deck. "I need to see the sun for a bit, I think," he grinned and stretched.

"Sure, leaving me with the freezing temps of midnight, I see."

"It'll help keep you awake, don't you know. Besides, you young'uns need to let your elders have what little perks there are, that's the right way of the world."

"I suppose. I mean, you're what? Forty? You're sure starting to look decrepit!"

"Hey now, I'm only thirty-three."

"Yup, getting up there."

"Hey now! You're a Michigander, and even if you are from the Lakeshore, you should know better than to mess with a Flint boy."

"Ooo, shaking in my boots."

"Do I have to pull this sub over and separate you two?" Ed said, smiling.

"No sir," I said, "There's nowhere nice enough to stop around here!"

Everyone erupted in laughter. Then, before I could move, Teddy stood up, grabbed a set of binoculars, called "Topside!", and dashed out of the room.

Plotting is tedious work at best, and when constant readings are being called from Sonar, Radar, soundings and bearings from the deck, it quickly gets exhausting. The time just seemed to crawl by until 2030 hours, when I would relieve Teddy topside and get a chance at some fresh air myself. Half an hour before, I put on my red goggles to dilate my eyes and prepare them for night lookout duty. It leached all the color from the Control Room, turning the brass and copper pipes, the dark green linoleum floor, and steel wheels various shades of blood red and black.

COB Hudson, stood in the Control Room, watching over his crew. Two of our seamen were manning the Planeswheel stations in case Captain ordered a crash dive. Electricians continuously checked the circuits on the starboard wall, while others checked the pneumatic systems for the ballast tanks. Men strode through the room in a semi-constant stream of traffic to and fro, often in their stocking feet, ostensibly to cut down on the noise that could be picked up by enemy sonar in an emergency. Despite that, sound reverberated all around me. I heard the hum of the ice cream machine, the slap of cards in the Mess Hall, Turner and Clyde cleaning and removing dinner and setting up the late-night snacks, and men moving about to chat with one another on their off time.

Dorricott and our other yeoman, Jimmy Elder, were chatting in their tiny office a few feet away, while typing and filing the immense amount of paperwork and records the Navy required on each patrol. Someone had moved one of the record players and was blasting

Duke Ellington from Crew's Quarters or beyond. Excited chatter seemed to bubble all around me, and underpinning it all was the growling vibrations of *Flier's* engines and the swish of the water sliding past her hull.

I packed up and stowed my navigation tools and stretched.

"Lookout duty?" Asked Hudson.

"What? The red goggles didn't give it away?" I grinned.

"Lucky dog," he said, as I mounted the ladder to the packed Conning Tower.

The sounds from below were now overlaid with the sounds of a submarine's business: the rustle of charts, the whine of the radar, the rustling sea sounds picked up by the sonar. As I climbed up to the Conning Tower, my crewmates crowded around me. Knapp stood at the Torpedo Data Computer, adjusting trajectories for any moves *Flier* made in case we had to fire a torpedo quickly. Howell and Tremaine had their backs to me, their faces buried in the Radar screens at the back of the room. Next to them, Pope was listening at the Sonar Station. Crowded on either side of the ladder to the bridge was Russo at the helm and Jim at the plotting table, where they could quickly relay messages and respond to orders to and from the bridge. I slid between them and scrambled up the steel rungs to the bridge. A moment later, all sounds of sub life vanished completely under the evening wind.

Captain stood next to Ed, who was the Officer of the Deck, on the bridge outside, straining their eyes and binoculars over the bow. The island of Balabac loomed ahead, guarding the channel. High overhead the enlisted lookouts leaned over their guardrails: Gerry Madeo and Baumgart were the aft lookouts watching the stern of the boat with me, while Wes Miller and Gene Heller covered the bow with Ed. Teddy stood alone on the aft bridge deck, next to the 40 mm gun, scanning our wake for any sign of danger.

He was so intent on what he was doing, he didn't hear me walk up behind him, and jumped slightly when I tapped him on the shoulder before saying, "I am ready to relieve you sir."

He recovered quickly however, and continued the ancient ceremony, "I am ready to be relieved." He looked at me and said in a quieter voice, "I'm sure you know our position. Balabac is straight ahead, but no lights or enemy has been sighted yet. Comiran has not been sighted yet."

"Radar hasn't reported it yet either, though it should be of our port bow soon, according to the charts," I told him.

"I guessed as much. Everything is quiet. No planes, not so much as a fishing boat."

"Thank you," and in a slightly louder voice I said, "I relieve you sir."

"I stand relieved," Teddy intoned. "Attention Bridge, Ensign Jacobson has the Conn."

"I am Ensign Jacobson and I have the Conn."

"Thanks Jake," Teddy said, in a lower voice, the formalities finished. "I'll see you in four hours." He grinned at me.

"Thanks Teddy."

I handed him the red goggles, clapped him on the back, he crossed the deck and dropped below. I never saw him again.

Sunset had just passed, and the last dying rays colored the high clouds overhead a blood red, while dark storms built themselves over Balabac's mountain.

I quickly fell into my pattern, watching the skies and sea for a plane, a wake, anything that said we weren't alone, but it remained quiet.

Flier cut through the sea with ease, her engines humming happily, vibrating the deck beneath my feet.

"We should be coming up on Comiran in a few moments, sir," I heard Jim's voice, a half hour after I had come out on deck.

"Begin taking continuous soundings." Captain told him.

The clouds started to build and thicken to the west, pushing overhead, obscuring the few stars that were appearing.

An hour after I replaced Teddy, a lookout called out, "Captain, there's a light off the port bow, sir."

There was a tiny point of light barely visible in the darkness, as I turned and looked quickly.

"Ensign Jacobson, pass me the Conn." Captain called back to me.

"This is Ensign Jacobson, Commander Crowley has the Conn."

"I am Commander Crowley and I have the Conn."

So, while unusual, Captain was going to control the engine speed and direction from this point forward, and, I suspected, for the remainder of the Balabac passage.

Moments later, he called out, "Battle Stations."

Two pairs of feet strode quickly across the deck, and Phil Mayer and Bill Reynolds, climbed onto the deck, Reynolds watching over the starboard side, Mayer the port.

"Ninety-Five fathoms" Jim's voice boomed out from the bridge hatch.

No one spoke. We just all kept straining to see any threat to our boat.

"Sixty fathoms, with Radar reporting Comiran Island 7800 yards ahead off the port bow, bearing one–seven–four true."

I suddenly realized that the rushing of the water was now competing with the rushing of my blood in my ears. I took a deep breath, rubbed my eyes quickly and dropped into the starboard seat of the 40 mm deck gun to steady my binoculars as I concentrated on seeing in the gathering darkness.

"Comiran Island 6700 yards ahead bearing one–nine–zero true," Jim's voice drifted back to me. "Sounding, seventy-one fathoms."

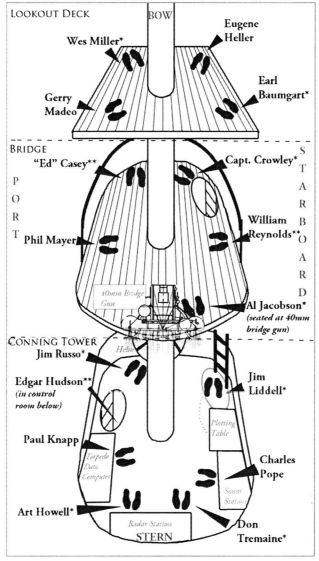

LOOKOUT DECK BOW

Wes Miller*

Eugene Heller

Earl Baumgart*

Gerry Madeo

BRIDGE

"Ed" Casey**

Capt. Crowley*

P
O
R
T

S
T
A
R
B
O
A
R
D

Phil Mayer

William Reynolds**

40mm Bridge Gun

Al Jacobson*
(seated at 40mm bridge gun)

CONNING TOWER
Jim Russo*

Helm

Edgar Hudson**
(in control room below)

Jim Liddell*

Paul Knapp

Plotting Table

Torpedo Data Computer

Charles Pope

Art Howell*

Sonar Station

Radar Station
STERN

Don Tremaine*

This chart shows the probable positions of the Flier crew at the moment of her sinking . During the investigation into Flier's loss, Capt. Crowley testified who had been on the Lookout Deck, Bridge and in the Conning Tower as well as which stations were manned. Those marked with a single asterisk testified to their own position. Those names marked with a double asterisk had their position stated during the same investigation. Those without were recorded as being on duty on the deck on which they are shown, though their exact location may never be known for certain. The layout of the conning tower is based on USS Cod, a sister submarine built at Groton only a few weeks before Flier. Those not shown were deep inside Flier.

Minutes ticked by, as I continued to take deep breaths to steady myself. I turned to look around for a moment's rest. Balabac loomed ahead still, illuminated by the flickers of lightning that shot through the storm clouds. There was a faint shadow of the mountains of the main island, Palawan, to the north, and Comiran was easily seen on her own off the bow. The darkening sky was turning a deep shade while the sea glowed as it always did moments before night truly fell. Whenever my family and I had sailed Lake Michigan, this had always been one of my favorite times of day. Despite the danger, it was the most beautiful scene I'd ever witnessed, and for a moment, I just took it all in.

"Forty-one fathoms." Jim's voice sounded urgent.

"Forty-one?" Captain questioned, crouching down to the bridge hatch. "Are we drifting away from course?"

"Not according to the charts, sir. A finger of a reef might extend here, could be all. We could be in deeper water in moments."

"Can we turn south a bit to adjust and find deeper water while maintaining sea room in case of a surface ship?"

"I believe so, if we adjust head…"

It happened so fast.

Flier suddenly bucked and thrashed violently to port, throwing me off balance against the gun. Reynolds crashed into me, and we tumbled together in a tangle of arms and legs. Air was roaring from somewhere. *Flier* groaned.

"Aaah! My side!" Reynolds shouted.

"Lie still!" I shouted back, extricating myself. "Hang on a second, I'll see what happened."

Mayer pounded past us in two strides and threw himself over the guardrail.

I could hear screaming erupting from behind me, accelerating in terror and volume, and the roar of the ocean was now too close. A moment later, *Flier* drove herself under the sea, dragging me twenty feet down in the space of a hastily gulped breath.

'*The screws!*' I thought, panicking. I could imagine them shredding my body in moments, a bloody mess for the sharks.

I tore for the surface, pushing myself as hard as possible from *Flier's* deck even as she fell away beneath me. Her props, still drumming at full speed, agitated the water and threw me like a rag doll, spinning me around until, lungs bursting, I suddenly broke the surface of the water.

I gasped, heart hammering, and thrashed about in the sludge for a moment before I could face the horrifying truth.

I was shipwrecked, and it had taken only seconds.

4

DEATH BELOW, AND ABOVE

I floated easily in the warm sea. The oily sludge that had been *Flier's* lifeblood now weighed down the waves and coated my head and face. I ducked my head again and again to try to clear my eyes, but couldn't rid myself of it. It clung to every part of me.

I slowly became aware of the sounds of splashing and yelling. At least I wasn't alone. I scraped my eyes clear as best I could, and saw heads bobbing in the dark water. The blood was still pounding through my ears, and voices I should recognize sounded strange and muffled. Suddenly, Captain's voice roared, "Men! To me!"

In the distance, one shadow appeared to be waving.

I tried to swim, but my clothes impeded my movements and my shoes couldn't push the water around like they should. *'If you're ever stranded in the ocean, kick off your shoes and remove your clothing, it will make it easier to swim for extended periods,'* my drill instructor's advice from boot camp rushed back.

I kicked my shoes off, and shed my shirt. I tried to grab my knife out of my pocket, but it slipped out of my grasp, when I fumbled with my belt. Fortunately, my binoculars had apparently survived the sinking, and floated next to me, attached to the strap around my neck.

"Men! To me!" Crowley kept calling. I kicked over to him, and heard a babble of voices in front of me.

"Roll Call!" Crowley ordered, when most everyone had gathered around him.

"Liddell!"

"Baumgart!"

"Casey!"

"Mayer!"

"Pope!"

"Knapp!"

"Tremaine!"

"Miller!"

"Madeo!"

"Russo!"

"Howell!"

"Reynolds!"

"Jacobson!"

The names tumbled over each other. With Captain we were just fourteen men…no, fifteen.

A brilliant bolt of lightning streaked overhead, and for a split second, I could see, wheezing in the water, so bloodied and bruised I could barely recognize him, Edgar Hudson. He gasped and groaned, one arm floating dead beside him, obviously broken. His hair was matted with streaks of oil and blood and his face was already swelling to grotesque proportions. Miller and Baumgart supported him as best they could. "Sucked…from…Control Room … beneath… the ladder," He gasped. "Don't … remember … much…"

'Blasted through two hatches,' I thought in horror. Other stories spilled over each other.

"I pulled on the periscopes to get to the hatch where the air was rushing out." Pope said.

"Blast tore off my shirt before I landed in the water," Jim said.

"I was thrown to the aft deck and she sank under me." Crowley muttered.

"There was no one on the bridge when I got up. I called 'Abandon Ship'" Tremaine said.

"I dove overboard…"

"…saw men tangled in the guardrails…"

"…where's Gene?! He was right next to me!"

"…didn't know where I was…"

"…happened so fast…"

"ENOUGH!" Captain yelled over the accelerating din.

Just fifteen men remained out of the eighty-four men who had been eating, working, and sleeping, just moments before. Fifteen…and now fourteen. Hudson gave a long sigh, and relaxed in the waves. "God go with you, son," Captain murmured as we released him.

"What now?" someone muttered.

"Jim, what's our chances of finding land?" Crowley asked.

"There's land on three sides of us. There's nothing east. Comiran Island is the closest land to the south, probably only a couple of miles away, but it's tiny and if we miss it in the dark, it's fifty miles to Borneo, the next island to the south."

"Anywhere else?"

"Balabac is west, some ten miles away, but the Japanese are there. Our last option is Palawan Island and the little cluster of small islands to the north. Depending on which one we find, those are anywhere from…" he thought for a moment, "maybe nine to thirty miles away."

"Where *is* north?" Pope asked.

We said nothing, but looked around. High on *Flier's* deck, even without the lightning, Balabac at least was easily visible, as well as other islands. But now, I only saw water from horizon to horizon.

In the last few minutes, the clouds had finished blanketing the sky, covering any stars we could have used for bearings. We were hopelessly lost.

Lightning streaked overhead in a huge fan, and for a moment again, I could briefly see everyone, covered in oil and blood, floating in the fouled sea with fragments of cork and debris around us, but no land anywhere.

"There!" Jim pointed. "If that storm is still mostly west of us, that way," he gestured, to the right, "should be north."

Lightning flashed again to the "north", then the "west", and then all sense of direction was gone.

"We can get lost this way," someone behind me muttered.

"We can't stay here," someone else said. "What if what hit us was a Japanese sub? They could be on their way here now to check for survivors."

"Moon rise is at three." Captain broke in, "That's four hours from now, and we can take a definite bearing then. Comiran is too risky, if we miss it, we're done. Balabac is nearby and large enough to easily find, but is also a known Japanese stronghold. I put the question to you men: do we risk the longer swim for the unknown islands to the north, or the shorter swim where we know we'll have to deal with the enemy and their networks of garrisons?" Captain asked us.

"I'd rather die swimming north than risk being captured by them." Russo said.

We all agreed. The rumors of Japanese prison camps that circulated in the pubs and halls were enough to give anyone nightmares. Better to drown in the ocean, or starve on a distant island than that.

"If we swim north," Jim Liddell said, his voice projecting away from us, probably still facing the "north" he had figured out earlier, "the current seems to be forcing the waves to slap us east to west. If we can swim, keeping the waves hitting us on our left side, we will be going north to…whatever there is."

"Agreed," Captain said. He paused, then took a deep breath, "One more thing, we have no idea how far we will have to swim, or how long. Some of us are stronger than others, some might be injured, but to insure as many people as possible reach our goal, and home…" he took another deep breath "…our swim needs to be 'every man for himself.'" He paused, allowing us to take this in. "Are we agreed?"

Captain was the oldest of us by far, around thirty-five, and a notoriously poor swimmer. He was acknowledging that he may not make it to "safety" by morning as much as any other man and barring us from helping him, if it got the rest of us home.

One man, who was clutching his side, pushed himself away from another man who had been supporting him and muttered quietly, "Agreed." It was Phil Mayer, who had run past Reynolds and I and over the guardrail. He must have hit something on the way down. We each took stock of our own strength internally, but very quickly the new rule was agreed to by everyone. I was not injured, but still wondered just how long we would have to swim, and if it would be long enough to find land.

"Let's go then. Try to stay together if at all possible," Captain said.

As the men began to splash away, I noticed one veering off slightly. "Hey," I called out, "north is this way."

"Jake?" The swimmer stopped and turned...past me, then thrashed back and forth in the water. "Jake, is that you?"

It was Ed, swimming with no direction, no sense of...sight?

"Ed, it's Jake, follow my voice." I came up behind him. "What happened to you?"

"I was blinded in the blast," he grunted, turning to face me, "hot oil in my face. I think I hit something on the way down too, I can't lie on my stomach."

"You're still fully dressed, let me help you."

"Wait, my knife, grab my knife." His knife came out of the pocket easily, but without a way to strap it to myself or keep it, I soon lost it too.

"No matter, I'm sure someone else has theirs." I said, hoping it was true. I steered Ed around until we faced the crew, swimming away. "Here, just follow me, and I'll keep you going straight." Since Ed couldn't swim on his stomach, he had to rely on his strong back and side stroke. We soon caught up to the others.

We swam in silence, conserving our strength. Opening our eyes and mouths for a time was horrible as the diesel oil coated the surface of the water. Time became meaningless. I was still wearing my watch, but in the darkness I had no idea if it still worked. The recent events seemed a distant memory rather than minutes or hours ago. I didn't even notice the thinning oil slick until it disappeared.

I switched between the breast, side, and back stroke as needed, all the while keeping an eye on Ed, who occasionally needed to be called back to the group as he swam.

'The Lord is my shepherd…Yea, thou I walk through the valley of the shadow of death, I will fear no evil: for thou art with me…' Strange, I hadn't read that psalm in ages. Still, repeating over and over in my head was Psalm 23, a glimmer of hope in the dark.

Sometimes, lightning struck in the west, and I could see the tip of what we hoped was Balabac Island. If it wasn't…I thought that only once and refused to think it again.

'He leadeth me beside the still waters…'

My hand struck something hard in the water, and I recoiled. What was that? Something else brushed against my side, and I grasped at it even though I also shuddered. I missed it in the dark. Then, the sea around me was thickly coated with a layer of thick, scorched oil.

"Ugh! Are we going in circles?" someone yelled.

"I don't think so," Jim's voice was surprisingly close. "The lightning has stayed left of us, this could be moving with the current, and caught up with us."

I struck something again, and grasped it quickly, seizing it as well as I could in the slippery muck. It was a thin layer of cork, and with a sickening lurch, I realized that this was the insulation that had covered *Flier's* interior. They were useless; not even large enough to help with floating, even if my skivvies had pockets to put them in.

I tried not to imagine them down there, but I couldn't help myself. Just a while ago, we had been working, watching movies, playing poker, waiting for the morning when the "action" was supposed to take place. Had Clyde and Turner started on the morning's bread since we were surfaced and could let the steam vent? Had Doc been tending some seasick kid, or writing home to his family? Had Ken Gwinn, been obsessively tinkering with his "Tin Fish" in the Forward Torpedo Room when it happened? Did he even know what happened? Walter Dorricott would never even see a photo of little Medric. How long before his young wife was told he was never going to come home? We were not due back for six more weeks and no sub was considered "overdue and presumed lost" for about six weeks after that. It was August now…dear God, it could be past Thanksgiving, then, before any of our families found out we weren't coming home.

No. I shook my head. I was going to go home. I was going to hug my mother and father, and sisters, and tell them what happened. I wasn't going to be the one that didn't return, not now that I had a second chance.

"How much further?" Pope's voice rasped. He sounded like he was in severe pain. We were back in clean water, the oil slick mercifully behind us.

"Not far." Jim's voice called from ahead now, and trying to sound encouraging, "Nine miles maybe."

"To hell with this," Pope muttered. He stopped swimming. Lightning flashed, and for a moment, I saw the exhaustion and hopelessness on his haggard face. He had already trailed far behind the group, and now watched us swim on. Moments later, when I glanced back again, he was gone.

I turned away and kept swimming northward. There would be time later.

'I will fear no evil, for thou art with me'

We stuck to the rule, "Every man for himself" with one exception: me. Ed kept swimming to one side or the other, lost in his blindness. I kept calling him back to the group, checking on him. He was my mentor and my best friend in the submarine force. I refused to fail him.

My first days on *Flier* had been difficult. I had been assigned to her fresh out of Sub School, and traveled across country to reach her at Mare Island, where she was in the final stages of the Midway repairs.

"Ensign Alvin E. Jacobson, reporting for duty," I announced myself from the dock to the Officer of the Deck, Lt. Ed Casey. "Permission to come aboard?"

"Permission granted. Welcome aboard, Ensign Jacobson," Ed said, looking over my paperwork to make sure I was who I claimed. The Submarine Force was Top Secret, after all.

"Everything's in order, welcome to the *USS Flier*, one of the newest boats of the fleet."

"Thank you sir, she's a beautiful sh—BOAT!" I realized my mistake almost instantly, and Ed laughed.

"Rule number one, kid, this is a boat, NOT a ship. To a submariner, a ship and a target are the same thing!"

Though *Flier* was beautiful and practically new, the crew was deeply divided. I heard some of the rumors about the Midway incident, and how Captain had nearly lost his boat, and now, he and the XO refused to work together, the XO threatening to leave the Submarine Force altogether rather than patrol on the *Flier*. Experienced men were needed so desperately that a lot of the original crew had been reassigned during *Flier's* renovation and most of us that had been assigned to her were unqualified. The few of the crew that remained started to believe the *Flier* was jinxed…was she? That idea quickly spread through the new hands and made the crew as a whole nervous and anxious.

I stepped into all of this, 21 years old, expected to be responsible for men older and more experienced than me, all while studying for my qualifications. It was a lot to manage, especially when I hadn't been the most studious person to begin with.

Ed was a graduate of the Naval Academy with all its rules and regulations, and so at home in this environment. He quickly took me under his wing and became my mentor; helped me study, learn how to be an officer and take responsibility for others while not losing my own mind or sense of humor. It was like having my older brother back.

He did this for many men on the *Flier,* and was the favorite officer of the crew, I knew. In a way, he was the heart of the boat.

He was also swimming the wrong way again.

"Ed!" I called out as I swam over to him, "Ed! You're swimming the wrong way." I didn't say "again".

He stopped swimming but didn't turn towards me this time.

"Ed," I gripped his shoulder which bowed wearily in the water, "come on, let's rest a moment, then I'll push you back to the group."

"No." he breathed and slipped out of my grasp. "Every man for himself. We all agreed on that."

"Let me help you back to the group. Just put your feet on my shoulders, I'll push you."

"I don't need pushing Jake. If I can't find my way, then I can't find my way."

"Ed, please. Just follow my voice, back to the group."

He hesitated for a moment. "You're not going to leave, are you?"

"Not a chance, I'm not going to let Betty Ann and Ricky down. You still have to get Ricky his birthday gift. If we're lucky, it'll be you." If he really was blind, they'd send him home for good, but now wasn't the time to say that.

I heard him take a deep breath, and saw his shadowy figure nod. "Just don't…don't push me, I'll keep up, if you guide me."

We began to swim back, and I cast around in my head of any idea at all, to distract him from the idea of giving up. "Come to think of it, you still owe me a party when we get back to Fremantle. You promised me you could throw a better party in your sleep than the ones at the hotels I was going to."

"I did, didn't I? Guess I'll have to raid the Emu Brewery too, if you're going to hold me to my word. And I'll have to find you a beautiful girl. Unless you got serious about one in Freo and never told me."

"No one in particular. Despite everyone's threats and attempts, I managed to stay unmarried during R&R. All of Perth and Fremantle may be populated with beautiful women, but no one has managed to catch me yet."

"I'll find you the second most beautiful woman in the world Jake, and she'll catch you."

"Second?"

"You can't have Betty Ann." I could hear the smile in that voice, weak though it was.

We kept talking, his voice low and hoarse with exhaustion, though sounding much more optimistic as we swam back to the group. A few shadowy figures turned at our approach and nodded a greeting, too tired to talk. Ed's breathing was labored, and I was exhausted, though I would not admit it to anyone.

"Thanks Jake. You can stop talking now. It's not fair for you to weaken yourself on my account. Every—"

"Man for himself. I know Ed, but it's not a big deal."

"I can hear you kicking the water when your feet or hands break the surface. If you keep ahead and to the side of me, I can follow you. Just don't splash me in my face, got it?"

I swam slightly ahead and to the side then rolled on my back and kicked the surface gently. "Can you follow that?"

"Sure can. Thanks Jake. I'll make sure to find you a gorgeous girl when this is all over."

I heard Ed swimming quietly just behind me for a while.

The storm had died away, and the clouds overhead were separating into wispy threads that showed the stars in small clusters. I saw the cluster Jim taught me was the "False Cross", and from my own days sailing in Michigan, I spied Capricorn and Sagittarius, but the clouds to the north stubbornly refused to reveal the Dippers or North Star. We were still only guessing at the direction. It was breathtaking, and brought back the 23rd Psalm in full force.

The Lord is my shepherd; I shall not want.
He makes me to lie down in green pastures:
He leadeth me beside the still waters. He Restoreth my soul:
He leadeth me in the paths of Righteousness for His name's sake.
Yea, though I walk through the valley of the shadow of death
I will fear no evil: for Thou art with me.
Thy rod and thy staff, they comfort me.
Thou preparest a table before me in the presence of mine enemies:
Thou anointest my head with oil; my cup runneth over.
Surely goodness and mercy shall follow me all the days of my life:
And I will dwell in the house of the Lord forever.

It must have been an hour later when I realized I didn't hear Ed's breathing or splashing anymore. "Ed?" No answer. "Ed!" I rolled over and looked around me. "ED!" The ocean behind me was empty.

I turned and kept swimming after the guys. The war forced a strange familiarity with death. You had to harden yourself to it, before you went crazy. It was worse on the submarines. They often simply went missing with no reason, or known grave. Every time I was in port there were more notices of boats "overdue and presumed lost". Friends just vanished into the ocean and you had to force yourself to keep going while promising yourself you would think of them later. Anything else and you'd go mad.

So later…I would think of Ed later.

I flipped over again onto my side. My muscles burned dully, and I had to switch positions more and more often, trying to rest them in turn.

I looked at the other men and realized that in my concern for Ed, I hadn't noticed that we seemed to be two more men short. It was impossible to see who it was in the night. I twisted in the water, trying to recount. "They're gone," I heard the wearied voice of Paul Knapp next to me. "Phil and Bill are gone." Bill Reynolds, who landed on me on *Flier's* deck, was gone, as was Phil Meyer who had pounded past us over the side.

I changed position again and just thought to myself, 'Keep going, just keep swimming." Paul swam beside me for a while, but we drew further and further apart. I barely noticed the distance until I realized he too was gone. He must have felt his time was up and quietly left us for the few moments of privacy I desperately tried to delay or deny Ed. It was courage as I had never seen: to die alone and quietly, without distressing the rest of us, giving us the chance and hope to reach some sort of safety, and get back home.

The water grew slippery with *Flier's* oil again. I was growing tired of the grisly reminder. It was like she was chasing us, or we had been wasting hours of effort. I didn't like either option.

The moon finally rose, slightly to our front and right sides. We'd been swimming northeast, but now we had a concrete bearing. The rainbow threads of the oil faded as I turned true north, and, quickly thinking a prayer for my shipmates, I also prayed that I never saw it again.

No one talked; the energy and concentration couldn't be spared. My arms and legs felt like lead, but after so many hours, the swim strokes were automatic. I refused to think of the miles between me and some island, or I'd give up, I knew. I pushed myself to think of nothing but the next stroke taking us to safety, even freedom. Thoughts of family, friends, the *Flier*, the missing men, I violently pushed aside. Just think about the next stroke, the next, the next.

The moon was still low in the stars when the sky began to lighten at the horizon, telling me that it was at least six hours that we'd been swimming together. I had hoped to be practically on an island's beach, but in the pre-dawn light, I couldn't see any indication of land.

I kept going, trusting God would see me through one way or another again. 'Be Prepared,' I remembered my Eagle Scoutmaster telling me. This was about as unprepared as I had ever been, but I decided I would continue swimming until my heart gave out, and no sooner. If it were up to me, *Flier's* fate and those of her crew would be told.

Keep going, just keep going.

"We swam the wrong way!" Madeo suddenly shrieked.

"Madeo, wait, we may see more with the sunrise." Crowley called. His voice was hoarse, strained and exhausted. "We may be nearly there."

I heard Madeo thrashing around in the water, "There's no land anywhere!"

"Wait for the sunrise Madeo," Captain called back, his breath sounding labored.

I clamped down hard on anything except the determination to keep going.

When the sun finally blazed across the sea, Madeo was gone. Miller too.

Captain had been right; land was on the horizon, a low black mass of safety, provided the enemy wasn't waiting there for us too.

-5-
DESERT ISLAND

"Make for the island as best as you can, don't try to stay together if you can make better time." Crowley's hoarse voice called out from behind me.

In the morning light, I could see Russo, younger and an excellent swimmer, far ahead and quickly pulling away from the group. Baumgart and Howell were within yards of me, and someone was swimming far to my right.

My muscles were screaming with pain and weariness now, I had to change positions every few minutes and even pause to rest, but still the island seemed to perversely, stubbornly stay on the horizon. As the light grew brighter, I could make out the dark green of trees, but little else.

Only the sun climbing higher in the sky told me that I had been swimming for hours on end. The warm water and warming air was so soothing, I started to fall asleep, sometimes mid-stroke. I shook my head, and dove deep into the cooler water beneath me to keep awake. The lapping of the waves only compounded the problem. I forced myself to think about the island, food, anything to combat the fatigue, but that too seemed to blend in tempo with the waves.

At times, I felt as though a bee buzzed around my head softly.. I shook my head, and waved it off with my hands, but the noise didn't come closer or further away, like a bee would. Stopping in mid-stroke, I looked up. The sky was dotted here and there with small clouds that clustered near the southern horizon, but the buzzing, slowly growing louder, was coming from nearby. There was no boats, no animals, no distant ships, just the few of us and our island. What was it?

I thought I saw something dark flicker for a second out of the corner of my eye. I glanced up, and saw the dark flicker again on the horizon. I grasped my binoculars and pointed them to the sky, searching for what I hoped was just my imagination.

Then, "God help us...PLANE!!!!" I roared as loudly as I could. I had seen the Red Disc on the wings: a Japanese Zero.

As the plane drew nearer, we tried to stay as still as possible, waiting until she was nearly on top of us. "NOW!" I yelled, taking a deep breath and slipping under, kicking as deeply as I could.

Not soon enough, the shadow flickered overhead, but I stayed under until my lungs were ready to burst. Heart pounding, and all sleep a distant memory, I finally shot to the surface, exploding through to the air, gasping painfully. The plane had passed over the island and was a distant speck already, flying placidly away. Baumgart and Howell's heads blasted out of the sea, and they shook the water from their hair and eyes. For a second, we all panted, too tired to do anything else.

"Figures," I finally grinned at them, "see a plane and every submariner in the area dives in seconds, sub or no sub."

They chuckled wearily. If we could laugh at that lame joke, we might just make it.

At least the island finally appeared to be getting closer, though with agonizing slowness. My muscles trembled with the effort, my breath dragged raggedly in and out of my lungs. Only a little farther, I told myself. Just keep swimming....

A pristine white beach spread itself beneath the trees and I thought, for a moment, I saw a house sitting on the beach. I blinked hard, forcing the sea water out of my eyes, and shook my head. My vision was strained and blurry from the hours of sunlight glaring off the water's surface, and now, all I could see was a green blur on top of a white streak.

"Hey, is that a boat?" Howell croaked excitedly.

There was a low, dark shape in the water, with what appeared to be some people sitting at one end. I couldn't see movement, but quickly lifted my arm and waved frantically. "Hey!" I rasped, "Hey! Do you see us?"

Howell and Baumgart started waving and hollering too, but no one moved, or even acknowledged our existence. They sat so still, it was unnatural.

"Do you think they're friendly?" Howell finally asked.

"They have to see us from this distance." Baumgart said, waving his arms over his head in wide gestures.

"If they won't help a guy in need, we'd better give them a wide berth." I said, "No telling who they are, or if they'll report us."

We swam away from it, and suddenly, my hand smacked the binoculars, still floating beside me! *'Oh geez, how tired am I?'* I thought, sheepishly bringing the glasses to my eyes. Seconds later, I burst out laughing. "It's a palm tree! It's just a stupid palm tree!"

Caught in the current, it came for us rapidly. Sure enough, when it got closer, we could clearly see our "native boat" was an old palm tree floating in the waves, the "people" were the remains of its once broad fronds, now bent and broken at bizarre, twisted angles.

We laughed, slapping each other's hands and the waves in joy. It was the first bit of luck in the hours that we'd been in the water. We splashed over to it in excitement and clambered aboard, straddling our new ship proudly. Baumgart and Howell broke off some of the larger fronds for paddles, and, as the Commanding Officer, I straddled the rough trunk and scanned the water with my binoculars for the rest of our men.

Russo was too far ahead, and was already wading in the hip-deep water towards the beach; there was no point to trying to get to him. I scanned behind us, and saw Captain and Jim struggling feebly. "Men!" I pointed, "To the Captain!"

The fronds made for lousy paddles, and soon we knew they would have to swim at least part of the way to us, or we'd be out here another whole day. We stretched our raw, hoarse voices to our limits, yelling, whistling, throwing sheets of water in the air to get their attention, while trying to steer our "ship" out to sea to get them. They glanced our way once or twice, then suddenly stopped and stared in amazement, before laughing, and pushing hard for our tree, as we kicked and paddled our way to them.

"I had almost given up," Crowley croaked out when he joined us. Despite the hot sun that was burning me, his face was nearly grey and dead-looking. He didn't even have the strength to haul himself aboard for a few minutes and simply hung onto the trunk weakly. "Almost given up hope," he panted again, "when this bizarre vision yelled at me. By God, I never thought I'd be grateful to see one of these again."

"At least this time, it really WAS a ship, sir!" Jim laughed.

"You'd been at the periscope, what was it, five hours chasing that so-called ship last patrol? You thought it was a sailboat, then two sailboats?" I said.

"Yes, then it was a massive sail ship with men in the riggings," Jim replied.

"…and about everything else under the sun, until we surfaced and there was a…"

"FLOATING PALM TREE!" All three officers chorused, and everyone laughed.

"All right, all right, we'd been at sea for days, and I was a little tired. At least that incident didn't make it into the official records." Captain was laughing as hard as the rest of us.

"Nope," Jim said, "but I made you get off duty and go for coffee…or was it to bed?"

"Both," Captain admitted, grinning. We laughed lightly, too tired to do much else.

We hauled Captain and Jim aboard the "*USS* Palm Tree", and

proudly started to pilot her to the beach. Russo was staggering up the last few feet of surf, but Tremaine was struggling in the water far to the east. We screamed and hollered at him until he turned and waved, but kept pushing on to the far end of the beach. We watched him go, confused, but with no more Fliers in the water, we paddled for the sand, using all the fronds as paddles as well as our hands and feet.

Now, sitting above the water, and closing in on the island, I could see that there was no house or any man-made objects, just a smooth white beach spread beneath the tall jungle. It looked like the perfect tropical island, and also perfectly isolated.

The water beneath us was crystal clear and covered with colorful corals and hundreds of fish darting about, a scant few feet beneath us.

"It's looking like we're going to have to wade the last bit in," I said.

My feet brushed a large chunk of coral as it passed under us, and a moment later, I grunted in pain.

"Jacobson, what happened?" Liddell asked.

"I'm not sure sir," I said, reaching down to examine my sole. There was a thin, clean cut, neat as though carved with a razor, with a watery trail of blood trickling from it. "I think I might have cut my foot on a coral."

We all had cuts on our feet and legs by the time the Palm Tree shoaled a couple of blocks from the beach, and we were forced off. I clenched my jaw when my feet landed fully on the coral, slicing open my feet and ankles, the saltwater carving in deeper, and just forced myself to take every step forward.

It seemed like hours later when I finally dragged myself onto the powdery beach and collapsed, too tired to move further. I heard the thuds of other bodies striking the beach around me, as we all gasped and panted. I could feel the water streaming off of me, and the warmth of the blood on the soles of my feet.

A few moments later, I became aware of the sound of ticking; a very rhythmic, precise ticking. By some miracle, I had forgotten completely about my watch, and despite it all, it was still ticking! I squinted at the face, wondering if it was merely moving, or if that really was the time of day.

"1530?" Captain asked me, glancing at his own.

"That's what mine says," I replied.

"Same here," he dropped his arm and lay on the beach, shielding his eyes from the mid-afternoon sun.

We'd been in the water for seventeen hours.

Russo had been the only man on the beach when we got there, and was still lying flat out on the sand, breathing deeply. "'Bout time," he said, "though I like the improvised ship."

"How long you been here?" Jim asked.

"Dunno sir, ten minutes?"

Jim looked around, "Have you seen Tremaine?" None of us had noticed when he had vanished, only that he was no longer here.

"I couldn't see anyone except you guys after I landed." Russo said, sitting up and squinting around him. "I didn't see Tremaine at all after the sun rose."

"He was here only an hour or so ago, drifting east." Jim muttered. He sighed, then struggled to his feet, and trudged eastward. I may have drifted off then, for it seemed like only a moment later, Jim returned with Tremaine in his wake.

"You were on that native canoe?" He said when he got close enough to talk without straining his voice.

"It was a palm tree. You saw us; you waved at us when we hollered at you." Baumgart said.

"I couldn't hear anything. I thought you were native fishermen waving at me, but if you weren't friendly enough to come help a guy out, I wasn't going to take my chances."

We laughed feebly, and together limped up the beach and threw ourselves onto the shaded sand. Every one of us was stripped to his skivvies, burnt red. The fine grains of sand clotted our bloody feet, but worked themselves in deeper with every step. I kept taking deep breaths when I stepped, to keep from showing signs of pain.

Tired, wounded, hungry and thirsty though we all were, we had to make some kind of shelter quickly, before the sun set. Getting soaked and battered by a storm would only weaken us further. Captain quickly organized us into a construction crew, and we scavenged everything we could: driftwood, palm fronds, the fibrous vines that covered the trees.

Despite my hopes, we quickly discovered that somewhere on the bottom of the ocean lay all of our knives. With no alternatives and light running out, we hauled with all our strength to wrench those blasted vines from the trees and bushes. By the time the sun touched the horizon, we had a sorry excuse for a shelter. I suspected a stiff breeze would have no trouble dismantling it, but in the rain, it was better than nothing.

"How about some dinner?" Howell suddenly said, holding up a coconut. "I managed to snag this on the way to shore. Now if only we can…well…"

"Open it?" Tremaine said.

We smashed it against tree trunks and rocks until it cracked open. The smell of sweet coconut milk flooded my nostrils, making me nearly dizzy with hunger. We passed that small coconut each taking a small swallow of the milk, then shattered the shell for the meat. I scraped it off the shell with my teeth, savoring every bit.

Minutes later, my stomach clenched painfully. I ran from camp and pitched towards the sand, losing my meal and then some. My muscles trembled and I curled on my side, hearing the others also lose their dinners. We would get through this, I promised myself. No matter what, we would get through this.

The sun vanished over the horizon, and soon, the temperature dropped. Shaky and weak, we walked back to our shelter and huddled together for some warmth and sleep. I couldn't stop shivering and despite the fact that my sunburn was already serious, I wished for sunrise if only for the warmth it would bring.

No one even suggested building a fire. We all knew the Japanese were still camped on Balabac, and it was more than possible that a random patrol may see a fire here on the beach, so we did without.

No one had slept well when the sun broke over the horizon the next morning. We trembled and stumbled into the early light, trying to warm as fast as possible, even walking up and down the beach, swinging our arms.

Howell had gasped and groaned when he tried to stand. His knee, was badly swollen, mottled with deep bruises.

"I think I banged it on the bridge hatch when…" he shivered.

"Up you get," Tremaine told him, seizing Howell's arm and ducking under his shoulder, lifting him bodily. Russo dashed forward and grabbed his other shoulder, and together they hobbled out into the sun. The unspoken submarine culture was unbroken: we were in this together.

We'd been on our own for a day and a half. Today was Tuesday, August 15.

"Men," Captain said when we had all stopped shivering badly. "We're as rested as we're going to get today, and we need to take stock of the situation and explore the island. We need food and water, and to know if we're alone here. Howell, since you're unable to walk, you will be in charge of trying to reinforce the shelter. Do I have volunteers to stay with him?"

"We will, sir," Tremaine and Russo said, and Captain nodded his acknowledgement. "Okay, that leaves Jacobson, Baumgart, Liddell and me to explore. Liddell and I will head east and Jacobson and Baumgart will head west," he looked at us and we nodded our assent.

"Very good. You three," he said to the camp crew, "watch the strait and search this area when you're done with the shelter. We need water and food. If we can't find it, we'll have to weigh our options from there. I have a watch and so does Jacobson, so try to return no later than 1800, agreed?"

"Yes sir," I said.

"Don't strain yourselves too hard, we can't risk anyone overheating when we have no reliable source of food or water. All right, dismissed,"

I left my binoculars with the shelter group, and Baumgart and I headed west, with the sun behind us. In the early morning light, before the humid haze rose high, I could easily see the dim purple shadow that was Balabac Island. To the west, a couple of miles away, was another island. It looked larger than ours, and also heavily forested. Compared to these giants, we had landed on a spit of sand.

The fine, silky grains of the powdered beach, which worked their way deep into the cuts on my feet, was quickly giving way to broken chunks of coral and my feet were soon raw and bloody again. I longed for my shoes. I could have tied them together and slung them around my neck, couldn't I? Maybe tuck the knife inside them?

"Is it just me sir?" Baumgart grunted as he too limped beside me, "or is this whole island intent on killing us slowly?"

"I'll side with you on this one," I replied. "Seems to be deserted too. I hear birds and the occasional monkey, but there are no signs of people."

We limped and grunted down the beach, as the rising sun caused the humidity to shimmer above the waves, until Balabac was hidden. Another patrol plane buzzed overhead around nine in the morning, but we were already under the spreading fronds of several palm trees, so just watched it pass.

We rounded the end of the island, and what little of the beach that was left vanished into a pile of coral chunks that covered the short distance from the trees to the shore. But washed up on these weathered razors were hundreds of coconuts.

"You think they're any good?" Baumgart asked me, eyes alight.

"I sure hope so."

"Let's break one open and make sure, before we lug these things back to camp." Baumgart said.

We each grabbed a coconut, and banged them against tree trunks and the shattered rocks until they finally cracked. The sickening sweet smell of rot assaulted me.

"Ack!" I hurled the rotten nut into the trees, and clutched my stomach, gagging for a moment. "Okay, okay, there's dozens of coconuts on this beach, there's got to be some good ones."

"You'd think so," Baumgart croaked out. "But I'm from Milwaukee, I'd never know a good coconut if it bit me."

"Well, I wouldn't eat the one that bit you," I joked, "might be a bit too fresh." We laughed wearily. "But I know what you mean. I'm from Grand Haven," Baumgart looked at me questioningly, "across the Lake from you actually, just south of Muskegon."

"Where the lake ferry docks," Baumgart said, "No kidding. So we're practically neighbors."

"Yeah something like that. So I wouldn't know the good ones either. Should we…knock on them like melons?"

He chuckled. "Your guess is as good as mine, sir. It's at least worth a shot," he said, nudging one with his toe and picking up another one.

We picked our way carefully along the shore, knocking on coconut after coconut until we found one that sounded whole and hollow, but it too was rotten inside. We kept going, cracking open one after another, choosing only the most inviting sounding or looking coconuts, but each time, the smell of rotten coconut overcame any hunger pains we had.

Baumgart slumped beneath a palm tree. "We're never going find anything to eat."

"Nonsense," I replied, keeping a laugh in my voice. It was the first rule of survival: don't panic. Panic or resignation wouldn't help anyone. "One hundred coconuts down, one of these has got to be good. Come on."

Another patrol plane flew overhead at around three that afternoon. This place might have been deserted, but it was certainly regularly patrolled.

I was about to suggest to Baumgart that we turn back for camp, when I spotted a human figure emerge from the trees some distance ahead. I hauled Baumgart into the shelter of the trees at the same time he tried to shove me under cover, and we landed in a heap behind a screen of thick fronds.

"Did he see us?" I asked as we untangled ourselves.

"No idea. I don't think so." We peered out at him from behind some thick palm branches.

"If he has, he sure didn't show any signs of it." I said.

"What do you think, sir?" He asked me.

"Dunno. It's got to be a native or an enemy scout. Doesn't seem to be in much of a hurry, does he?"

The man was meandering all over the beach, occasionally prodding a coconut with his foot. He didn't seem to be armed.

"It can't be a scout. I heard that those bastards never go anywhere without being armed to the teeth." Baumgart said.

"Could be scuttlebutt though."

"Scuttlebutt is still usually correct."

"True."

Who could he be? I wondered. I heard no Japanese soldier ever went unarmed but at the same time, I had heard that they sent small patrols to check islands that did not have garrisons on them. He wasn't walking like someone who had a purpose like hunting or fishing, or even looking for something. His gait was stiff, like he was old or had arthritis.

Regardless, if he kept going, he was going to find camp. I started to root around for a large enough piece of coral, or a stout branch, or something.

"Are you thinking what I'm thinking sir?" Baumgart whispered, as he started to quietly root around too.

"Well, whoever he is, we can't let him find the camp, and I don't know about you, but I don't think I can chase him down with my feet like this."

"Same here. Let him pass then get him?"

"Unless you've got a better idea. I don't want to attack an unarmed man, but we can't let an enemy, armed or unarmed, find the camp, and we won't know who he is until we take him."

We watched him continue his slow walk towards our hiding place. He appeared to be limping.

I wished fervently for my binoculars, which would have helped me see him better. My eyes were still weak from the glare of the sun yesterday

Baumgart and I waited, rocks and branches in hand, breathing deeply and quietly behind our cover, watching, waiting for our quarry to limp ever closer.

"Wait a second..." Baumgart raised his head a little higher to get a better look at him from over the palm fronds. "Wes?" he breathed. The figured limped closer. "Oh my God, Wes!" He yelled, stepping out from behind the bush.

The man leapt a mile in the air and then staggered in our direction. "Earl! Thank God! Are you a sight for sore eyes! I thought I was the only one that made it!"

It was Wes Miller, who had vanished before dawn the day before.

"Where have you been?" Baumgart asked.

"The current must have swept me to the other end of the island. By dawn yesterday, I was nearly past here and swam to the beach. I'm so relieved! I thought I was the only survivor left!" He laughed.

"You nearly swam PAST this island?"

"Sure did."

"Well, I think that beats Russo's record for fastest swimmer then," I said, "what do you think Baumgart?"

"Without a doubt!"

"Russo's alive? Where is he? Are there more than you two or three?"

"No, there's seven of us, eight with you." I told him.

"I'm so relieved," he repeated. "Last night it was so cold, I didn't know what to do, I couldn't believe I was the only one left. I was just looking for food or water, can't even find a coconut around here," he said in disgust.

"Well that answers that question then," I told Baumgart. "But I think the others will like what we found on our half of the island better than coconuts anyway."

"Who all is left, sir?" Wes asked me.

"Of the officers, there's only myself, Captain, and Lt. Liddell. Besides you and Baumgart here, we also have Don Tremaine, Art Howell, and of course, Russo. Howell got banged up pretty badly when it happened, and he is back at base with Russo and Tremaine. Baumgart and I were sent by Crowley to scout this island for food, water or any supplies. I take it there's nothing further down the beach."

"Not unless you want rotten coconuts," he grunted, kicking one away with his feet. "I spent most of yesterday cracking the damned things open to find nothing. No water on my end either."

He turned north and pointed to a small point some distance

away. "I landed just around the corner from that point. The beach up there is rocky, mostly broken-up coral, with little real sand, tore my feet up badly, in fact, coming on shore," he looked at our feet. "Apparently it's the same on your side too."

"Only if you count very small razor blades as sand," Baumgart said.

"I spent the day hoping to see someone from *Flier*. I couldn't tell if I had been swept east or west or further forward or farther behind. I thought it was just possible that I was the only one who made it. But I couldn't find food or water, so I made up my mind this morning to explore, and if I had to, head for that island," he pointed to the large island next to us. "It didn't look that far away, but boy! Am I ever glad to see you fellas."

"I guess that's it then," I said, standing, "We have to head back."

The air was now heavy and saturated with humidity, and the breeze did little other than re-distribute the sweat on our bodies. In the distance, I saw rain squalls form and dump rain on the ocean. I licked my rough tongue over my cracked lips and wished one would sweep over us.

The rocky shore slowly gave way back to the sandy beach as we turned to the southern edge of the island. After hours negotiating the razor rock, it felt almost soft.

Hungry and dehydrated, we tired quickly, and had to take frequent breaks, usually in a shady patch of beach.

We were the last to arrive at the base, and Wes, for fun, hid behind Baumgart and me for effect.

"Find anything?" Howell called out, looking at us through my binoculars.

"Nah," Baumgart hollered back, "Just some guy."

They all looked up in alarm: Enemy, native?

Wes walked out from behind us with a grin. "Hey guys!"

Everyone shouted, grabbed Wes, shook his hand, clapped him on the back, and asked him where he had come from. Captain greeted him briefly, then signaled me aside.

"Anything to report besides Wes?" He asked.

"I'm sorry sir, there's nothing on the other side of the island. From Wes's report, he landed on the north-western corner, and he found nothing there all day yesterday, hence why he was coming down the beach looking for other things. We found about a hundred of rotten coconuts, but that's about it."

Captain nodded his head. "I was afraid of that," he muttered.

"Nothing on your end then, sir?"

"Nothing that will let us stay here."

"There was a large island sir, directly west of us, you can see it from here in the morning. It looks larger and more substantial than this one, if we have to migrate."

"Any driftwood?"

"Uh, no sir, nothing to speak of."

He nodded, his forehead furrowed, then said, "Thank you Jacobson, I'll keep that in mind."

"Thank you sir."

I had to retrieve my binoculars from Howell. I felt too exposed without them today, and there was that outside chance I almost didn't want to admit to myself…

Howell was sitting down again, while the rest of the guys were gathered around Wes swapping stories about what happened to them. His leg was propped up on a large piece of driftwood, taking the strain off of his knee.

"Hey Howell, how's the leg?"

"Just fine, sir. I'll be up and around in no time."

"I'm sure." I replied. "Still have my 'binocs?"

"Yes, sir," he fished them out from a pile of palm fronds behind him. "There you are sir, good as new, or at least in the same condition you gave them to me."

"Thanks Howell." He'd been the one watching the strait all day. "You didn't happen to see anything, or anyone…" my voice trailed off as I glanced at Wes.

"Sorry sir, I didn't."

I sighed, "It was a long shot anyway, I just thought maybe it was just possible…" It sounded stupid even as I tried to explain what I was thinking by not explaining it.

"Lieutenant Casey, sir?"

"Yeah, I suppose," I laughed a little nervously at my foolishness. "After we found Wes, I guess I thought if a miracle can happen once, it might happen twice."

"It's not going to for Lieutenant Casey sir, I'm sorry."

"How…how do you…? Are you sure?"

"Yes sir," Howell said, looking out at the ocean. "I heard you talking to Lieutenant Casey when you guided him back that last time. About the party in Fremantle, you know? I was behind both of you. After a while, Lieutenant Casey kept falling behind, but he was quiet about it, so you didn't notice. He ended up near me.

"He was trying really hard to keep going, but he was in a lot of pain, something was wrong, and he couldn't swim on his stomach. I offered to push him. He was a great guy, and my favorite officer…no disrespect to you, sir," he said quickly.

"None taken, he was one of my closest friends too. Everyone on *Flier* liked him."

"Yes sir, he was the one who personally invited me to serve on the *Flier*.

"Anyway, he let me push him, and I tried, and tried, but we kept falling further behind…" he paused and took a deep, shaking breath. I knelt beside him in the sand. "He was still talking about home and trying to keep my spirits up, but you know, in the end, I just couldn't push him anymore. I…I told him I was so sorry, but I just…couldn't. I was so tired, I didn't think I'd make it. His voice was so quiet by then, I think he was in pain, or maybe even losing consciousness. I don't know, it was so dark, I could barely see him. He said a quick prayer, and put himself in God's keeping. The last thing he told me was… 'It's okay Howell, save yourself.' Then he…I watched him sir, I had to watch him sink beneath the water."

Howell's head dropped and we both sat silently next to each other. I had known Ed was probably gone, but to hear it like this was just dreadful.

"After that sir, I just kept going," Howell resumed. "I wasn't going to give in even with my knee after that. Lt. Casey told me to save myself, I wasn't going to disobey his last order."

"I'm sorry I wasn't closer to you, Howell, I would have helped."

"I know sir, I saw you retrieving Lieutenant Casey several times, while I was helping Ensign Mayer, not that that mattered in the end either…"

There was nothing to say. We both understood, but there was nothing that could ease the pain.

The joyful reunion going on nearby seemed unimportant now, as Howell and I sat together, remembering Casey, and by extension, all the others. Despite everything, death never got any easier, not matter how close and familiar you were forced to live with it.

Later, as the sun was very low in the sky, we gathered on the beach, enjoying the cooling temperatures before it became uncomfortable. The humidity was dissipating, revealing the large islands to the southwest and east, with smaller ones peeking through here and there.

The captain stood in front of us and said, "It's come to this. If there had been food and water here, I would wait a few days to gain our strength back here, but there isn't any. We have only one choice left: to leave. But which way?" He knelt, took a small broken stick and drew a rough map in the sand as he talked. "Balabac Island is southwest of here. We sank about seven or eight miles off its western coast near Comiran." He punctured the sand, the tiny island not even worth drawing of an actual "circle." "We know that the Japs have garrisons and outposts on Balabac, which is why we decided to swim north when we had the choice that night. We don't know much about this string of islands here, since they're surrounded by reefs and often are exposed during low tide, which is why subs general avoid this area."

I nodded. On a submarine chart, there are markings for depth, currents, exposed areas, reefs, and anything else a sailor may need to know, but islands were often just blank spaces marked with names and possibly a rough description. When we had passed these islands two days ago, I noted only that it was surrounded by shallow waters and other areas marked "Passable at high tide" or "exposed at low tide". With orders to stay in the 600 foot areas of Natsubata, I hadn't given them a second thought.

"We can see Balabac Island over there," Captain said, pointing over his shoulder, "but there are other islands to the east and the west of us, both of which are large enough that we're more likely to find food and water, though there are no guarantees. The large western island is within a mile or two away. The eastern island is a bit further away, with a string of small islands like this one between it and us." He drew this out on the sand. "According to Jacobson's search party, Wes was the only thing worth retrieving on the western shore of this island." We all chuckled, and Captain continued, "The only thing worth mentioning on the eastern shore there is a large pile of driftwood.

"If we take another swim, we may be pushed apart from the currents, so we're going to build a raft out of the driftwood. It can't be too big, or it'll attract the attention of the regular patrols buzzing overhead. But if we hang on to it, while swimming, we'll stay together.

"The only question left is: west, east, or south? The western island is closer, though we'd have to drag the raft to the western shore or raft all the way around this island to reach her. The small islands between us and the eastern island are fairly close together, but we'd have to walk around each island as it came."

"Of course sir, if we find food or water on one of those small islands, we can rest and recuperate there." I suggested.

"Exactly. The western island is also going to be close to, if not bordering, the North Balabac Strait, which means it will most likely have some Japanese forces on it. The eastern island is a complete blank. It may be patrolled by entrenched forces, or it may just be left alone since it does not guard any significant passages or resources we know of. Of course, it may have no food or water as well.

"And we could, of course, head for Balabac Island, where we know is food, water, and enemy garrisons and patrols we'd have to avoid.

"We're in this together, so this choice has to be all of ours. Would you men prefer to head for known food and water with enemy forces to dodge to the south, likely food and water with likely forces to the west in one long swim, or several short swims to an island we know nothing about to the east?"

"Sir," Wes said, "after all we've gone through thus far, I'd rather take my chance with the unknown again, than try to play hide and seek with an enemy that knows the ground far better than we will. I'd go east."

"Chances are better that there are Native Filipinos there than Japanese anyway," I said. "The Japanese would be on Balabac because it forms one side of both Balabac and North Balabac Straits. If I remember the chart correctly, that western island does guard the North Balabac. The eastern island doesn't guard any critical passage except what native boats probably cruise around here. If there are natives we may find sympathizers, or they may choose to leave us alone entirely." They might also turn us over, but I didn't say that, we all knew that was a possibility

"I'd rather take my chances with the unknown than the known enemy." Baumgart said.

"Agreed," Russo spoke up.

"Same here, I'll take my chances." Tremaine said.

"I'm not ready to turn myself in." Howell agreed.

"It sounds like the crew is decided Captain." Jim finished, glancing at me for a reassuring nod. "We'd rather go into the unknown than take our chances with a prison camp, or worse."

"It's settled then." Captain paused for a moment, looking at the horizon. "It's too late to begin tonight. We'll start in the morning, if we work fast enough, we can launch as soon as that patrol plane makes her afternoon run."

The sun was just touching the horizon now, throwing long shadows onto the white beach. My family used to have driftwood fires on the beach and roast marshmallows this time of day. I wondered if my parents and sisters were carrying on the tradition tonight in our stead.

Suddenly, I saw a tremendous explosion throw water high in the air just at the horizon, near where *Flier* went down. "Look!" I yelled, pointing, before ramming my binoculars to my eyes.

The eruption was tall and violent, the water churned into a frothy foam suspended in mid-air for a few seconds before falling back to the ocean to be absorbed. Was it another ship fallen prey to a mine, or *Flier* herself collapsing under the weight of the water?

Captain tapped me on the shoulder. "Jacobson, may I?" I handed him the binoculars as the muted thunder of the explosion, which much have been deafening at the source, rumbled to our ears.

We were silent, crouched there on the beach, watching and listening to the spectacle.

"Do you suppose it was her?" Russo asked.

"Or a mine." Jim said.

"Did we hit a mine out there?" Baumgart spoke up.

"I don't know. Even at forty fathoms, Japanese mines should have been too deep to catch us running on the surface." Jim replied. "Could it be a battery explosion?"

"No." I said, "The batteries had already been cleaned for the day when I reported for duty. If they were going to explode, they would have done so then."

"Enemy Submarine?" asked Miller

"We never saw one in the area on Radar and no one surfaced to check for survivors or trophies," Tremaine said. "Pope would have heard the scream of a torpedo before it hit, but he never mentioned anything."

"Did we go too fast and get off course?" Wes asked.

"We erred on the side of caution and accounted for speed. I don't think it's possible." Jim retorted.

'Was it?' I wondered.

We stood and watched the horizon for several minutes, each lost in his own thoughts, until, one by one, we turned for our lean-to and bed.

Before sleeping, remembering the rain squalls I had watched pass by all day, I scavenged dozens of seashells and placed them, hollow-side up, in the sand. There had been another squall building in the west just before sunset and I prayed fervently that by morning, we'd be able to slake our burning thirst.

-6-

INTO THE UNKNOWN

Even huddled together for warmth, I could barely sleep for shivering. The others tossed, turned, curled into balls, each struggling to find a position that was relatively warm and comfortable.

Though wide-awake and exhausted when the sky finally began to lighten in the east, I knew I had slept some because I dreamt about my family in Grand Haven.

By now, my mother would have received the letters I had written during *Flier's* first patrol, and that rug and boomerangs that I had sent. She knew that after a few weeks of letters, they stopped, and that meant I was on patrol for a few weeks. I wondered how long it would be before she suspected something was wrong.

Of course, I reminded myself, Ed's family doesn't know about him either, and if none of us made it back…I shook my head. *'Don't think like that,'* I told myself sternly. *'We're going to make it back and I will hug my mother again, and tell Betty Ann about Ed's end,'* I promised myself.

The sun crested the horizon, and we all moved to the sunny edge of the beach, stiffly stretching sore, cold muscles. My stomach cramped painfully, but I tried to ignore it, since there was nothing to help it. Though I had heard the distant rumbles of thunder occasionally that night, nothing had fallen on our island, leaving our seashells as dry as before.

We staggered to the east following the Captain and Jim.

The jungle seemed just as impenetrable here as the eastern end, with nothing that looked remotely useful to eat…or build a raft. That is, until I spotted a small piece of canvas tangled in a low bush. It was dirty and quite tattered, but I grabbed it, hoping there was enough beneath the leaves to make a sail for the raft. It crumbled and fell away at my touch, and despite being as gentle as I could, when I finally extracted the last of it from the bracken around it, I knew that dream was impossible. The piece was too small and slashed with holes in it everywhere. There was no way we could use this for a sail or anything else, so I left it behind.

I scraped my feet open on a partially buried chunk of coral, ripping open a new raw spot on my foot. After cursing my luck under my breath, I grabbed that piece of canvas in a fit of inspiration. I tore it in half and wrapped it around my feet, tying the ends together in a rough sandal.

I took less than ten steps before I had to stop with gritted teeth and rip it off. It had been rubbing on the sores on my ankles and heel, driving dirt further in. I re-wrapped it again, being careful to avoid binding those areas tightly and set off again. But after a step or two, I wrenched the cloth off my foot and yanked a small vine off a nearby tree. I folded the cloth and placed it under my foot, tying the vine around, leaving the top exposed to air and uncovered.

I wrestled with that fabric again and again, wanting some protection from what I knew had to be coming, but no matter what I did, the burning ache of my bare feet was more soothing than the stabbing pain of the rough canvas rubbing all the sores.

I left the canvas scraps behind and walked quickly to catch up to my crewmates.

The island's beach curved to a point, and just beyond that, we saw a large pile of driftwood

"We're going to need vines or something to tie these together," I said to myself.

"I'm sure we can find some in the jungle here," Jim said.

"I'll join you sir," Russo volunteered.

"We've got some nice straight lengths of bamboo too," I mused, pulling aside some strands of seaweed. "That should make this somewhat easier."

"Have you ever built a raft from scratch, Jacobson?" Captain asked me.

"Kind of, sir," I said, "I was an Eagle Scout, and my siblings and I were always building things during our summer vacations on Spring Lake, so I can probably pull something together."

Soon, we were in teams, pulling the long, spars of bamboo out of the twisted driftwood and seaweed and dragging them under the shade of the palm trees that overhung the beach. Here, we could build the raft away from the eyes of the morning patrol, and conserve our energy

It had been over two days now with no food or water, and dehydration was taking its toll. My movements became increasingly clumsy. Sticks and vines would slip through my fingers, without the slightest warning, and sometimes I found myself tying the same knots over and over without pulling them tight. My lips were cracked and my tongue swollen, and the constant beating of the waves against the beach was agony. They reminded me of the fresh water of Lake Michigan beating against the shore, but here, I couldn't just take a drink. It was torture.

The raft started to take shape: about four feet wide and seven feet long, there was a "deck" in the center just wide enough for two of us to straddle, and an outrigger frame the rest of us could hang on to. Captain split two lengths of bamboo halfway, and tied a number of crosspieces, forming primitive paddles.

Jim, now that he had pulled down a number of vines, was standing at the shore, throwing twigs into the water and making scratches in the sand. Since the others were busy lashing the deck together, I checked on him.

"Hey Jake," he said as I approached.

"Hi Jim, what are you up to?"

"I'm trying to calculate the current between these two islands," he tossed a small stick into the water, and watched it float away, while holding a watch to his ear counting off seconds. "I'm estimating the distance of course, but there's at least a six-knot current flowing between here, which is going to be too strong to fight to get to the next island. We'd waste our energy."

"I think that if we leave just before slack tide, not only will the current be slower, but there's a good chance that it will also change directions before we get to the next island. So if we get swept away, we may get swept back shortly thereafter."

"Any idea when that might be?"

"I watched the tides a bit yesterday. I think slack tide will be in four hours or so, but I'll keep checking and narrow the time. Tell Captain that."

"Okay, I'll also tell him where his watch is," I grinned.

"What? You think I slipped this off his wrist when he wasn't looking?" he joked back. "With all the salt and grit stuck to our skin, I had to practically sand his hand down to the bone to get at this!"

We finished the raft, the paddles and even found two poles in case we needed to pole our way across. Now all we had to do was rest and wait.

Time crawled. Sometimes the buzz of insects seemed ear-splittingly loud and the sea far away. I must have drifted off, for I woke up suddenly, feeling the sand stick to my skin like a coat. The humidity was almost palpable.

"It's time," Jim said from the shore.

We lumbered to our feet. Baumgart and I grabbed the raft, Captain the paddles and Miller the poles. Howell was helped to the shore by Tremaine and Russo. The shock of the salt water rushing over my feet and into my wounds made me clench my teeth and suck in my breath. It was a good thing I knew, for the salt to wash my feet clean of dirt and sand, but for a moment, the pain was nearly blinding.

Captain and Howell were going to ride for the first shift, at least until the water was deep enough for Howell to swim without putting too much stress on his bad knee. Jim joined us, and we began to walk, haul, and swim our way towards the new island. After a few minutes of little headway, the sand beneath us dropped, and we were free-swimming with one hand grasping the raft's frame, eyes fixed on the distant beach of our target. It was going to be a long swim, and already, the island was slipping north of us, as the current dragged us back to the sea.

"Listen!" Howell suddenly called. The low buzzing of the plane was almost imperceptible under the sounds of the ocean, but quickly grew louder. Captain and Howell tumbled into the water with us and waited tensely. The tiny dark shape of the plane appeared over the horizon to the south west, and slowly grew larger. I grabbed my binoculars and scanned her, hoping and praying to see the white star of an American fighter we could signal, but, as we expected, it was the scheduled Japanese Zero. "Enemy patrol," I confirmed, dropping the binoculars and waiting for the right time…

"Wait for it….wait for it…" The Zero came closer and closer while we tensed for the orders. "Now!" Captain said and we dove under the raft, shielding ourselves and praying the Zero only saw some driftwood in the waves. The shadow streaked over us and departed north without deviating. My heart hammered as we surfaced, but the immediate danger was over. Within moments, we had the raft loaded again and kicked off.

We didn't talk, the salt water got into the mouth when we tried. Swimming while hanging onto the raft was not mentally taxing and I found my mind wandering back to *Flier*, and the first days I had been on her. Then her first kill…

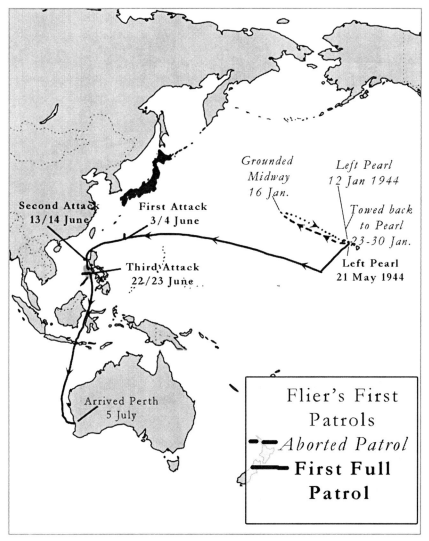

This map shows Flier's first two patrols. Between the first and second patrol, she was overhauled at Mare Island, California.

We had been fruitlessly chasing a northbound convoy that the *USS Silversides* had reported to us when we intercepted a different convoy heading south.[20] The glass-like sea made a daylight periscope attack impossible so we tailed them from a distance, waiting for night.

Two hours in, Joe Pourciau, sitting on Sonar in the Conning Tower said, "I'm detecting a distant depth charge attack, sir. Three… four… five… they're raining down heavily."

"Is it our convoy under attack?" Captain asked.

"Unknown sir, but I have not detected any other ships in the area."

"Periscope depth, slow to five knots," Captain ordered, raising the attack periscope only enough to clear the eyepiece two feet above the floor. He crouched, gripping the handles, and peered intently through them.

He quietly counted the ships and smokestacks.

"Twelve depth charges now, sir," Pourciau said.

"Thank you, keep me informed." Captain said, shifting slightly from his position.

"Sir?" Liddell asked.

"They're not behaving as if they are under attack, but they're too far away for me to see the ships, only the smoke trails. Those are not bigger, or more than they were before, and do not appear to be moving as if they are under attack," he muttered.

Over the next several hours we waited for updates or orders to engage the target or leave the area. Pourciau kept a verbal tally of the depth charges.

"Eighteen now, sir."

"Twenty-two now, sir,"

---

[20] These events took place July 3 and 4, 1944 south of Formosa, or present-day Taiwan

"Still twenty-two, sir."

"Final tally sir: twenty-two. I did not detect any large explosions indicating a damaged vessel."

Captain, Jim took turns on the periscope, raising it up for a momentary glance at the advancing target, then a full sweep of the area, before sending it descending back down. We relied mostly on Pourciau's sonar to tell us what was happening. At one point, we spotted a lone vessel heading north at high speed, too far away to identify or pursue. It was heading in the direction of our convoy, and might have been reinforcements.

After six hours, Captain ordered *Flier* to turn away from the target in preparation for surfacing in the open range. He raised the periscope again, and reported, "Target bearing one–zero–nine." We recorded the position, tracking the convoy while Captain did the three-sixty, when he suddenly said, "Wait...wait a moment..." He peered intently, increased magnification once, then again. "I have a second target, bearing..." he checked the gyroscope repeater,[21] "two–one–zero. Thus far, it appears to be one ship."

We watched both targets carefully, taking readings on heading and position every two minutes. The new target, which proved to be a convoy, was approaching faster than the first target, and was coming closer.

"Which one Captain?" Jim asked, pointing at the two tracks of our targets.

Captain looked over the chart for a moment, then, "The new target. It's closer, we have a more favorable position, and that other convoy may be under attack. I'd rather not run afoul of someone else's prey. Change course, turn to heading two–seven–five until the target convoy is at approximately bearing one–six–five. I want them

---

[21] A gyroscope repeater or gyro repeater is a navigational compass that uses a gyroscope, located in the control room, to identify true north.

on our starboard flank coming at us, then hold that position. Prepare for surface."

The moon was nearly full and illuminated everything for miles, when Captain, four lookouts, and I climbed onto the bridge, searching the horizon for our convoy. They were behind and east of us now, nearly ten miles away, and now we could see the eight ships, four freighters and four fully-armed escorts, zigzagging in the standard anti-submarine pattern. Whatever cargo they carried was valuable, for this was far beyond the standard escort.

A low rumble of thunder reached my ears, and I trained my binoculars on the dazzling firefight from our first convoy over thirty miles away.

BOOM!

One of our new target's escorts roared back with her big guns, firing in the direction of the original convoy, but then sped north, towards us, ignoring any further plight of their fellows.

We watched for an hour, when the convoy suddenly changed direction, heading straight for us.

"Radar! Watch them, see if this is a zig or a base course change," Captain ordered the Conning Tower.

A zig meant they would zig back in a few minutes, and we'd have to decide on a strategy, but if they had just changed course, they were literally going to sail right into us.

Minutes passed, and they kept coming. Ten minutes passed, then twenty minutes. Then the convoy changed direction, but not back onto their original course. "That had to have been a base course change sir!" I heard a muffled voice excitedly call.

"All right then. Rig for Dive!" Captain shouted, grabbing the dive alarm and pulling it twice. We were all down the hatch and had it dogged shut in moments, and soon heard the waves slapping and gurgling on the other side of the Conning Tower walls.

The lookouts went below, but Captain and I went to our stations in the Conning Tower, where Jim was working on the map table. "ETA?" Captain asked.

"Providing they maintain their current eight-knot speed, they'll be in range in forty-five minutes."

"Good, Jacobson, assist Liddell on navigation and get Howell up here to man the Radar for a Radar approach."

The Conning Tower was quiet as we waited, while Howell peered intently into the SJ Radar, watching the convoy approach. They were moving fast, and it wouldn't be long now...

"They're changing course Captain!" Howell called out. "New course is..." it took several minutes for the surface convoy to complete their turn, "The new course is one–nine–two sir."

"One–nine–two?" The convoy was now heading almost straight south, directly away from us and their new course. "Periscope depth," Captain announced shortly, raising the periscope and gripping the steel handles as they emerged out of their well in the floor. He spun around, until he swore. "Maybe that wasn't a base course change after all. Keep an eye on them."

Half-hour later, it was obvious our optimism of an early, easy, first kill was premature. They were back on their original course, passing south of us over nine miles away. We were going to have to run fast on the surface to catch them.

By the time I went on lookout duty, they were south-west of us now, almost to our side, steaming safely in the night. Captain and Jim watched them for a few moments, then had a short whispered consultation. "I heard the words "End-Around Starboard", then Jim went back downstairs, and moments later, *Flier* turned sharply starboard, and roared north-west, racing the convoy. "Jacobson!" Captain's voice roared back at me, "Tell me if they change their base course!"

So we were doing an end-around. *Flier* was going to race ahead of them, cut off their course, and wait for them to come to us.

I signaled my lookouts to keep scanning the water, horizon, and sky for other enemy patrols, and I trained my eyes on the convoy. We were so close that through my binoculars, I could make out the details of every ship in the convoy quite clearly, down to the flare of a match lighting a cigarette, and the many glowing tips of other cigarettes the sailors clenched in their teeth as they went about their work. Teddy relieved me after an hour, and I went downstairs to work at the map table as we continued our chase.

Flier flew at top speed for three hours, and the convoy slowly lost ground, dropping behind us, blissfully unaware they were being stalked.

The moon was setting at 0320 hours when we turned neatly around to wait for the convoy to catch up to us. I relieved Teddy on the deck, but half-hour later, Captain, satisfied that our convoy would cooperate this time, muttered, "Beautiful," then, "Rig for DIVE!"

We jumped down the bridge hatch and dogged it shut once again, with a sense of déjà vu, as we waited, listening to Howell's report as they zigged, zagged, and kept coming on.

My watch said 0447 hours when Howell announced, "Target twenty-one-hundred yards out."

"Periscope depth," Captain replied.

The periscope came up from the floor again, and Captain gripped it and swung it around, before giving a low whistle. "Oh perfect." We waited quietly for the next order. "They've split into two columns, and one is going to pass our bow, and one our stern. If we fire all tubes with proper timing, we can take out all four freighters before the escorts know what's happening. Ready all torpedo tubes, and battle stations."

"GONG! GONG! GONG!," sounded the General Quarters alarm. I heard the pounding of the feet below us as men ran to their stations. The floor shuddered sharply as a water-tight door slammed

shut, then another, and another. In less than a minute, all was quiet again, and the lights flickered from white to red.

The lack of a moon was an advantage, making our exposed periscope head all but invisible. Captain could hardly keep his voice steady from the excitement as he started to track his targets, two spreads of three torpedoes from the bow and two spreads of two torpedoes from the stern. We counted down, three…two…one…

"Fire One!" Captain called on the intercom, clicking the button clenched in his hand.

"One away!" Ken Gwinn's excited voice responded over the intercom.

Seconds later, "Fire Two!"

"Two away!"

Captain quickly fired all six, watching the bubbling trails stream away to our targets with satisfaction, the swiftly swung around the periscope to finish final calculations on the stern targets.

"Dammit!" He swore, "The targets are too close to us to safely fire right now, we may miss this shot."

Howell announced, "Torpedo one hit sir!"

Captain swung back around, and grinned, "She's smoking amidships!"

I mentally counted down torpedo two's trajectory. '*Three…two…one…*'

"A hit on torpedo two!" Howell crowed.

'*Three…two…one…*'

Nothing.

"Miss on three," Howell reported, then, moments later, "A hit on four!"

"We've got the second ship!" Captain said, pressing his face to the eyeglass. "And she looks like she's dead in the water!" He swung to a quick one-eighty then, "SEND HER DEEP!"

He sent the periscope shooting down in its well, as *Flier's* deck tilted sharply, heading for safety. "We've got the two trailing escorts coming on us," he announced to no one in particular. He looked around the room and spotted me. "Jacobson, how long have you been on duty?"

"Since 1350 sir," I replied.

"Sixteen hours?! You're relieved, send a replacement,"

I dropped down the ladder and headed for my cabin, undogging and re-dogging the door on the way there. No use arguing with Captain about the fact that he'd also been on duty longer than I had.

I didn't know what to do, I'd only heard stories of what a depth charge attack felt like. My cabin was empty, since my roommate Herb Miner was apparently on duty, so I sat nervously on the edge of my bunk, waiting.

Flier's deck leveled out gently, then the air conditioning sputtered and died. We'd gone "all quiet", turning off all systems that were not absolutely necessary for life. Her engines off, *Flier* sat and waited for the inevitable. The temperature quickly rose and the red lights made it seem hotter than ever. Sweat began to pour down my body, and I stripped off my uniform leaving only my sodden skivvies as I waited alone in my cabin.

Rumble.

Flier barely quaked in the first depth charge attack, too far off to do much damage. I crouched on the floor, keeping all my joints loose and unlocked as I had been taught, wondering if this was going to be so bad after all.

Rumble. RUMBLE.

They were closer, but still, *Flier* barely felt them.

I waited, not moving, trying to keep so still that the surface boats' Sonar, if they had it, couldn't find us. I heard nothing for several minutes.

Click!

"Oh my—" I never finished my whispered prayer.

WHAM!

Flier violently threw me into the wall of my cabin and dropped me to the floor. I heard the crash of dishes in the Pantry and someone groan there. I shook my head to clear my eyes of the stars, vaguely aware of the sounds of stocking feet racing down the hallway, as the fire crews checked for damage.

"*Click!*"

WHAM!

I hugged the floor, braced my feet on the wall and the bed frame, but *Flier* tossed me like a rag doll, cracking my head against something hard. I groaned, looking up at the walls and ceiling, and the bed frame lying next to me. The photos of Miner's wife and son, as well as my family, fluttered down, landing on my face. Water from the super-humid air was condensing on the metal walls, running down to the floor. In the red light, it looked like *Flier* was bleeding.

"Jake!" An urgent whisper, sounded in the hallway. "Jake, you okay?"

It was Ed, crawling from his cabin down the hall.

"I think so," I whispered, rubbing my throbbing skull, "no blood at least."

"Get in the wardroom, move!" He hissed back, crawling further down the hall. "Anyone in here?" I heard him whisper in the next cabin.

I belly-crawled out of my cabin, hugging the green linoleum floor, pushing past Ed's legs, when there was a moan from the pantry.

"Turner!" Ed's whisper was urgent, and he crouched and stepped into the pantry. "You all right man?" I heard him ask.

"Yes sir," he muttered.

"Come on, get in the Wardroom with Jacobson and me."

I was in the Wardroom now, peering through the pass-through window to the pantry, and saw Ed help Turner get up. I whipped the nearby curtain open and grasped Turner's other shoulder when he stepped in. "Need help?"

"No, thank you sir, I'm all right, just hit my head is all," he said, settling next to me on the bench. "That tiny room covered in metal drawers and cabinets is a hazard to anyone's health."

"Okay you two, listen to me," Ed said, settling in the bench across from us. "The trick to riding this out is to not fully extend any joint, or you'll get hurt. Grab the edge of the table and push your spine into the back cushion, curl your head down and tuck your chin to your chest."

We quickly braced ourselves. "Now what?" I whispered back.

"Now we wait."

I started shaking in shock. This was the worst part. I had never understood the older hands saying how the waiting was the worst, and now I did. To just sit, helpless, praying that the next one would fall just far enough away to survive one more explosion, one more…

Click!

WHAM!

Flier bucked, but I pushed back, and rode it out. It wasn't until we let out our breath as she drifted to a stop that I realized any of us were holding it. There was a strange sound above us though: a swishing, bubbling sound.

"What is that sound?" I whispered to Ed, afraid it might be a leak somewhere.

"Just all that water swirling through the superstructure under the deck. Nothing to worry about. If we can hear the swishing, we're still alive."

"Click!"

WHAM!

Swish, swish, gurgle, gurgle….

We panted for a moment, as the red lights flickered, then went out. We were left in the pitch black, waiting.

"That's seven thus far." Ed's voice whispered.

I tried to keep count of the depth charges. Nothing I had experienced before prepared me for this. Ten, then fifteen, then seventeen explosions rattled and tossed the sub around like a tennis ball.

Every part of my body ached, even my jaw from the unconscious clenching. Sweat poured off my face, dripped off my nose, and into my eyes. My head throbbed painfully. Cramped, I sat in the dark praying that there would be no more.

The red lights flickered back on feebly, and I glanced at the clock. We had been under attack for over one and a half hours. We watched and waited as ten minutes passed, then twenty, still braced, and still waiting.

The white lights flashed on, and the air conditioning rattled loudly, blasting us with a welcome breath of stale air. *Flier's* deck tilted gently up and headed for the surface.

We unclenched everything and sighed, looking at each other with relief.

"Congratulations you two," Ed said, "You've survived your first depth charge attack." He peered at me and grinned, "You know, I think that tan of yours is gone, you're whiter than snow now!"

"You sure you're not talking about me?" Turner joked back.

We laughed in relief, as we stood, stretched and cracked back into shape.

Despite being sweat-soaked, I dressed and reported back to the Control room. Everyone was picking up and putting things back in position, and nursing bruises, aching joints, and bloodied faces. Jim sent anyone needing Doc out of the room, and put me to work in the

Conning Tower with the Captain.

Under the harsh lights, his face looked deathly white, with dark circles under his blood-shot eyes, as he looked at me stepping into the room.

"Jacobson, how many do you see?" He said, pointing at the periscope.

I shoved my eyes against the glass and squinted at the dark images, then magnified them twice. Our convoy was fleeing north, but there were not as many of them as before. I counted quickly, and stood up.

"Seven, sir," I replied.

"That's what I count. We got at least one then."

The rumble of thunder brought me back to the present. The rain squall that had been building before we left swept over us, pouring down in thick, fat drops. We opened our mouths to the sky like baby birds, trying to capture a drop or two, but the rain seemed to splatter everywhere but my parched mouth. It was quick and heavy and soon over, crossing to our island. I thought longingly of the shells we had left out on our old beach, now undoubtedly full, and wished that someone else had spread several on the beach on the new island.

We were three-quarters the way across now drifting south with the weakening current when the tide changed, sweeping us north to the lee of the island. We pulled and struggled but the island drifted further and further south, and the light from the setting sun began to wane.

"Pull men!" Captain yelled from the front of the raft.

The sun set behind the trees, and the island faded from brilliant white and green to a dark shadow. My feet struck ground and we slipped and stumbled to the silvery grey beach, dragging the raft behind us above the tide line.

Painful bits of broken coral littered the sandy beach. "Get rest wherever you can men," Captain rasped out, falling to sleep quickly on the beach.

It was easier said than done. The rapidly cooling night air whisked the water from my skin, leaving the crusty salt behind. I burrowed into the still-warm sand to keep warm, piling the sand on top of me like a blanket. The grains grated against my skin, but the shallow sandy blanket kept the wind off me, and let the heat seep into my muscles.

But I couldn't stop shivering. Ten minutes later, I'd shaken the coating off, and burrowing deeper only exposed wet, cold sand. I tried to sleep, banks of sand piled beside me to shelter me from the wind, but it seemed like moments later, I was wide awake, shaking so hard I was nearly convulsing. I struggled to my feet and paced up and down the beach, slapping my arms against my chest, trying to warm myself up.

The moon was halfway up the sky, revealing that I had slept for quite a while. Under her light, I could see the shadows of several of my crewmates, most who seemed to have followed my lead, and burrowed into the sand, and promptly shivered everything off, leaving a little wall of sand around the human-shaped trough. One trough other than mine was empty.

I stamped my feet as I walked, trying to pound life back into my numb legs, sucking my breath in through clenched teeth when they came to life again with fiery shock.

"You too?" I heard Jim's voice rasp. His shadow limped out from under the trees.

"You mean the inability to sleep or the pain in my feet?"

"Does it matter?" Jim said.

"Not really," I said, blowing and half expecting to see the fog of my breath. "If only I could get warm, I'd be able to sleep."

"Same here," he said, blowing into his cupped hands. "I'm trying to walk enough to stop shivering and go back to sleep."

We paced up and down the beach, vainly trying to warm ourselves. I had no idea what the temperature was now, but it felt colder than it should have been this close to the Equator. We walked back to the huddle of the crew and though we both had stopped shivering, neither of us was warm.

"Well, good-night Jake, I only hope I don't start shivering before I can fall asleep."

"Jim? What if we buried ourselves together? Combining body heat with the sand, we may warm up and stay warm for the rest of the night."

"You think?"

"Well, sharing body heat is a common survival skill. It's a treatment for hypothermia."

"We're not freezing."

"No, Jim, but it might keep us warm."

"Anything's worth a try, I suppose."

We quietly plowed the sand out of the trench until it was long and wide enough for Jim's frame. We lay back to back, finding neither was warmer than ourselves, and the sand, no longer warm from the sun's heat, was like being buried in an ice-block. We began to shiver again.

"Come on Jake," Jim's voice carried a note of amusement "Shake in unison, or we'll lose our blanket faster than before."

We were surrounded by our sand wall in a few minutes.

"Oh well, good-night Jake," Jim said, and lay still beside me.

I shivered myself to sleep, and when I came to again, Jim was gone, the moon was low, and Earl and Howell were pacing the beach, trying to calm their shakes.

I prayed for the sun's rise. I was already dangerously burnt, and would continue to be burnt, but sunlight at least meant warmth, and cessation of shivering.

We were all awake by dawn, but being on the west side of the island, we only saw the colored sky, the sun itself was hidden in the trees. The effect was the same however, the air quickly warmed and shimmered with the tropical heat, and I felt myself relax.

"What the hell happened to you, Earl?" I heard Wes exclaim.

Earl's body was covered in hundreds of red pockmarks from his neck to his feet. "Something kept biting me all night long! I couldn't believe the rest of you slept so soundly!" He looked at us closely, but no one else had the marks on our body. "How—?"

"Where were you sleeping, Baumgart?" Captain asked, with a smile hovering on his lips.

"Over there," Earl pointed at a trench that was closer to the water than anyone else's.

Captain, an Annapolis native, walked over, poked the sand at the foot of the trench and grinned. "Ever hear of sand crabs, son?" He said, holding the minute thing in the palm of his hand.

"Oh hell!" Baumgart groaned, scratching at the welts all over his body.

"Next time," Captain said, clapping his hand on Earl's shoulder, as the rest of us laughed, "sleep as far away from the water as possible.

"Okay, slack tide will be this evening again, so we're going to have to walk to the launch point on the east side of the island. Only question is, long way around," he pointed south-west, "or short way?" He pointed north east.

"Sir?" Howell said, "I REALLY don't like the look of those rocks." He said, thumbing towards the east.

I didn't either. The beach, currently a mix of sand and stone, graduated to solely jagged rocks a short distance from where we stood.

"I vote for the long way around," I said, "We may be able to see an American ship using the Straits and get picked up. Not to mention the coconuts seem to wash up more on the southern side, we might find a good one today."

"Oh, food…" Wes said.

Everyone quickly echoed the long way around idea, and Captain nodded "Everyone take it easy then and keep to the shade whenever possible. I don't need anyone pushing too hard and getting heatstroke."

We set off to the south, rounding the point to the powder soft beach. Here in the shallows the coral was covered with a luxurious coat of seaweed that cushioned the feet. Immersed in the cool water, despite the salt sting, my feet felt better than they had in days, but the sun beat down on my already burnt skin mercilessly. Soon, we were taking shifts, some dragging the raft through the soft surf, and others shielding themselves beneath the trees.

I scanned the sky and horizon with my binoculars but never saw a sign of another ship of any nation. We may as well have been at the end of the world for all the traffic we had seen since *Flier's* demise.

We were soon wading through coconuts, but most were obviously split and spoiled. The few that were not were soon smashed open, spewing the sickly-sweet rotten milk over us. We stopped talking, our raw throats in agony, searching for even a swallow of saliva that had long since dried up.

We collapsed on the far side of the island as the afternoon patrol buzzed overhead. We heard it coming a long ways away this time, and were well under shade when it passed, but I was starting to wonder if the pilot even looked at these little islands

"No food, no water, we're never going to survive this," someone grumbled.

That bothered me. If we were ever going to get home, then we couldn't think like that.

"Hey," I said. "If you start talking like that, we'll never get home. Whatever comes, comes, and whatever doesn't, well, okay. The only way we'll get out of this is to keep pushing on."

"Jacobson's right," Captain said. "Just focus on the job at hand, and let the chips fall where they may."

We dozed under the over-hanging palm fronds, taking turns watching the current for slack tide, and hauled ourselves out to the surf for the swim when the call came. We held on to the raft, but the water here was shallow, and we had waded nearly a third of the way to the tiny rock between us and our large island before the sea floor finally dropped out from beneath us and we started swimming.

Jim, behind me, poked me in the shoulder, then pointed to the north. I looked, and saw three dark dorsal fins circling in the water not far away. I did not know what type of sharks lived around here, but I just stared ahead and kept swimming. *Whatever comes, comes* I reminded myself.

It was nearly sunset when we staggered on the western beach of this tiny third island, and promptly burrowed into the warm sand to attempt to warm up before trying to sleep for the night. I spent that night much like the previous three: wishing for the sun and warmth, even though it now hurt like hell to move, and the skin on my shoulders and neck were blistering.

I ached all over when I woke the next morning. My hands and feet felt like ice cubes, and my heart pounded with the slightest movement. It was our fifth day since *Flier,* and tonight, we would be on the big island that loomed just east of us. I just hoped it had fresh water near where we landed.

We started around the southern shore without talking about it today. No one seemed in the mood to talk, and I wondered if I could. My tongue seemed to have swelled to the size of my mouth, and was bone dry.

This island was rounder, with a point on the south-eastern tip which we were planning on using as a launch-point. It also kept us shielded for as long as possible, in case someone was watching from the island.

"Hey, what's this?" Wes pointed.

It was an old dugout canoe, punched with holes in the hull. It was too far gone to be of use, but there was no mistaking that someone had been here not too long ago.

"Jacobson, survey the area," Captain quickly rasped, kneeling down for a better look, but not touching a thing.

He gave more orders while I searched the jungle for any signs of further occupation of this island. Had natives been here, or had this been a Japanese outpost at one point? I saw no signs of recent habitation at all and the rest of us Captain sent on short scouting missions around the dugout reported back that nothing looked like anyone had been nearby.

But someone had been here at one point. There had been people in the area, but the question was: friend or foe? "Be on your guard, all of you," Captain ordered, "No matter how seemingly trivial, keep an eye for the enemy."

Several yards down the beach, Baumgart grunted at me through his cracked lips. "What do you make of that, sir?"

It looked like a clear path, leading into the jungle. I had roamed many like these in the woods and dunes near home, most of which eventually came to nothing, but given the dugout, we really couldn't afford to take the chance.

I informed Captain of what we had found and he halted the parade to let Baumgart and I check it out. Everyone waited on the beach for our return.

The powdered coral quickly gave way to hard rock, and the bracken and debris were not cushion enough against further damage to my feet. It lead upwards and certainly looked clearly marked, but

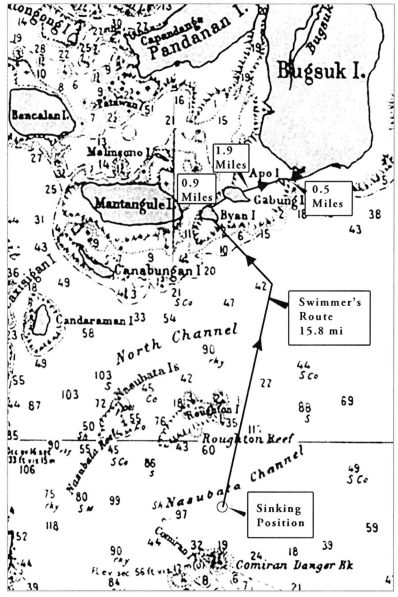

During the escape, the men did not know the names of the islands on which they landed. This map shows the approximate route as plotted by Jacobson. (Original map from the family of Al "Jake" Jacobson)

after walking a few hundred feet, the path abruptly ended, and Baumgart and I were left standing, surrounded by the jungle and the shrieks of monkeys that leapt over our heads.

"Nothing after all then," Baumgart muttered.

"Given some of the other options this could have been, I'll take 'nothing'." I replied.

Captain simply nodded when I told him it seemed to be a naturally-forming path that led nowhere, with no more evidence for human occupation. He nodded shortly and signaled the group to move on to the point.

We trudged on, and the sun rose higher. It was almost noon and we were walking through the coconut fields again. With little hope, I grasped yet another seemingly good one, and pounded it against a tree trunk. Thud, thud, crack, it opened, spilling milk into the sands. I braced myself for the rotten smell to roll over me, but the milk streaming over my hands and down my legs smelled sweet and clean. "A good one!" I announced as loudly as I could, though still barely a hoarse whisper. "I've got a good one!" I quickly flipped it over to retain what was left of the milk and pried it open, but all of the milk was draining in the sands.

"No matter," Jim said, grinning, "At least it's food finally. We're almost to the point, we can eat it there."

I cradled our hard-sought prize and stumbled after the group, most of whom were grinning at me and the coconut. It was wonderful to have a bit of luck again after five days of desperation.

We reached the point and looked with satisfaction the big island, our goal for the evening. It was almost mountainous and covered in dense jungle. I saw birds flitting through the trees and fishing near the beach. It looked so promising that I...wait a moment. I stared suddenly at one point near the water's edge. It was almost hidden in the trees. I blinked, shook my head and stared again. It was still there.

"What the—?" I heard Jim breathe.

I passed the coconut to him in a daze, and grabbed my binoculars, shoving them against my eyes. It was still there.

"Jacobson," Captain held out his hands for the binoculars, which I swiftly handed to him.

"You see what I see?" Russo asked no one in particular.

"A house. It's a house!" Tremaine breathed.

7

SIGNS OF CIVILIZATION

The plan had been to wait for slack tide again, but with the evidence of habitation so close by, we were leery of arriving there while we could be easily seen. We dragged the raft high off the beach and threw it under a bunch of undergrowth, and kept to the shadows as much as possible. My binoculars were passed from person to person as we scanned every inch of the island. I thought I saw some other structures hidden in the trees, but under the tree shadows, it was impossible to see clearly. The one house was weathered to a silver-grey, and appeared unkempt, with shutters hanging wildly and broken branches lying haphazardly on the roof. The structure itself appeared solid, no sagging lines, or leaning walls, so it might have been abandoned only a short while before. Or it might be disguised to look abandoned.

"If we leave during the height of slack tide, and keep low to the water, we'll arrive near sunset." Captain announced to us after a couple hours of watching. "That will hopefully give us enough light to maneuver to somewhere we can set up camp tonight, and still make us difficult to see if anyone is watching. Questions?"

"We're eating first, right?" Wes asked.

We all laughed. The coconut was smashed against a tree and we scraped the meat off the shattered husk with our teeth. It was hard work for not much gain, but it tasted heavenly after the past few days. I let it roll around my tongue, trying to suck as much flavor as I could from it, hoping that doing so would make me feel fuller.

The afternoon patrol buzzed overhead, and we dozed in the shade, conserving what strength we had. All too soon, it was time to start out again.

Jim, Captain, and I studied the terrain near the house. It sat at the head of a small sheltered bay, the other side made up by a small, jutting peninsula. We decided the safest route would be to land on the opposite side of that peninsula, then hike all the way around the bay to the house. If someone was there, hopefully, they wouldn't see us while we walked around the bay and checked the area for enemy or natives. We also could, if necessary, return to the raft and keep going. It wasn't much of a plan but it was what we had to work with.

Slack tide arrived and we dragged our little raft down to the water for what we hoped would be the last time. The water was shallow, and we had to crouch, while hanging on to the raft. No one rode, it was too visible.

It took four hours to finish crossing the short distance, fighting the swift currents all the way. The sun was low in the sky when we finally landed. We would have a couple of hours to round the bay and reach the house before dark.

We pulled the raft onto the shore and made our way quietly along the peninsula trying to stay out of sight. At the end of the peninsula we found ourselves in a coconut grove. Strong, well-maintained trees soared to the sky in neat rows, each absolutely laden with coconuts. Just behind the trees lay the remains of a small village.

It was impossible to tell if it had been abandoned voluntarily or forcibly. The walls, made of bamboo, leaned drunkenly in every direction. Grasses and small bushes peeked out of doorways and windows, showing that no one had lived here for at least a couple of years. Tremaine and Russo pawed through a particularly thick patch of grass, pulling up the remains of a woven rattan fence that had fallen down. The whole place smelled damp and decayed, but there were no indications of bones or blood.

Baumgart and I began collecting coconuts while the rest continued on to the main house that we had spied on the previous island.

"Spread out and search quickly. See if you can find any signs of recent inhabitants," Captain ordered. "In pairs."

While the path between the coconut trees was well-worn, Baumgart and I found no indications of recent traffic. However, I did notice relatively few coconuts on the ground.

After gathering about a dozen coconuts and seeing no signs of anyone else, we rejoined the rest of the Fliers around the big house.

The windows of the house were empty and dark, and any glass that once may have been there was long gone.

The rest of the group had finished their searching and crowded around a large cement object. As we approached, Howell looked at us and said. "It's a cistern. It's water!"

Dreams of a coconut and water feast filled my imagination.

Captain addressed us, "Jacobson and Baumgart, I realize you're dying of thirst, but I advise you to take only sips for now. We don't know how drinking a lot of water now will affect us, and I'd rather not have any of you out of commission because you got sick on too much water."

Howell looked a little guilty and confided to us later that after finding the cistern he drank as much water as he could stand.

The cistern was about six feet square and the main part was about 4 feet high. Although warm, stale and smelling sweetly bitter I savored liquid in my mouth. The first trickle down my throat felt better than I had ever imagined, and I had to fight myself to not follow Howell's example. To eliminate the temptation, I forced myself away from the cistern into the house to explore.

Despite the light musty smell, the house appeared mostly dry and sound. Most doors sagged sadly on broken hinges or had been wrenched off and now lay flat. Small strips of paper were thrown haphazardly, about. I picked one up and saw they were receipts, written in English. One was for the sale of a load of lumber, another for several head of cattle, and both were dated in 1941. As I continued to read, I noticed that none of the receipts were dated any later than mid-1941. Whoever had owned this house must have been a prosperous business owner or merchant, but had vanished right before or after the Japanese invasion.

"Sir?" Baumgart's voice echoed in the empty rooms. "There you are. We're going to crack open the coconuts for the feast now, unless you want to give me your share?"

Our dreams of a feast faded as we began the arduous task of removing the husk from the coconut. While cracking open the brown nuts we had found washed up on various shores was relatively easy, the thick, fibrous coat on these coconuts thwarted our initial efforts to open them. We tried pounding one against the ground, the walls, and the corners of the walls. Finally, searching the ground, I found a broken rock with a sharp edge. We braced that against a wall, and taking turns ramming that coconut onto that rock, finally managed to cut into the fibrous coating and start peeling it back. We cheered quietly as the hairy brown nut was finally freed from the husk, and quickly pounded a hole in the eye, each taking a swallow of the sweet milk before smashing the nut apart to scrape the flesh from the shell with our teeth. No one felt up to the task of trying to break open another one.

The last bit of light was fading, and more than a handful of stars were overhead when we finished our meager, but still welcome, meal. "I'll take first watch tonight," Captain said as we entered the house, "and we'll all have to take turns tonight, just in case. Wake your replacement when your time is up." We nodded sleepily, most of us past caring anyway. I claimed a door I had seen earlier, and as I stretched out on it, fell quickly into a dreamless sleep, more comfortable than I had been in days.

A groan woke me suddenly. In the moonlight now spilling through the windows, I saw Howell doubled in agony, his teeth clenched. Captain and Jim woke and were at his side in a moment.

"What is it?" Captain asked.

"My stomach is killing me. My head is throbbing, and my hands and feet feel like they're being stabbed with hundreds of needles." He was trying to keep quiet, but the rest of us were awake and alert already.

Howell suddenly rolled over and retched all over the floor, losing most, if not all of his meager dinner.

"I told you not to drink all that water," Captain mildly scolded.

"Try to rest, you'll be fine by morning." Jim said. "If you haven't taken a turn on watch, I'll take it. Just rest."

He sounded confident, but I wondered if he believed Howell get better. We had no medical supplies, so all we could do was keep Howell as comfortable and relaxed as possible. He was going to have to try to pull through this on his own strength.

By this time, everyone was up and surrounding Howell. "Who's on watch?" Captain asked.

"I am sir," Tremaine said. "I had just gotten up, so I can keep going for a little while."

"Good," Captain said. "Try and keep quiet and let Howell sleep, and the rest of us will try to do the same."

"Yes sir," Tremaine said, leaving the room.

"We'll need our sleep for the morning gentlemen," Captain said.

"I'm sorry to be a bother sir," Howell grunted.

"No bother son. We're in this together, just like always."

"I'm right here Howell, if you need anything," I said, dragging my door over to him.

"Thanks sir,"

I lay down, and before I knew it, Howell and I were asleep.

The sky was a pre-dawn gray when I jerked awake. My crewmates were still asleep. I quietly crawled towards Howell. He was sleeping steadily.

I shook his shoulder gently, but he groaned and rolled over. Another shake and he flicked my hand away from him, muttering "Leave me alone, ma."

"How is he sir?" Baumgart said, walking into the room.

"Well, he thinks I'm his mother, so he's either blind, or better."

"Oh that's good," Baumgart said, visibly relieved. "Have you had a turn on watch yet?"

"Not yet," I replied.

"I just got up myself, and am too awake to go back to sleep at the moment."

"Everything in order then?"

"More or less."

"Then if you're fine here, I will explore the grounds."

"I'll let Captain and Lt. Liddell know where you've gone. I know Captain would prefer going in pairs, but…"

"We need to know what resources, if any, we have besides the cistern. I'll stay in sight of the house."

"I figured as much, sir. Just didn't want trouble with the Captain."

"Understood."

Three sides of the house were surrounded by woods, but I was interested in the side that faced the water. We'd seen that side first, and anyone coming to inspect the house would likely land there rather than come the way we had.

The house sloped quickly down to the beach, where two large launches lay. Each had been about thirty-eight feet long when they were built, but both were unserviceable. One had been destroyed, its sides caved in by the heavy blows of an axe. Nothing remained of the engines or props, not even the mounting brackets. The other had never been finished.

There was still room on the beach for someone to land, and we would have to watch this area closely, but the boats were useless to us or anyone else, so I turned to explore the grounds.

Several patches of cleared land indicated former gardens, and a small, clear stream flowed into the water. Fish swam lazily, and I wondered if we could rig up some nets to catch them. I took a sip of water, and spat it out quickly. Being this close to the sea apparently meant that the water was too salty to drink.

When I returned, the rest of the Fliers were up and sitting outside, enjoying another breakfast of coconut. Even Howell was outside, enjoying the morning sun, with his knee propped up, joking about being accident-prone.

"First things first," Captain said, "We should spend several days here and recuperate before we decide what to do next." We all nodded. "We'll need supplies, and between the coconut farm, the fish, and the cistern, we're finally well off when it comes to supplies.

"But this house and the village prove that there were people here not too long ago, and we don't know if they're still in the area, so we'll need to set watch in addition to foraging. Any natives in the area may find us and they may be able to help."

"Or turn us in," Baumgart said.

"Yes, that's a risk," Captain acknowledged, "but we'll need their help if we're to get home. Subs and ships don't pass close enough to this island to signal for help, and we don't know how long it will be before the Allies re-take these islands.

"For today however, we need food and fire, and we'll work in pairs. Howell, once again, you've earned the right to sit on your backside and tend home camp." We all laughed, including Howell. "In this case, making and tending a fire and keeping watch."

"Wes is taking the magnifying glass out of the binoculars and I'll use that to light the fire," Howell said.

"Fine. Then Miller, when you're done with that, I guess you can fetch firewood. I'll go back to the coconut grove with Tremaine and gather more coconuts while Baumgart and Jacobson do some more scouting. That leaves Russo and Liddell for the fishing."

At that moment, two native boys stepped out of the jungle. We stared at each other for a moment, and the boys began calmly walking toward us. Since there was no hiding from them, we followed suit and went to meet them.

"Good Morning," Captain said to the boys. They glanced at each other, but made no response. Captain glanced at us, but met blank stares, no one else having any other ideas. Finally Captain tried, "Americans or Japanese?"

The taller boy smiled. "Americanos!" he said with a big, white toothy grin. Then he said, "Japanese" and made a violently quick motion like slitting his throat. He pointed at us. "Americanos?"

"Yes, Americanos." Captain sighed in relief, as we all quickly echoed, "Americanos, Americanos."

The smaller boy, in an apparent effort to be useful, pointed at the cistern and said, "No drink water." Captain asked him why, but both boys looked at us blankly. Remembering our policy of "letting come what may," we just accepted it.

"Food?" Captain asked.

The taller boy grinned and said "Rice" while patting his stomach. He motioned us with his hand to follow them back through the jungle, and then disappeared into the woods.

We were too astonished to follow for a moment, it was all surreal.

"Captain?" Liddell asked.

"Well, we've been warned that not all Filipinos are on our side, and to be especially cautious of those who don't speak English, but we don't have many options at this point."

We all agreed. The prospect of food and friendly faces overcame what would have been our trained distrust.

With a rustle, the older boy appeared on the trail again, looking at us quizzically, then motioning us to follow him again.

"Here goes nothing," I heard Captain mutter to himself.

The boy turned into the woods and glanced back several times to make sure we were following. The other boy was waiting for us at the foot of a great tree, with a bundle wrapped in a handkerchief tied to the end of a stick slung over his shoulder. It reminded me of my brothers and me taking off for an afternoon fishing expedition. The larger boy, in one fluid move between steps, grasped his own pack off the ground, and slipped around the tree with practiced ease, and vanished into the woods, the younger boy in his wake.

My feet had been sore during my morning exploration, but I had been able to ignore it when moving at my own, slow pace, but these two fairly flew through the woods, their worn sandals slapping against the soles of their feet, and we struggled to keep up. I felt my feet open again, but bit the insides of my cheeks and tried harder to find the deepest pads of leaves to walk on, rather than the coarse broken soil. From the quickly smothered gasps of the others, I knew all of us were in for a rough time.

We staggered behind them through nearly invisible jungle trails, panting with effort. Occasionally, I felt dizzy, stars floated past my eyes, and I had to rest for a gasp or two before continuing.

The jungle gave way to another clearing, dominated by tall, tasseled grasses. The boys stopped here and motioned us to sit. I gratefully flopped to the ground with a thud, wheezing. They withdrew huge, curved knives from their belts and swiftly cut the grass down and stripped the leaves from the central stalks. The taller one held the first yard-long piece out to Captain who took it gingerly. "Eat" the boy said, nodding and smiling. We looked at each other, puzzled. "Eat," the boy repeated, and gnawed on the end of the piece he was stripping in his hand. Captain gingerly licked the end of his stalk and his eyes lit up. "Sugarcane!" He laughed. "I must be sugarcane."

It was sweet and moist, though exceedingly tough. After a few moments, my jaws ached from the effort of chewing, but I wasn't about to stop. I could feel energy returning to me. After giving each of us a section, the boys sat too, chomping on their own. After a half-hour, they picked up their packs, motioned us to follow them, then vanished into the woods again. We scrambled after them, and after another fifteen minutes or so, entered a field, overgrown with tall grasses and wildflowers. Sitting in the middle of the field was a raised platform covered with a roof open on all sides, like the picnic shelters in parks back home. Weathered, old fashioned benches with attached desks stood in rough rows facing what must have been the teacher's desk before the war.

The boys motioned us to sit down on the benches and faster than I could have started a fire with matches, they had whittled a spindle and started a fire by spinning it in their hands on a notched chunk of wood. Moments later, they had a cook fire going. The older boy pulled out a small pot from beneath the platform, filled it with water from a nearby stream, and set it in the fire to boil. The other grabbed a small burlap bag out of his pack and poured a pound or so of rice into the water.

When that was done, the older boy grabbed a large machete and started chopping down broad leaves from a nearby tree, the other, pulled a small metal cup from a pack, filled it at the stream, and brought it to us.

"Drink," the boy said. I could see the water was very muddy and unappetizing. Captain took it with a smile, but looked at it worryingly. "Drink," the boy repeated, taking the cup back and drinking some himself. He handed the cup back to the Captain, who took a cautious sip. "It's all right," he told us. "Tastes a bit like mud, but I'm not going to complain now."

When he finished, he handed the cup back to the boy, who took it, grabbed another from his friend's pack, and raced to the stream, bringing water back and forth until we had our fill.

The older one returned, laden with broad leaves, which he laid near the fire and boiling pot. He stirred the pot with a wooden spoon, said something to the smaller boy, and began to ladle out hot, steaming balls of rice onto the glossy leaves. The smaller boy scrambled to his pack, took out a bundle wrapped in more leaves, and with a flourish, laid a portion of small smoked fish on top of each pile of rice. The exquisite smell made my stomach groan loudly, and mine wasn't the only one. They picked up the leaves and raced back and forth between us and the fire, laying their food offering before each of us with a smile.

I pinched some rice between two fingers and began to eat. The hot rice made me cough and suck in air to quickly cool my mouth before it could burn. The boys laughed, and showed us how to eat the rice using their hands, the customary way of eating, around here.

I resisted wolfing everything down in one gulp and tried to eat somewhat slowly to give my body time to adjust to the first real meal in days, carefully stripping the meat from the skeleton of the smoked fish. I started to relax. We had found friends, were eating hot food, were off our feet, and shaded from the sun. Life was looking up.

A rifle cocked. We froze. A dozen men stepped out from under the shadow of the trees, armed with rifles, machetes, and blowguns, all aimed at us.

The boys stood up next to us and grinned. "AMERICANOS!" they yelled, pointing at us.

8

THE BUGSUK BOLO BATTALION

We were betrayed.

There was no escape. The clearing was large enough that we would be shot before we had run more than a few feet. I glanced at Captain, and saw his shoulders sag in defeat. We were done for, and would be carted off to a POW camp.

The apparent leader stood in front of the group, his deeply tanned skin stretched over sinew and muscle. He looked keenly at the boys, who bounced up and down, pointing more animatedly.

"Americanos! Americanos!" They chanted.

He suddenly smiled, and said, "Hello!" He walked quickly to our shelter. "My name is Pedro Sarmiento, and I am the leader of the Bugsuk Bolo Battalion."

He shook all of our hands while we stared in stunned silence. Was this another trick? The other guerillas, while lowering their weapons, advanced slowly, watching the surrounding trees warily. One spoke rapidly to the boys who replied in their own language, and our guide pointed back into the woods.

"Sit, please, you look tired, and you're going to need energy soon." Sarmiento said, motioning us back to our seats.

"I'm sorry," Captain began, "but what is going on? Why should we trust you?"

"Well, to answer the second question, if you give me a chance, I will prove my trustworthiness. As to what is going on, this is the Bolo Battalion stationed on Bugsuk Island. We are Filipinos defending our own land, and since you are Allies, we have orders to take you to a safe point until you can be rescued."

"How do you speak English so well?" Captain asked, eyes narrowed, apparently debating on whether to trust the stranger.

"I was educated in Manila as a schoolteacher. Before the island was taken by the Japanese, I was the overseer at the plantation near the big house, and the schoolteacher of this school. Part of that education is teaching English." He replied calmly.

"How did you know where to find us?"

"We have lookouts surrounding this island day and night, keeping track of enemy and allied patrols, landings, anything that could be useful. Around sunset, a lookout near the big house reported seeing eight men swimming to the island, and it was impossible for him to tell if you were Japanese or American. They sent runners all over the island to gather the battalion." He swept his arms to indicate the armed men around him. "This morning, we surrounded the house, and sent the boys to find out who you were. If you were friends, they were supposed to lead you to this place."

"And if we hadn't been?" Captain inquired.

"Then they were to pretend they were going on to the coconut grove, and every one of you would have been killed right there in that courtyard."

I felt the hairs on my arms and neck stand on end. Sarmiento had said the last sentence with cold finality.

"Come Mr…."

"Crowley. Commander John Crowley, United States Navy." Captain replied, giving his name but not our boat's, just as we had been taught.

"Commander Crowley, we've had ample to attack you if that was our intention. Now please, eat and regain your strength."

Captain stood still for a moment, then looked at us, nodded his head, and seated himself in front of his banana leaf of food. We followed his lead, and I quickly resumed my meal, though it was quite cool now.

We ate peacefully for a few minutes, while two of the Battalion patrolled the perimeter, and the rest sat in the shade of the schoolhouse watching us with open curiosity. The boys were now cooking more rice for the guerillas over their fire.

"One more question, if you do not mind," Captain said, "the boys told us not to drink the water. Since they thought we were friends by that time, why would they not want us to drink from the best source of fresh water available?"

Sarmiento smiled and said, "When the owner of that house heard that the Japanese had taken Manila, he assumed he would be chased out of his house at some point. So he hid his tractors and machines deep in the forest, destroyed what he couldn't move and took his family away to safety. Then, in case the Japanese did come, he laced his cistern with arsenic. Our lookout watched all of you drink from there, and that's why we were surprised to find you still alive."

We stared at Howell, who looked shocked himself, then laughed. The tension was finally broken, and everyone relaxed. Sarmiento accepted his portion of rice from the boys and quickly scooped the mounds into his mouth. He finished quickly, and gave instructions to the boys, who ran off in the direction of the house.

"Now look," he said, turning to us, "we don't have a lot of time. I have standing orders from my headquarters that any allied survivors are to be brought to Cape Baliluyan on Palawan. We're going to have to walk north across Bugsuk to get to the kumpit boat I had readied in case you were allies. It's only about eight kilometers. But we have to leave soon because the Japanese patrol is due to land at the great house shortly."

"How shortly?" Captain asked sharply.

Sarmiento looked at the sky, "they usually get here late morning or early afternoon, so they will land anytime now." We looked at each other in alarm. If we had stayed, we would have been captured. Sarmiento must have misinterpreted this because he quickly added, "Don't worry, they will only patrol about a mile inland, then spend the night at the great house. We don't let them patrol much further, so you'll be safe once we get moving."

Captain brushed his hands together in an attempt to rid them of the starchy rice paste and said, "We're ready to move."

Sarmiento smiled. "Not so fast. You have to finish eating, and so do my men. Besides, I have to wait until the boys get back, they are checking to make sure you left nothing at the house that might reveal your presence to them."

My stomach, so long cramped from the lack of food, now felt grossly full from just the handful of rice and bit of fish. The morning sun was warm and nearly lulling me to sleep as insects buzzed lazily around my head.

I must have dozed a bit because the next thing I remember is with the two boys returning and handing Sarmiento with a small item. "What's this?" he said, exhibiting the small piece of glass.

"Oh no," Miller said, as he flipped my binoculars over and looked at them. "That's the magnifying glass from Ensign Jacobson's binoculars. I had just re-assembled them when the boys found us. I must have left that behind."

"Not wise," Sarmiento said, handing the glass to the Captain. "The Japanese may have noticed that and hunted down someone, anyone, to figure out how that got there." His eyebrows knitted in frustration as he attempted to light the pipe in his teeth.

"Mr. Sarmiento—" Captain began.

"Pedro." He corrected.

Captain gave him the magnifying glass. "As a thanks for finding us and very likely saving our lives."

Pedro took the glass, considered it for a moment, then walked into the sunshine and lit his pipe with it in a few seconds. "This is going to come in very handy," he said. "Thank you."

"Now," he raised his voice. "We start." With a few more

commands in his native tongue, the other men leapt to work. In less than a minute, the camp was cleaned, brushed, and restored, all evidence of food, fire, and men gone.

Half of the men, including both boys, were apparently locals who lived nearby, and they departed with a cheerful wave. Pedro placed us in the middle of the rest of the guerillas. Three men in front cut a path for us, and those behind guarded our rear.

"It is not far to the mouth of Bugsuk River," Pedro announced. "If we walk steadily, we should make it by nightfall. Let's go!" He started off, swinging his machete in wide arcs up ahead.

Bugsuk Island was heavily forested and sloped gently uphill, but the wretched coral was always only a few inches beneath the leafy forest floor. We tried to keep up, but exhaustion and our shredded feet quickly took its toll. Pedro and his men tried to hustle us along, but after an hour, it was obvious that we were in too sorry a state to keep a pace that would get us across the island in one day. Eventually, Pedro took mercy and called a quick break to regroup. He spoke some words to the guerillas in the front and they took off.

"You're obviously not going to make it today," he told us, "so I'm making arrangements for us to spend the night in a little village ahead. Hopefully, we can start again in the morning and get to the river tomorrow evening."

"Thank you," Captain panted, and we echoed.

"We can't dawdle too much as we'll need to get at least half way through the island today."

It was 1700 when we finally staggered into the village. Even though we had walked for eight hours, we had travelled only two and half miles. Despite this, I barely noticed it when we entered. Someone guided the eight of us to a hut where bamboo mats were laid out on the floor. I was asleep before I was aware that we had really arrived.

"Come on, get up, get up," Pedro's voice intruded.

"They've cooked dinner for you. It would be impolite to refuse."

We stumbled out of the hut, and I saw the sun in the final stages of setting. The small village, no more than a dozen people, was lit primarily by firelight. Scrawny chickens pecked around the clearing, looking so sick and weak, you couldn't have given them away in the States. There were four huts, constructed of bamboo clustered around a central fire. The people smiled at us, and ushered us to the fire, where glorious smells wafted from a cooking pot suspended by a tripod over the flames.

An older man, who Pedro told us was the village leader, sat down next to us, and at a signal, the women scooped the contents of the pot into coconut shell bowls and handed them to us with shy glances.

"This smells like chicken soup," Russo said, "it reminds me of home."

Pedro smiled and repeated the remark to the village leader. He smiled and said something to us, while gesturing for us to eat. "Meat is rarely eaten here," Pedro told us when he was finished translating. "It is usually only cooked on special occasions, like when they are hosting honored guests."

"Please tell them we are very honored by their meal, and we thank them." Captain said.

Pedro translated for us, and soon, the whole village was joining in the meal, talking to one another, and relaxing. We began to relax with them and started talking amongst ourselves and to our hosts with the help of Pedro.

"They woke you?" I suddenly heard Jim say to Captain, "I didn't hear a thing."

"Believe me, I resisted the attempt too, but I guess once you join the Navy you're never truly free of paperwork no matter where you go."

"Oh?"

"Yeah," Captain sighed. "Pedro needed our names and where we were stationed in order to make a formal report."

Pedro chimed in, "Paper is one of the rarest things on the island, but I still must submit formal reports to headquarters."

The village's water came from a small stream, only about four inches deep, and less than a foot wide. The villagers carried water to us in five-foot long bamboo pipes. Though muddy, the water seemed all right, and at least it was refreshing.

Thankfully, we were sent to bed again after a dessert of wild honey, with assurances from Pedro that he would post guards around the village to warn us of any incoming Japanese.

The next morning Pedro was impatient to move on, so we waved our good-byes to the people of the village and continued our march north.

Though the sleep had helped to revive my energy, my feet continued to burn with each step. I was soon panting and straining to keep up, and we had to rest more often than Pedro was comfortable with.

"Come on," he was urging us. "I've even arranged for a noon meal at another village. If we can possibly get there before noon that is."

"Now much further?" Baumgart asked.

"Not far. Just another kilometer."

Twenty minutes later after a hard uphill climb, Russo gasped out, "HOW much further?"

"Just another kilometer." Pedro said, smilingly.

We looked at each other, but kept going. We were reaching the top of Bugsuk now and had to occasionally pull ourselves up using trees and the vines that twined around them. Colorful birds winged through the trees, trilling. I wished we were not so hurried or exhausted. It was truly an incredible landscape and that was only the impression I got when stopping to gasp and glance around me at every rest point.

"I thought this village was only another kilometer." I told Pedro after we had been walking for over an hour.

"It is."

"Lemme guess, just another kilometer?"

He grinned, "Exactly."

I rolled my eyes and heard several of the guys groan.

Despite our protestations and frequent breaks, we did reach the next village around noon. There were no chickens here, and only one large hut, but they offered us a large pot of blue rice. While surprising to look at, it had only a slightly different flavor from the brown rice, and I was learning to enjoy rice by this point. Our dessert was a tasty concoction of more rice, mixed with wild honey into an incredibly sweet paste.

Pedro allowed us to rest for an hour. The owner of the hut gave us a very large basket of rice, which we later learned was a great sacrifice for him and how the guerillas remained supplied with food. One of the guerillas hoisted the basket onto his back, and we continued our trek.

Five agonizing hours later, we came across a solitary hut on our trail, and the man living there, seeing the guerillas insisted we stop and share a meal of rice with him. My stomach still felt full from lunch, but he insisted.

He cheerfully seated us at his cooking fire and served us another meal of rice. We ate, smiled our thanks, and Pedro excused us to resume our march as soon as it was polite.

After another hour of walking, Tremaine, grinning, called out, "How much farther to this boat?"

"Guess."

"JUST ANOTHER KILOMETER!" we sang out. At least we

were now going downhill.

The sun was hovering over the western horizon when we broke through the jungle onto the banks of a river. A small sailboat rested in the water and a tall man with the most mischievous eyes and smile I'd ever seen, bounded off of it. He greeted Pedro and us in his language.

"This is Sula LaHud." Pedro introduced us quickly. "He is going to take you to Palawan to join the main body of guerillas."

"You're not coming with us?" Captain asked.

"No, I'm needed here. LaHud will take good care of you."

Captain looked unsure of this plan.

"Pedro," he said hesitatingly. "We sure would appreciate it if you could join us. Having someone with us who can translate would be a great help."

Pedro looked at us thoughtfully. "You make a point. While I trust LaHud to get you there safely, I would hate for an emergency to happen and have a language barrier make it worse."

He said something quickly to one of the guerillas, took the basket of rice, and settled himself on the deck. LaHud looked only a little surprised and motioned for us to embark.

The sailboat, or "kumpit" as they called it, was about sixteen feet long, with a pointed bow, six-foot wide beam, a four-foot square stern, and a smooth, round bottom. The deck of the kumpit ran flush with the gunwale from the stern to the mast and was used as storage. Racks ran along each side adding even more storage space. Forward f the mast sat 2 native boys, whose names we learned were Tom-Pong and Kim-Jon.

More supplies were loaded on the kumpit in addition to us. In the end, with twelve people, supplies, and despite all my experience on sailboats, I was amazed to see this thing float, much less make any speed under sail.

LaHud leapt easily onto the stern of his vessel and barked an order. One of the boys untied the kumpit, pushed it into the middle of the river and jumped back aboard. They then affixed two oars and began rowing. It was 1800 hours.

9

GUERILLA HEADQUARTERS

The river was narrow with steeply cut sides on either bank and towering trees hovered over the water. The night sounds of tiny croaking frogs and singing birds began.

The sun was setting on the horizon as we reached the mouth of the river. Suddenly, Kim-Jon, stood, yelled, and pointed at the beach. Sailor heeled the kumpit around and headed for it. I grabbed the edge of the kumpit, while straining my eyes in the falling darkness, but couldn't see anything or anyone. My crewmates also looked tense, and Pedro seemed alert.

The kumpit slid into the beach. Both boys jumped off the boat and began picking up something dark on the water's edge. They handed it to LaHud who started talking and gesturing with it.

Pedro translated. "It's a type of seaweed," he said handing some to each of us. "A doctor told him that it is good medicine, so he always stops to pick some up if he sees it."

It was difficult to see in the twilight and appeared almost black. It tasted like a bitter sweet pickle laced with iodine. The boys, after gathering a mass of seaweed, pushed the kumpit back into the water and deftly climbed in.

They then raised the sail as LaHud quickly maneuvered the kumpit around and off into the dark sea. He and Kim-Jon navigated the hidden reefs, in the dark, with very little strain.

I vaguely remembered, from the charts aboard the *Flier*, that this area was riddled with reefs and large areas that read "exposed at low tide". Several times I saw waves breaking over reefs just feet from the kumpit as it glided past. There was little chance that the men and I could have gotten through here if left to our own devices.

"You're an amazing sailor, LaHud," I said visibly impressed.

"I'll say," Jim said. "I wouldn't dream of navigating anything through this area in the dark, especially without charts of the area."

When Pedro translated, LaHud smiled and shrugged his shoulders, as if to say 'Ah, it's no big deal.' After that we all began calling him "Sailor" or "the Sailor", as a sign of our respect for his ability to sail and navigate simultaneously.

"If all goes well, we'll be at Baliluyan before dawn." Pedro told the Captain. "The reefs and the passages during the low tide tonight are forcing us to go several miles north before we can turn south for the cape. But LaHud is the best, and we should be there and under cover before the morning patrols can see us."

"Wouldn't the Japanese think this is just a fishing boat?" Captain asked.

"Not with this many passengers aboard," he replied. "We'll be searched the moment we're seen."

Sailor suddenly barked a command, and I jumped. So did Tom-Pong and Kim-Jon, who thrust their oars out and pushed the kumpit away from an exposed coral mound that suddenly loomed out of the water.

The time passed quickly, and soon Palawan's dark bulk loomed ahead of us. The wind died about halfway across and the boys had to row the rest of the way there. The kumpit gently slid up the beach at Baliluyan around 0300. The boys leapt over the side and hauled the boat in further in as armed men swarmed down from the trees, calling greetings to Sailor.

They quickly hustled us off the kumpit and ashore while others pulled the boat in closer and hid it under layers of palms and bracken. There was a narrow, twisting path under the trees, which I stumbled along. I could barely make out a roofline looming overhead when my hands were grasped and planted on a ladder in front of me. I climbed up and into a hut. The floor seemed to be bamboo or whole branches laid side by side. We were guided into a room, and

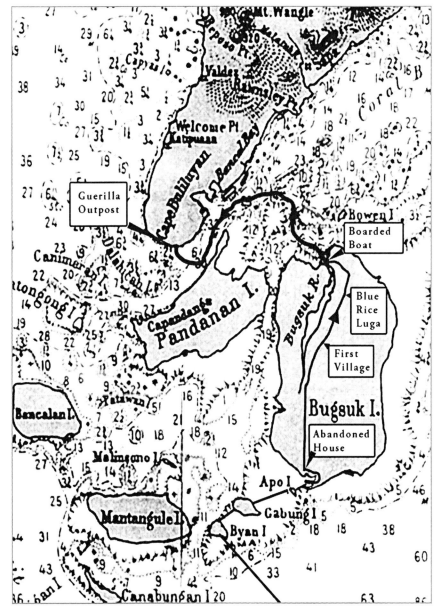

This map shows the approximate route the Fliers took from rafting to Palawan. Original map from the family of Ens. Al "Jake" Jacobson

what little light there had been outside, vanished. I heard the grunts of my fellow Fliers, when suddenly a match flared and lit an oil lamp. I could see we were in a small bamboo room, full of many men.

"Hello," a Filipino greeted us in perfect English, holding out his identification, "My name is Sergeant Pasqual de la Cruz of the USAFFE[22]. These are my men. Most of us were educators, though now we are full-time guerillas. We man Cape Baliluyan for the war effort." His men quickly introduced themselves by name, before inviting us to sit on the floor near the tables and handed us bowls of rice sweetened with sugar cane. "Can we get you anything right now?" De la Cruz asked.

"Our feet are torn up pretty bad," Captain said. "Do you have any medicine?"

De la Cruz went to a small shelf in the corner of the room where he took down a small round jar. Inside was whitish salve full of bugs and dirt. "I'm afraid this is all we have." He said.

Captain politely declined, and I let out a mental sigh of relief. I wasn't sure whether that salve would be worse than the seawater and dirt we've experienced thus far.

"Tomorrow night, all of you will be transported north to Brooke's Point where a contingent of US Army Coastwatchers will take charge of you."

"And from there?" Captain asked.

"I don't know," de la Cruz replied, "but there are at least three other military men waiting for rescue there. With the addition of all of you, they may be able to convince someone to come and pick you

---

[22] USAFFE: United States Armed Forces in the Far East. In July of 1941, as tensions in the Pacific increased, President Roosevelt ordered the Commonwealth of the Philippines military to be absorbed into the American military with MacArthur as the head. These armed forces where therefore one military with one commander, so there could be no infighting over coordinating two militaries in the Philippines should an invasion occur.

up."

We soon learned that these guerillas were all locals, and had friends and relatives scattered up and down the southern part of Palawan. The family members helped with food and supplies, and if the Japanese decided to take over this part of Palawan, they could easily blend in and disappear.

They primarily watched the North Balabac Passage, tracking the movements of ships and submarines. They would then transmit that information north where it could be recorded and transmitted to GHQ as needed.

Despite their in-depth knowledge of the area, most of them had been cut off from all news of the wider world as they had no radios or newspapers since the fall of Manila four years prior. They were eager to hear what was happening in the war, and how things were going. We were more than happy to repay their efforts with all the news we had heard before leaving Perth: the fall of the St. Petersburg siege, the advance of the Allies in Europe after landing in Normandy, and the failed assassination coup on Hitler. In the Pacific, we told them about the re-taking of Midway, Guadalcanal, the Battle of the Coral Sea, and the most recent battles in the Mariana Islands, including the huge naval battle in the Philippine Sea, the sinking of a massive Japanese aircraft carrier, and the re-taking of Saipan. Everyone cheered and laughed and clapped, excited to hear that the war was going our way after all.

De la Cruz, noting the time, dismissed his men to their duties and sent us to bed. The only place left to sleep was on the tables. We didn't mind though, as long as they didn't mind eating breakfast outside, because none of us were likely to wake up soon.

We woke up at around 9:30 that morning, to the sound of men working outside. De la Cruz walked in the room, his arms loaded with piles of clothes.

"Good morning gentlemen." He heaved the clothes onto the

closest table. "I don't know if we'll be able to help all of you, but the men and I scrounged all the spare clothes we had. Figured after wandering around in your underwear for several days, you may appreciate having something..." He paused, and looked over the pile, "well, something a bit more decent to wear."

We sat in stunned silence at their generosity, until Captain said, "Tell your men, thank you very much, from all of us."

"You're welcome," de la Cruz grinned. "Um, they're all different sizes, so good luck. We found more pants than shirts, and of course, our shoes and boots long since have fallen apart, so you'll still have to go barefoot. But we hope this helps. I'll be back in about a half hour with breakfast."

We all ended up with a pair of pants when we were done. Mine were light tan, cotton, a little threadbare in the seat and knees, and so large I had to roll the legs up three times. The shirt I found was about three sizes too small, and couldn't be buttoned across my chest, but I felt more human and definitely more presentable.

De la Cruz returned with bowls and a pot full of rice for breakfast. While we were eating, he questioned us in order to fill out his records and reports. We willingly told him our names, ranks, and serial numbers, as trained, but after that, it became a battle of friendly wits.

"Name of boat?" He asked.

"Classified, I'm afraid," Captain responded.

"I thought as much. Submarine though, that much I can tell."

"What makes you say that?"

"Deduction, mostly. The relationships between the officers and enlisted that I've seen in your group is too close and friendly for a large surface vessel. Also, we would have seen a surface ship in the area, especially one sinking. You showed up unexpectedly, and we've received no word or record of anyone seeing your ship. So you had to come from a sub, likely making a crossing at night." He paused, and Captain did not deny his deductions. "You cannot tell me your mission either I suppose."

"Sorry, but no I can't."

"Can you tell me if you were heading out to sea or back to a home port?"

"No."

"How long you've been to sea?"

"No, sorry."

De la Cruz looked a little frustrated, but understanding. It was the nature of our business. We were trained to give nothing about our boat away, lest the information somehow fall into enemy hands. We trusted de la Cruz, but one never knew. The Japanese could capture him and he could reveal something under torture. It was safer for us and him if he knew as little about us and our now-doomed mission.

De la Cruz, glanced at what appeared to be his records, and on top I spied a small slip of paper with our names, ranks, and serials written in miniscule handwriting. That was Pedro's list, I thought, and de la Cruz's brow furrowed as his ticked us off one by one on it. He then looked again at the Captain.

"The hazards of working in covert and top-secret missions," he smiled wanly. "If you cannot tell me the name of your boat, can you tell me where were you sunk, how long ago, how many got off, do you think there are any other survivors, and did you see any indications of other life?"

"I can't say where we were sunk, except that we could see Balabac, Comiran and Palawan moment before we sank," Captain said, skirting the issue. "There were fifteen men that called muster moments afterwards. At least three were definitely lost at sea, and the other four were likely as well. I don't think anyone else could have survived."

"Unless..." I said quietly.

"Yes Jacobson?" Captain said and both he and de la Cruz looked at me with interest.

"Sir, you know the depth of the water we were passing through. She wasn't necessarily crushed when she went down. If the crew was able to shut one or two of the bulkheads, it is possible that some of those in the stern were able to get out using the aft escape hatch. It's a long shot, but still a possibility. And they may have gotten out after we left the area."

"It *is* a long shot," de la Cruz conceded, rifling through his papers, and removing one. "You should be aware that fourteen days ago, the Japanese were transporting 4 prisoners to Puerto Princessa prison camp from Balabac City. We know that the prisoners were on a submarine and that at least six survived the sinking. However, all were captured and two were killed on the island. Is this the same submarine?"

"Fourteen days you said?" Captain questioned sharply.

"Well the transport of the prisoners was fourteen days ago, yes."

"We've been shipwrecked for only nine days, so it must be another sub."

De la Cruz looked again at each of us, and sighed. "Damn it. Now I have TWO submarines and TWO crews to looks for." He jotted a few notes down on his papers and looked up. "All right then. I'll send Pedro back to Bugsuk to search the small islands again for any more survivors. I'll send another group to cover Mantangule and Padanan Islands, and I'll also notify my people on Balabac to keep a sharp watch out."

"Do you use radios?" Howell asked.

"Not since the fall of the Philippines have we had radios. I once got to visit the Coastwatchers when they were stationed on Mantangule and listened to their radio. It was the first time I had heard from anyone outside the islands in nearly three years.

"Then how do you communicate?" Howell perused.

De la Cruz signaled a young guerilla. He couldn't have been more than a teenager, spoke to him quickly in the native tongue while giving him several pieces of paper. The young man departed with startling speed and was out of the hut in a moment. "We have our ways, and you may find they are surprisingly fast considering we don't use a radio. As the Coastwatchers will tell you, radios are risky too. The Japanese can triangulate your position if you send out enough signals. This way, we stay under the enemy radar, but by nightfall, half my teams will know my message, the other half within a day or two. It's sufficient."

"Wait a moment," I said. "Last night, you mentioned sending us north to the guerilla headquarters this evening, but now we're going to Mantangule?"

"No," de la Cruz straightened his papers and stood, "The Coastwatchers actually started on Ramos Island near Balabac, but moved to Mantangule for safety. That turned out to be too dangerous too, with their radio dispatches, so we helped them move north where we already had a contingent of guerillas. You'll see it tomorrow at dawn, if we're lucky. Despite being closer to the prison camp, it's actually safer there than the other places.

"Until about 1500, you're on your own. I have work to do, but you are welcome to explore this area if you like. Keep off the beach and don't wander out of sight of these barracks, please. After the afternoon patrol flyover, it'll be safe enough to start out, and we'll have dinner before leaving."

After the rapid march of the past two days and the cramped conditions on the kumpit, I decided to take a leisurely stroll through the camp to stretch my legs.

I explored the guerilla's outpost. Its layout was something I later found to be a standard pattern for these kinds of settlements. The house was made of bamboo and built on stilts about six feet high. Trenches for defense and fighting, ringed the building, bridged in places with simple planks, easily removed in an emergency. Chickens pecked around a small coop nearby.

There was a sugarcane field and a large cast iron cauldron behind the house where the guerillas boiled down seawater for their salt. Everything was functional, some things even doubly so. The roof of the house was pitched so the rainwater ran to one corner and collected in a cistern for drinking.

We rested for most of the afternoon, and the various guerillas came and went as they went about their jobs.

Dinner was a feast. They gave us a thinly sliced jerky of what they called carabao, which I later learned was a type of water buffalo. It was salty and delicious, but was so tough I could barely tear it with my teeth. The Filipinos, who enjoyed watching our attempts at this unfamiliar food, tore and chewed with a relish. This was a special dinner that was not often served, and they were enjoying it. They also had a paste made of coconut and honey which tasted great.

The zero flew overhead on schedule shortly after 1500, and we prepared to go. There was another, smaller kumpit next to ours. Pedro, with his assignment to look for more Fliers and the other submarine's crew, was returning to Bugsuk with Tom-Pong on the smaller boat, while we would go on the larger kumpit with Sailor and Kim-Jon. Another young man, Kong, replaced Tom-Pong in the rower's place. Also coming with us was Sergeant de la Cruz. We said good-bye Pedro and his party, and set sail for Brooke's Point

Once again, Sailor steered us so quickly and skillfully I almost looked for an outboard motor. For over two hours, the heavily loaded kumpit flew lightly in front of a strong wind. The land raced smoothly by and we settled down for an easy trip.

The sun's rays glittered across the water, the humid air rising in waves. The sky transitioned so smoothly to sea at the horizon that it was nearly impossible to see the difference. I closed my eyes against the bright sunlight.

The calming movement of the kumpit, slicing through the waves, rocking back and forth, and the warmth of the sun, relaxed me, and I drifted off into my thoughts. I had always found something comforting and soothing about the motion of a sailboat on the water. It was quiet, perfect. *Flier*, under battery power, had been like this, smooth and quiet as a whisper, except for the voices of eighty men talking, the background hum of all the electronics, the beeping of the radar, the crackling of the radio, the various noises from the sonar, and, of course, the creaking of the sub under pressure, which produced a sound like no other.

"I got a possible target bearing 015 true. It appears to be approaching."[23] Captain, eyes buried in the periscope, announced. We were heading south along Luzon's western coast, dodging the nearly ceaseless Zeros patrolling close to Japan's Filipino stronghold.

"All stop."

The sea's glass-smooth surface made using the periscope nearly impossible without causing a wake unless we were not moving. Even so, the strong sunlight could cast a gleam or shadow that was easily spotted. The Target Acquisition Periscope whirred up through the well and the captain's eyes buried themselves again into the eyepieces. "I've got smoke columns. One, two…three…oh boy, this is going to be a biggie."

"Sir." Radioman Paul Barron, at the Sonar station, held the headphones tightly to his head as he spoke quickly. "I can distinguish six distinct prop noises with a background mish-mash of at least three, possibly more."

For a quarter of an hour they approached. In all, eleven freighters

---

[23] These events took place June 13, 1944 off of Cape Bolinao, Luzon Island, Philippines.

and six escorts, bristling with guns, and a nearly endless supply of depth charges advanced on our position. The escorts protected the freighters on one side while the shoreline prevented access from the other. That gave us two options. We could attack from the seaward side, shooting the torpedoes through the line of escorts to hit the freighters. While that would give us the most room to maneuver, the torpedoes were unreliable enough that we would more likely hit nothing or the escorts, neither of which advanced the Allied cause. If we wedged ourselves between the beach and the freighters, we would have a beautifully clear shot. However, that left us no room to maneuver once the depth charges began.

"They're coming straight at us." Jim reported to Captain, peeking through the periscope quickly, before sending it into the well.

"Ok. Three degrees starboard." He picked up the voice-activated telephone and switched the dial to the Forward Torpedo Room. "Mr. Lindeman? Ready all torpedo tubes." He twisted the dial again, this time to the After Torpedo Room, "Mr. Wall? Ready all tubes, and be ready for a quick turnaround."

"Angle *Flier's* bow towards the shore," Captain ordered. "We'll target that oil tanker in front. We'll fire all four stern torpedoes at that one and then turn around and aim the bow tubes. Hopefully we can get off all ten shots before they can react." He flicked the "Battle Stations" alarm, and the crew ran to their stations, with two more joining us in the very crowded conning tower.

Because of our close quarters and limited space to maneuver, Captain was going to attempt an attack while completely submerged, which was much more difficult than the standard, "Surface, Aim, and Shoot" attack that most submarines did. *Flier* smoothly banked and maneuvered to where her stern angled toward the unwary tanker, who was so secure in her escort and protection that she wasn't even zig-zagging like she would on the open sea.

As we waited quietly for our prey to come in range, *Flier* began to…drift. It was so subtle I didn't realize what was happening, attributing the slight sense of movement to a cross-current. Suddenly, her stern dropped. I had to grab onto the rail near the control room hatch to steady myself as we began diving rear first.

"Lieutenant Casey! What's happening?!" Captain yelled down the hatch.

I glanced down the hatch to see three seamen straining at the stern plane wheel, which refused to move. Ed quickly ordered men aft to check the manual controls and control her from there if necessary.

"I don't know sir." Ed said. "The stern places failed. We can't fix her here and we're going to try and control it manually in the stern."

"Blow stern ballast tanks to compensate!"

"Blowing stern tanks, aye!" I heard the hiss of the pressurized air as it flooded the stern ballast tanks. *Flier*'s stern leveled out then continued to rise to the surface again with increasing speed.

"Power restored!" Ed announced.

"Flood stern ballast tanks!"

"Flooding tanks, aye sir!" Commands bounced off each other. *Flier*'s stern settled back down, but only for five minutes before the stern dropped again.

"Blow tanks, Snyder!" Ed's voice was authoritative, disguising the hint of fear I knew was there. *Flier*'s stern dropped like a pendulum. I grasped the periscopes to maintain my footing, and heard the shattering of crockery and the yelps of pain as the men stumbled. Once again she leveled out, then began rising to the surface, rear first.

I could feel the pounding of dozens of feet as the men raced from nose to tail using their own weight to try and compensate for *Flier*'s buoyancy problem.

Minutes later, she stabilized, and Ed spoke through the conning tower hatch. "Power is restored to the stern planes, and the planes seem to be responding normally."

"Thank you, Casey. After the fight I want you to conduct a full investigation of what happened." Captain's voice was calm, but I heard the ragged edge to his breathing.

"Aye aye, sir," Casey said.

We were all shaky, and trying not to show it. This was the first time *Flier* had just inexplicably failed. We tried not to think about this happening during the attack.

Still unaware of *Flier*'s presence, the convoy continued to approach. We waited for thirty minutes for the convoy to come in range. The air almost crackled with all the pent-up energy. Every few minutes Captain would raise the periscope, quickly glance around, and lower it again in a practiced move. The Torpedo rooms were packed full of men, each tube loaded and prepared, just waiting for the final orders.

Captain began feeding coordinates, bearings, and speeds to Miner who then inputted the data into the Torpedo Data Computer. Miner then relayed the settings to the torpedo rooms, so the torpedo crew could adjust the trajectories.

Crouched at the periscope, which was just barely peeking above the surface, the Captain signaled to Jim who handed him the remote firing button for the after torpedo room. The lights for tubes seven through ten were lit up, announcing the torpedoes were prepped and ready to fire.

"Open up a channel to the aft torpedo room," Captain ordered.

"Channel open, sir,"

"…Fire seven!" He squeezed his trigger, enabling the firing button in the torpedo room.

"Seven Away!" Wall's voice sounded over the intercom.

"Fire eight!"

"Eight away!"

Nine and ten were soon sent on their way and for a brief moment, we could hear the banshee-shriek of their props as they screamed away to the tanker.

It should only take about two and a half minutes at this distance to reach the tanker, and I instinctively began my own countdown.

"Turn her around!" Liddell ordered the Control Room.

"Yes, sir!" Ed replied.

Flier banked quickly underwater. She turned as quickly as she could to keep away from the shore, and lined up for her next kill.

Captain raised the periscope and ducked reflexively. "Whoa! We went a little too far, the next freighter is only a hundred yards away or so."

"That's too close," Liddell said, "How's our sightline on number three?"

"Good enough for a narrow spread," Captain replied, turning the periscope slightly, "but I think we're out of time…"

We were. I heard Liddell mutter, "…three…two…one…"

There was a pause as we all looked at Barron, clutching the headphones to his head. He shook his head. The first torpedo had missed.

A space of a few seconds…three…two…one…

Rumble…

"Got her!" Barron said, pumping his fist in victory. Moments later, "Two good hits sir!"

KA-BOOM!

The tanker screamed as she tore herself apart, the shock waves causing *Flier* to quiver and groan, despite being over half-mile away.

Captain raised the periscope and whooped. "She's going down!" He cried, and *Flier* herself dove, "ducking" the periscope underwater. "What the? No!" Captain said, "Periscope depth, our target just went down, not us!"

"Sir?" Barron's voice sounded urgent. "Escorts are closing in on our position fast."

"Belay the last order, DIVE!"

Flier pointed her nose for the depths, and I started to swallow rapidly to pop the pressure in my ears that steadily mounted. The thrumming of the escort's props started their war beat through the hull, rapidly approaching and shaking our thin steel skin.

Flier hitched, then slipped again, her stern sliding towards the depths. I knew the eighteen or so men who were already struggling to reload the after tubes would now frantically be pulling at the manual levers, trying to force the planes back level.

WHAM!

The first depth charge shook us.

WHA-WHAM!

Flier held, though she wobbled side to side, and her stern seemed to slowly pick back up.

Snapping, groaning noises were easily heard through the hull. Whoever we hit must be sinking.

"All Stop!" Captain ordered. "Keep her level!" *Flier*'s props stilled, and we waited. After the last depth charge attack, I kind of knew what to expect, and grasped onto the map table, and bent my knees slightly. Already, the temperature was raising, and the sweat started to run down my back.

Barron looked up, panting slightly, his knuckles white as they gripped the headphones. "They pulled away sir, the convoy is moving away, but the escorts have stopped." A moment later, we knew why.

PING!

The escorts sent out their Sonar reach, looking for us, and seconds later, their engines started.

"Here they come, sir!"

I gripped, held on tight, and heard the vibrations of the escort's props even over the groans of our victim.

Click!

WHAM

WHAM-WHAM

WHAM!...WHAM!

Six escorts, I thought, *God, help us all.*

They worked us over thoroughly, then pulled away again. Barron announced they stopped, then started their pinging. Playing possum wasn't going to work this time.

"If they want to find us, let's let them know where we are. Head port, four-five degrees, full!" Captain ordered.

Flier gripped the water, and laboriously slithered left. Her stern planes were shaky, and tended to slip, but the guys in the back were taking care of us the best they could. "They've got a fix on us!" Barron reported.

"Heading!" Captain asked.

"Bearing one–two–zero relative."

"Helm! Turn one–two–zero starboard. Head for that sound. Planesmen, take her down, to two–one–zero feet."

Flier spiraled down, and we passed beneath our pursuers. Nearly a minute later, nearly a dozen explosions sounded behind us.

"All stop." Captain said, and *Flier*'s props stilled. "Mr. Barron, tell me when you hear them start again."

We waited again, as depth charges rained down on our former position. There was silence, then, "Active Sonar sir!"

"Tell me when they start up and their bearing."

Moments later, "Pursuing, at two–one–nine relative."

"Ahead full, bearing four–five to starboard!"

She turned, and we scuttled out of the way. Barron was driven nearly insane over the next three hours as *Flier* would settle, wait for the Active sonar to find us, then quickly shoot beneath, between, beside, or behind our pursuers, hiding our prop noise under theirs. They hit us with everything they had, dropping three to ten at a time, sometimes close enough *Flier* would rock in the shock waves, throwing my balance. If I hadn't practically grown up on sailboats, I would not have been able to keep my feet.

We risked everything in that tiny corner, trapped between the escorts and the corpse of our victim. Between attacks I had to chart our position and the escorts based only on Barron's reports, and had to make sure we were not about to ground anywhere.

Once, one of the escorts passed just feet above us. She traveled the full length of *Flier* so close, we heard the rumble of her engines and the thrum of her props. Everyone held his breath and watched the ceiling of the Conning Tower, barely daring to breathe, and *Flier* shook in the wash of her attacker's huge props.

She passed overhead, but the thrashing of the water was too loud to hear the splash of the depth charge. We waited, trembling, the suspense much worse again, than the actual attack.

My watch seemed too loud in the tense silence, as it ticked away the seconds, then a minute, then another…when would it come?

Wham

Wh-Wha—Wham

Wham…Wham…wham…

We collectively let out our breath and grinned at each other, the closest we could safely get to cheering. They were giving hell to some empty stretch of ocean behind us.

My head was ringing. I had been crouched in the conning tower for nearly five hours. My chart was scrawled with *Flier's* insane circular path, looking more like a child's first drawing than our escape route.

"We're too close to Manila," Captain grunted between his teeth, after another charge went off behind us, close enough to be clearly heard, but too far away to cause any significant damage. "They're only a few hours away, they don't have to conserve anything. They're going to give us every bit they've got."

"How many has it been? I've lost count," Earle Dressell asked from the helm.

"One hundred and five," Barron said from the Sonar station. He looked worn and pale from the stress.

"That's the largest number of depth charges in one attack I've ever heard of," Buddy Voight whispered, from where he crouched near the Radar screens

"It only counts if we live through it," Liddell whispered back.

But that was it. The escorts stopped their attack, moved away, and then, Barron couldn't hear them on Sonar anymore.

We stayed underwater, the boat now unbearably hot and humid. There wasn't a square inch of dry skin on me anymore, sweat dotted my chart. But still, we did not move. Rivulets of water were running down the pipes and periscopes, but still, we waited, watching Barron, who listened intently.

After a half hour, Captain finally ordered a very quiet "Periscope Depth."

Flier gracefully rose, her stern planes now behaving, and Captain raised the Attack Periscope and carefully looked around. We waited.

"Take her up, Mr. Casey," Captain announced.

There was a quiet cheer, as *Flier* soared up and broke the surface, suddenly bobbing up and down in the waves. With a nod from Captain, I climbed up to the Bridge Hatch, wrenched the wheel and stepped into the fresh air and twilight sky.

"Phew! What the—?" They heard me yell.

"What is it? What happened?" I heard several voices call up.

"Would you believe we've been stuck underwater long enough that fresh air actually smells bad?!"

Sailor started speaking rapidly and turned the boat towards shore. Kong and Kim-Jon nimbly ran from the bow to the mast, hauling down the sail. Within moments, she slowed to a crawl, and Kim-Jon and Tom-Pong grabbed the oars and began to haul her through the water. Sailor, manning the tiller, raised himself onto his knees, watching the horizon keenly. Something large and grey was out there.

"What's going on?" We asked.

"It's a Japanese ship," said de la Cruz. "They are less likely to see us with the sail down or care about a small fishing boat cruising near shore. Everyone stay low to the deck so they can't see how many are on here. If they don't pass quickly or move further out to sea, we may not be able to put sails up again soon enough to get us to Brooke's Point tonight."

The large destroyer continued its approach, and soon I could see every detail. Guam and Mariana, a thousand miles east, had been taken by our Marines just before *Flier* left, and now Japan was fortifying the Philippines, their last great stronghold before their own islands were at risk. We heard rumor before we left that the U.S. was planning a massive invasion of the Philippines for late this year, and Japan possibly next.

Sailor kept our kumpit hugging shore while watching the destroyer warily. The sun sank behind the island's mountains, throwing us in shadow, and then the destroyer. She continued on, though taking her time, never changing course, but close enough that we could clearly hear her engines.

When she finally passed astern, just as the sun set, we noticed something else: our fair wind had died. Kong and Kim Jong, who had been rowing during the hours the destroyer passed us, couldn't stop. De la Cruz and Sailor took shifts with the boys but until Sailor took the kumpit into free water, we couldn't help with the rowing since we didn't know the paths through the reefs.

Sailor was amazing to watch. He was an artist when it came to his boat. When Kim-Jon and Kong took up their second shift, he fished out a heavy steel plate, tripod, and cauldron from beneath the deck before settling himself and the new gear at the tiller. He lit a fire on the steel plate, set up the tripod over the fire, filled the cauldron full of water and hung that from the tripod, and proceeded to cook our rice dinner. While cooking he continued steering the kumpit with his foot, and rowed with another

After dinner the wind started up again, and the sail was quickly raised back into place. I hoped this meant we'd get to Brooke's Point by sunrise.

Sailor and De la Cruz kept watching the wind direction, the stars, and the progress of the crescent moon. Something was troubling them, especially Sailor. Finally, Sailor seemed to say something with a note of finality in his voice, and gestured towards us.

"Sailor says by the time we get to Brooke's Point, it will be broad daylight and well past the first patrol. It's too great a risk. He knows a place nearby where we can probably find food and a good night's sleep."

Sailor turned the kumpit into the mouth of a river, nearly hidden by the shadows of the overhanging jungle. Everyone took a turn rowing hard against the current for another two hours, in the dark, with only Sailor and De la Cruz calling out instructions. It felt good to be active, but too soon my arms and chest burned from the effort.

We finally pulled up to a pair of bamboo and thatch huts, and four people spilled out of the small hut that sat on stilts on the banks of the river. Sailor threw a rope to a young man, and he, with an older man, quickly helped haul us in and secured the kumpit to a tree.

We were ushered quickly into the house, and I was asleep on a bamboo mat before I actually realized it.

BROOKE'S POINT

The sunlight streamed through the windows as I woke up that morning. I could smell something fabulous cooking, and got up and ducked my head out of the hut.

Our host, an older man, saw me, smiled, and gestured me to the fire, where Captain and Liddell already sat. A pot happily simmered over the fire, and our host's wife stirred and sniffed it.

"Morning," Liddell greeted me.

"Morning sir," I replied. "What's cooking? It smells spectacular." The cook looked up, and I sniffed the air pointedly and smiled widely. She grinned back.

"It's coconut chicken stew," De la Cruz said, crouching down next to us.

"Oh," I felt conflicted. On one hand, I was grateful for the chicken they killed just for us, but I remembered how much of a sacrifice killing a chicken was for these people.

De la Cruz must have sensed what I was thinking. "It is a sacrifice, but it is one they gladly give. To refuse would be a serious breach in manners. They're glad to be able to help fight off the Japanese in any way they can."

De la Cruz then told us more about the family: the older man and woman were husband and wife, whose daughter had just married the young man we saw the night before. Everyone in the small family took time to make us feel comfortable while the rest of the crew woke up and came out to the fire. The stew was delicious and I enjoyed having something besides rice for a meal.

We spent most of the day talking with de la Cruz about the guerillas work and their history while waiting for the afternoon patrol. After noon, the father began talking to De la Cruz and Sailor, and seemed to be asking a favor of them since both acted slightly uncomfortable. They eventually agreed to it and the old man was overjoyed. He clasped hands with both men, then ran to hug his daughter. In moments, all four were talking excitedly and racing around the clearing.

"What's going on?" I asked De la Cruz.

"The hospitality given last night was freely done," he said, as he sat back down next to me, "but in return, it is polite to show another favor. The daughter and her new husband have relatives near Brooke's Point, and we've been asked to take them in the kumpit. If we could not take them, they would have go north on foot."

I heard a squawk, and saw the daughter gently bundling two chickens in a basket before securing the lid.

"We've accepted, but transporting them means transporting her dowry and household goods too." There was a thud as a large bag of rice landed next to the basket of chickens, which was now surrounded by bundles of clothes, and several pots full of more goods.

"This could get interesting." I mused.

By the time we had lashed and stored all the newlywed's worldly goods on the kumpit, we had only enough room left for each of us to sit cross-legged. The bride bid a tearful good bye to her parents, then boarded the kumpit, which now sat just a bare inch above the water.

"Where's Sailor?" Wes asked.

I looked behind me, and saw De la Cruz at the rudder. "Sailor had to take care of some things, said he'd catch up with us later if he could."

"Aw, gee, I'm going to miss him," Tremaine said.

We all will, I thought sadly.

Kong and Kim-Jon shoved us off and the kumpit labored northwards. Even with a good breeze we were now so loaded down that she could only lumber along instead of the free-flying feeling from before.

Everyone sat, lost in their own thoughts. Looking around in the daylight, I could now see that where we had spent the night was in a large bay. To continue north we first had to steer out of the bay, then around a large coral reef at the northern tip before we could head north to Brooke's Point.

A few hours into the journey, just after we had cleared the reef, we heard a shout, and saw Sailor swimming towards the kumpit. He laughed when he saw how packed down the kumpit was and carefully hauled himself up to the deck, trying to avoid the numerous items piled everywhere.

"I knew I could catch up with you later, the moment I saw the sheer size of this dowry that was coming with us." he said through de la Cruz, "She's a fast little thing, but not when this loaded down!" The bride suddenly looked both proud and mildly embarrassed, while the rest of us, even her husband, laughed.

"I took the opportunity to visit my wife and kids who live near here for a couple of hours." He continued through de la Cruz.

I was glad to see Sailor again. He was a remarkable man, completely at home at the sea, and amazingly dextrous. Later, I looked back to see what dinner was, and saw another amazing feat of multi-tasking. He again manned the tiller with one foot, and rowed an oar with the other. He adjusted the main sheet with his teeth, stirred the cauldron of rice with one hand and with his other hand he was sewing.

I craned and twisted my neck until I could see that Baumgart's pants were missing! He had apparently split his pants out the back and Sailor was fixing them, and for all this, Sailor always had a smile on his face.

Dinner that night was rice pancakes, fried to a golden crisp on the metal plate, just near the edge of the fire. Even without butter or any condiments, they were delicious, light and nutty tasting.

The sun set, and we continued north. Sailor planned on sailing all night, and arriving at Brooke's Point before the morning patrol. Weighed down, and with a less favorable wind, the kumpit seemed to crawl at times, though Sailor and his crew maneuvered through the reef skillfully. I tried to twist myself into a comfortable position, but with no room, I think I ended up leaning on Howell while sleeping.

Discomfort and light dragged me out of sleep the next morning, drenched with dew. I stretched carefully, trying not to knock anyone or anything into the sea.

Soon Sailor began shouting at some small sailboats off the port side and heeled the kumpit around to meet up with them. As we drew nearer, I saw that the sailboats were not much more than outrigger canoes with a mast and sail. De la Cruz called them "boncas" and told us that locals often used them for spear-fishing. I watched as a darkly tanned man leapt with practiced grace over the side, a short spear in his hand. Moments later he surfaced, with an eel neatly speared on the end. Another man surfaced with three fish on his spear.

The fishermen began chatting excitedly with Sailor. They were apparently having a good morning, for several canoes had baskets piled high with fish, eels, squid and other things. The first fisherman I had seen was apparently a good friend of Sailor's and handed him the eel on his spear, then retrieved two more decently-sized fish, telling us through gestures that it was a gift for all of us. Sailor thanked him on our behalf, and we went on our way again.

The fish themselves looked like a type of mackerel, but the eel, I wasn't sure about, until Sailor roasted it over the fire and passed it out along with more rice for breakfast. The fish was good, light and salty from the water. The eel though, was different. The bride and groom had cried out in excitement when the fisherman had given it to us, and now I knew why. It was fatty, rich, and very good. Sailor didn't have any seasonings on him, but this needed none.

About an hour after that, we heard someone shouting at us, and the sail quickly dropped to the deck. Another kumpit pulled alongside and held a quick, multi-layered conversation with de la Cruz and Sailor.

"That was a friend of LaHud's and mine," de la Cruz said as he carefully picked his way back across the deck. "He is coming from Brooke's Point. We asked if there were any patrols ahead, but there haven't been today. We should be in Brooke's Point in a couple of hours."

Thick, acrid smoke accosted my nose. I started to cough violently. The only description I could give it was that it smelled like campfire with a tire tossed on for good measure. Kong, rowing in the stern was taking deep draws on what looked like a cigarette. Russo and Baumgart, denied their smokes for days, looked at the cigarette longingly, and gestured at Kong until he understood that they wanted one too. He smiled and quickly rolled one for each of them, then held out a third for any takers. There were none.

A moment later, Russo and Baumgart began to cough and retch, heaving over the sides of the kumpit while Kong laughed. He said something, and de la Cruz laughed as well. "Funny how two American military men can't handle a Filipino cigarette!"

"Cigarette nothing!" Russo coughed. "I think that thing was made of..." he coughed again.

"Tar, Russo," Baumgart gasped. "That wasn't tobacco, that was some kind of hot tar or rubber tires or something mixed in."

"I could've told you that stuff will kill you," Jim said smiling, "you couldn't figure that out from the stench?"

"Apparently not, sir," Russo said.

Finally, just as I was starting to watch the skies anxiously for the

This photo, taken after WWII one mile south of Brooke's Point, shows how Brooke's Point looked during WWII. Jacobson said that only the Mayor's house remained on the beach. The rest of the village had been bombed and destroyed. Photo courtesy of the family of Ens. Al "Jake" Jacobson

afternoon patrol, Brooke's Point finally came into focus. The point itself jutted out into the ocean forming a small, protected cove. I wouldn't necessarily call it a bay, and it certainly wasn't sheltered enough for more than a few small boats like this one.

Sailor came about, slowing the kumpit still further, and directed Kong and Kim-Jon to start rowing. De la Cruz picked his way to the bow of the ship, where he stood tall, searching the jungle for the lookouts that were sure to be on watch. Unless he could secure our entrance, these lookouts might shoot us before we could disembark.

No challenge came as we rounded the point. De la Cruz began shouting and calling. Eventually, a sleepy-looking guerilla stood up and recognized us. After confirming that we were friends, he took off to rouse the garrison. De la Cruz and Sailor talked for a few minutes, and then the boys and Sailor rowed for the shore.

"We can land now," De la Cruz told us, "though we probably

could have anyway. I think that man was sound asleep when we came in. We should have been challenged first, without my having to call."

The boys gave a final, strong stroke with the oars, and the kumpit grounded on the shallow water near the beach. Several of us got into the shallows to haul her up onto the beach with them. After spending so much time curled up on the deck, I was clumsy with stiffness.

"Stay near the kumpit until the others get here," de la Cruz warned us. "Don't go exploring yet."

Several large, heavily armed men emerged out of the woods. One stepped forward.

"Nice to see you again, Cruz," He said in perfect, unaccented English. He turned towards us and started shaking our hands. "My name is Captain Nazario Mayor, USAFFE[24], and I'm the acting Commanding Officer of Section D of the Sixth Military District here in Palawan. I'd like to invite you all to my home, about two hundred meters in the forest."

Captain readily agreed, as did we all, but the bride and groom thanked him in their language, picked up their goods, and departed into the woods. I hoped, as I watched them trudge away, that they didn't have far to go.

Sailor, Kong, and Kim-Jon hauled the kumpit high on the beach away from the reach of high tide, lashed it to a tree, and re-joined us.

As we walked, Captain Mayor told us about himself. We learned

---

[24] United States Armed Forces in the Far East: Shortly before the war began, the Philippine army and air force were combined and put under the command of the United States Army in the Philippines, headed by General MacArthur. The American government paid for their training and supplied weapons and uniforms. However, these troops were still technically not United States soldiers, but the Philippine Army co-operating with the United States Army. After the fall of Corregidor and the surrender of all American troops on the islands, some of these soldiers took to the forest and continued fighting guerilla-style. Due to their heritage could easily fade back into to forest and take shelter with the civilian Filipinos.

that he was a native Filipino, but had gone to college at the University of Kansas and received a commission in the US Army though the ROTC[25]. After he finished his tour with the military, he returned to Bugsuk Island and had run a prosperous business there.

"How is my house anyway?" he asked us. "I understand from de la Cruz that you were found there."

"That was your place?" Captain asked.

"Yes it was. When I heard that Corregidor fell, I hid my big equipment in the jungle, destroyed what I couldn't hide, and laced the well with arsenic for any invading bastard. Sorry about that, by the way. I never expected Allies would come there, but I'm glad you're all right. Anyway, Brooke's Point is more defensible and has access to better hideouts should they come here. Is the house still standing?"

"Mostly. You're going to have a lot of work to do when you get back though," Captain told him. "The trees are taking over."

"That's all right. I'll just have to re-build someday, or maybe start all over. Who knows?"

Our feet were still very raw and wounded, and everyone else must have been as stiff as I was as we staggered up the path to Mayor's place. I thought to myself that we must appear very disappointing to the guerillas if they were expecting stellar examples of American military men. Hiking started to help with the stiffness, but needles of pain shot up my feet and legs, and I tired far too easily. It was beautiful country, and had I been fully healthy, like I was eleven days ago...was it eleven days already?

"Mayor!" A shout came from the forest.

"Ah, wonderful. You received my message." Captain Mayor

---

[25]ROTC: Reserve Officer Training Corp: A program for college students where they train for the military while in college. The military often pays a significant portion or the entirety of the tuition and board, and in return the graduated student becomes an officer in the military for at least four years upon graduation. Jake had also been the ROTC at the University of Michigan.

turned to us and said, "This is Mr. Henry Edwards. He's an American businessman who lived here at the point until the war broke out. His house is two miles up the mountain and much more defensible than mine. After we get you fed, we're going to transport you there to await further orders. There are already three more people waiting for evacuation, with the addition of eight of you, we may finally be able to get you out of here."

"Three more?" Captain asked.

"They've been here since December. George and Bill are from the Army and Charlie is a Navy boy, though from the surface fleet. You'll meet them soon enough."

Edwards joined the group on the trail and told Mayor, "Corpus is on his way down too, he should be here shortly, he just had to wait for one of his boys to return to guard the radio up there."

"Good, good." Mayor nodded, "Let's hope everything continues to go well."

The house was hidden in the trees. It stood on stilts like the one at the Cape. Inside, we found a pretty, dark-haired lady cutting up fruit and watching a boiling pot that emanated all sorts of incredible spicy and sweet scents.

"May I present my wife, Mary Ann." Mayor said, as stood up and smiled in our direction.

"Pleased to meet you ma'am," Captain said. He introduced himself and the rest of us while she nodded politely.

"I'm pleased to meet all of you," she said in English, with a touch of an accent. "I will have breakfast ready soon for all of you. Please, wash up, and relax, the children will help me."

She called her children in from the woods where they had apparently been playing, and after washing their hands at the well, quickly set the tables for everyone. Mrs. Mayor put on an incredible meal of game, some seasoned, salted fish, fruits and vegetables served over rice with a sweet and spicy sauce, some flat breads, and several items I didn't recognize, but all were incredibly good. I probably ate more than I should have.

A discrete cough silenced us and I saw a tall man with a slightly worried-looking face finish mounting the ladder to the veranda and stride inside. "Ah, Sergeant Corpus, welcome," Captain Mayor said as Mrs. Mayor hurried to find another cushion for him to sit at our low table. "Captain Crowley, may I present Sergeant Armando Corpus of the United States Army Coastwatcher unit. They are attached to the 978th Signal Service Company, scattered all throughout the Pacific[26]."

Sergeant Corpus was dressed in coveralls, and barefoot. He thanked Mrs. Mayor quietly and joined in the meal, or what we had left of it.

"I brought the cart and carabao," He said to Edwards, "and two boys to help drive them. I hope they will be sufficient."

"I'm sure they will, thank you. I don't think they'd have made the climb to the base in their condition." Edwards said, gesturing in our general direction.

"Which is the base then?" Captain asked Mayor and Corpus, looking from one to the other.

"I am the captain of the guerilla movement here in southern Palawan," Mayor said, "we've been independent of the United States

---

[26] Unlike the USAFFE, Coastwatchers were an official unit of the American or Australian military forces. Their job was to gather intelligence themselves or from native and guerillas groups in the area and radio this information back to headquarters. They had a nearly 65% fatality rate, because they faced danger from the environment, hostile natives who may have preferred Japanese rule, as well as the enemy themselves. Every radio transmission was a chance for the Japanese to triangulate their position and ambush. In the Philippines, Coastwatchers were recruited from American men of Filipino descent, chosen for both intelligence and the similarity of their facial structure to the natives. Oftentimes, however, having been raised in America, Coastwatchers spoke the native languages badly, or not at all. In times of invasion, their best bet was to hide with sympathetic natives and keep quiet. Due to the expanse of formal education in the English language under the United States rule from 1898 to WWII, many Filipino natives spoke at least some English, partially eliminating the language barrier.

army since the fall of Corregidor. We do the best we can in terms of supplying information and comfort to allies, and we do what we can against the Japanese while risking the locals as little as possible. De la Cruz works under me in Cape Baliluyan, and there are other groups all around the Philippines, some originally from USAFFE like me, and some who have never had any military training at all.

"However, the Coastwatchers are an official American military unit assigned with watching and reporting all enemy shipping, movements, weather reports, etc. Corpus and his men landed here…what, in May was it?"

"June. June 8th specifically. We were dropped off on Ramos Island just north of Balabac by a US submarine. We stayed there for a few days, until Ramosian Moro found me while I was scouting areas to set up a permanent station. Moro had escaped from the prison camp in Puerto Princesa here on Palawan. A couple of days later, the chief of his tribe showed up with a message from the island's owner telling us that Ramos was too dangerous a place for us to stay because of a Japanese base ten miles away in Balabac City.

"To top it off, a famine last year had also taken a hit on the Ramos tribes, and they came asking for food, supplies, blankets, and whatever we could spare. Since we didn't want word spreading about our being there, the island's owner, Mr. Rufo Samson, made arrangements for us to load all of our supplies on a couple of his boats and land on Mantangule, an island on the other side of the strait."

"So how did you get here?" Captain asked.

"Well, most of our stuff had gotten soaked in rainstorms, so while the men were setting up camp and drying out the electronics so we could contact HQ, I fulfilled a promise to some friends of mine and came to Brooke's Point. I told Mr. Edwards that his daughters had safely arrived in the USA, and I brought a few cartons of cigarettes, as well as magazines and luxuries for him and his family. When

Mayor found out who I was and where I had left my men, he insisted

Approximate route from Baliluyan to Brooke's Point. Path based on deep water routes in southwest Palawan waters.

on coming back with me to Mantangule and moving everyone here."

"I was actually shocked that they were still alive when we got there," Mayor cut in. "Especially when I found out they had dried out and fixed their radio. However, they hadn't sent any transmissions yet, which might have saved their lives. Mantangule is usually so hot with activity that I was certain that during the week he had been gone, the Japanese would have surely found them out and killed or captured them. I sent a message to the deputy governor of Palawan about my idea, and he showed up the next day with a small flotilla of kumpits and sailors to move us here. Took nearly a week."

"We have a small shack here near this house where our radio is stored in the hopes that it will work someday." Corpus finished. "We do have a working radio up in the mountains near Mr. Edwards' place, which is our main base. Mr. Mayor has kindly let us stay in his "summer home" as he calls it.

As soon as we can, we will send word of you to Australia, unless your mission is too top secret to risk sending word."

"Not that top secret," Captain said. "We'd like to be evacuated if possible. But first we've got to tell them to keep everyone else out of Balabac Straits." Captain said.

"Well, with eleven of you now, we may be able to get a plane or submarine here to clear you out. We'll do our best at any rate. If we get back to the mill before the next scheduled transmission, we'll imbed your message with it, rather than make a new transmission. Cuts down on the enemy listening in and thinking we're broadcasting more than weather reports."

"Has the enemy ever found you here?" Baumgart asked.

They smiled. "Only once," Mayor said, chuckling as he pulled a small, official looking book out of the small desk in the corner.

"Ah yes, here we are," he cleared his throat. "July 26. Japanese gunboat anchored 800 yards off beach and twenty soldiers landed. Enemy casualties, 20. Our casualties, sore trigger fingers."

We laughed. "They know we're here all right," Mayor said, closing and replacing his book, "but as long as we broadcast regularly and talk about the weather, they won't likely land again."

"The Coastwatchers gave us their extra arms and ammunition as a thank you," one of the guerillas said proudly, showing off his Army M1 Garand. "And as long as Kierson gets here soon, we'll have no trouble keeping ammunition coming."

I let the conversation wash over me, feeling completely safe and relaxed for the first time since we were left stranded on the ocean's surface. We were with friends, Americans too, who could obviously take care of themselves and now even had hope of rescue someday, rather than living my life out as Robinson Caruso.

After dinner, and thanking Mrs. Mayor and her family profusely, we loaded ourselves into the rickety cart lashed to a carabao.

Corpus and Edwards took off on their own assuring us they would see us when we got to the house. Howell ran up just as we were getting ready to depart for the mountains.

"Sir, I've been looking at their radio here, and I think I can fix it if given time. Captain Mayor said I'm welcome to stay down here with his men to work on it if you will give leave."

"It would be a great help to us if we could get that old thing up and running again, Captain," Mayor said.

"Well, Howell is a great radio technician," Captain replied, "if anyone can fix your radio, he can. He's obviously well protected here with your people, so if he wants to stay, it's all right by me."

"Thank you sir," Howell said.

"Thank you Captain Crowley. We'll send him along as soon as the radio is up and running."

I waved good-bye to Howell. De la Cruz and Sailor planned to head back to Baliluyan that evening, so we thanked them profusely for all their help and made our goodbyes knowing we would likely never see these amazing men again. After our farewells, the young boy entrusted with guiding the cart to Mr. Edward's place hauled on the carabao's rope and we rode away.

Though only three miles, it took nearly five hours to reach Mr. Edwards' home. A rainstorm the day before left the jungle dripping and sodden. Every time the carabao found a muddy puddle big enough to muck around in, he thankfully sank to his knees and wallowed happily. The boy, enraged because he had been charged with bringing us swiftly and safely to the settlement, would yell, kick and beat the carabao with his crop every time, but he might as well have beaten a stone. We tried not to laugh because the boy was very upset that he was unable to fulfill his duty as quickly as possible, but the carabao laid there in the cooling mud, ignoring his "master."

When the carabao decided he was rested enough, he got to his feet and moved on without any encouragement. It must have been a heavy rain because there were many mud wallows.

The panting boy finally led the mud-encrusted carabao into the settlement around dinner time. Two houses and a mill sat in a rough triangle in the cleared land, and trunks from the felled trees still protruded through the forest floor. Like all the others we had seen thus far, these houses were also made of bamboo and suspended on stilts six feet off the ground with grass-thatched roofs.

Mr. Edwards peered around the side of the mill, wrench in hand, glistening in oil and sweat. "Ah, there you are," he said, "I was starting to wonder." He looked at the boy and the carabao and said, "oh dear, I'd forgotten about the rain."

He said a few words to the boy, clapped him manfully on the back making the boy smile broadly, and sent him to fetch the others at the settlement. Soon after, Corpus along with several others emerged from the house and the nearby woods.

"You've met Corpus," Edwards said. "This," he gestured to a short, lightly-built man with a pleasant disposition, "is Sergeant Carlos Palacido of the Coastwatchers, and the three ruffians behind him are George Marquez and William "Red" Wigfield of the United States Army, and Charlie Watkins of the Navy. The rest of the Coastwatchers are all over the island right now, but they should be returning soon.

"There's also Henry Garretson, a civilian engineer turned guerilla. He's sick with malaria right now, and in bed. Part of the reason I hope you can convince someone to evacuate you is maybe they can also take Harry. His illness is getting worse, and beyond what we can treat."

He gave us a quick tour of the grounds. "I live in the big house you saw when arriving. George, Bill, Charlie and Harry are already staying there, so we can only take about three of you. The other house belongs to Mr. Mayor, but he only intends on using it if the Japanese ever land here in earnest, so the Coastwatchers stay there for now. It's also where we'll put the rest of you. Thankfully, with everyone out, we'll be okay in terms of space. You saw me coming out of the mill when you arrived. It's currently broken, despite all my attempts to fix it, and the radio shack is attached to it."

"When can we send a message to Admiral Christie in Perth?" Captain asked. "They need to close the Straits before another ship gets in trouble.

"We can only send messages to MacArthur's Headquarters in Brisbane. However, we can probably have them forward the message if we know who it should go to." Palacido said.

"The message needs to go to Submarine Task Force 71 in order for Christie will get it."

"We can do that."

"Do you have paper and something to write with?"

"Not really anymore. Sorry. Tell me the message and I'll embed it in the next transmission."

Captain thought for a moment, then said, "Tell them *USS Flier* struck a mine and sank in less than 30 seconds in Balabac Straits at 2200 hours on August 13. 50 fathoms of water. There are 8 survivors."

"*USS Flier*, struck a mine and sank in 30 seconds, 50 fathoms at 2200 on August 13 with eight survivors. Got it. It'll go out this evening when Sergeant Corpus makes the routine report."

Mrs. Edwards, a native Filipino, was a happy, smiling woman despite her small crowd of children and constant houseguests underfoot. She already had dinner waiting for us, which was coconut sprouts, rice, a citrus fruit she called Kalamansi, and a grapefruit-type citrus. Palacido and Corpus donated the last of their emergency rations to the feast: crackers, cheese, and coffee. They also brought better clothes, soap, sulfa drugs and first aid cream.

After dinner, I took a long bath in the cold stream, scraping and scrubbing off the salt from my skin and hair. I also shaved for the first time since the incident, and covered my clean feet in the cream, then wrapping them in clean bandages.

Clean and full of good food, I hadn't felt this good since *Flier* sank, and I slept peacefully and deeply that night, more hopeful than ever that I would get home.

IN THE MOUNTAINS

The night we landed Edwards sent a message to a local missionary family, the Sutherlands. They arrived the next morning, and at Captain's request, conducted a church service in the settlement. Mr. Sandy Sutherland, a native Scot, had been on Palawan since 1931. He administered medicine and saw to the locals' dental needs in addition to his ministry work. He and his wife Maise had two delightful little children, Alastair and Heather.

Mr. Edwards had also sent for a native lady they had trained to give haircuts and a native doctor. I wasn't too confident in the local's concept of medicine, and had more faith in the Coastwatchers' and Edwards' supplies. I could see from the other's faces, they felt the same, but he was kind and-well meaning, and we had problem with him changing the dressings around our feet.

Every evening, the compound tuned in to the radio for an update from the outside world. We listened eagerly to the continued invasion of France and the fight that now raged around Paris. How our troops had conquered North Africa and were crossing the Mediterranean into Italy and Southern France. The Allies had re-taken Pisa, and the Germans fled to Florence. The resistance had ended on Guam, and our submarines sank two ships in the Philippines.

Living in the shadow of the enemy, these nightly broadcasts were the only things reminding the guerillas and Coastwatchers that the war did progress. After days of being cut off from the wider world, I found myself listening avidly for every scrap of information, and understood why this was an important ritual to everyone involved.

The next morning, I woke up feeling better than ever. Two days of rest and good food had done wonders for me and I was eager to do something useful today while we waited for a response from

Australia. Palacido had been on the radio last night, and said there was no message for us, though Corpus looked haunted after looking through the pile of decrypted messages.

"Good morning Mr. Edwards, Mrs. Edwards," I said, grabbing some of the cooked rice and citrus for breakfast.

"Good morning Ensign Jacobson," they said.

"How are you feeling?" Mrs. Edwards asked.

"Much better. Tired of just sitting around all day. I was never good at doing nothing."

"I only wish I had your problems, I have to head back to the beach today to set up some things with the guerillas."

"I thought you were going try fixing the rice mill again," Mrs. Edwards said, trying but failing to keep the note of disappointment out of her voice.

"I know sweetie, I know. But it's got to be taken care of this morning. I'll try this afternoon."

"What's wrong with it?" I inquired.

"I think it might be drive belt, but I don't know enough about engines to fix it," Mr. Edwards admitted. "It's driven by a diesel engine that I salvaged from my old home, and I had some help setting it up, but everyone's been too busy to help me fix it."

"I can take a look at it if you like," I said.

"Really?" Mrs. Edwards sounded hopeful.

"Sure. I know a little about engines."

"Being on a submarine I'm sure you're familiar with all sorts of machinery," Mr. Edwards laughed. "When you're ready, I'll show you around and give you access to what tools I have."

Inside the shack where the rice mill was, I saw a jury-rigged setup, and while it was a mess, I thought I could figure it out.

"What do you think?" Mr. Edwards said, after showing me the room and the very few tools he had. "You don't have to, and I certainly don't want you to exhaust yourself, but if you think you can fix it, I'd be ever so grateful."

"I've got a few ideas," I admitted. "I'll give it a go."

"Great!" Mr. Edwards shook my hand. "I really have to get going down to the beach now, but if you need anything just ask Mrs. Edwards, one of my kids, or the Coastwatchers."

"Sounds good. Say Hello to Howell for me."

"I'll do that," he said, with a wave, and quickly vanished down the path to the beach.

Time passed quickly, and I hummed to myself as I worked on the mill. The other Fliers woke up and said good morning to me as I worked, then disappeared with other refugees to go fishing. The Edwards kids vanished into the forest to gather fruits and nuts for everyone, and before I knew it, it was close to noon, and the compound was quiet and deserted.

First and foremost, I replaced the bad belt driving the mill. When finished with that, I started tinkering and adjusting valves and timings to see if I could get the engine to run smoother. I then turned my attention to the mill itself and started working out how it operated.

Gradually, I became aware of someone watching me. I turned around and saw Palacido standing behind me and grinning.

"And here I thought you were dirty and disheveled when you arrived," he joked.

"That bad huh?" I said, rubbing my sweaty forehead with a grimy forearm.

"Well, if you wish to avoid the wrath of Mrs. Edwards, I would wash off before you dare enter her house."

"It's awfully quiet around here." I said, looking around.

"I think we're the only two. Mrs. Edwards went off a few minutes ago to wash clothes down where the creek is deep enough.

Don't get any bright ideas though, she'll know if you touch anything with those dirty hands."

"Hey, are you busy?"

"Depends on your definition of 'busy'. I'm not volunteering to be a grease monkey if that's what you mean."

"Nah, I've already finished here and was just playing. I was actually curious about something."

"Sure, what's up?"

I glanced around the compound, but still saw no one. "When we first arrived on Palawan, it seemed like we were mistaken for submariners from another submarine that must have sunk not long before we did. What happened?"

Palacido sighed, closed his eyes, and said, "We're still trying to figure this one out. Our means of communication on these islands are good for the technology we have, but sometimes we still have only fragments of information.

"Several days ago, we heard rumors that there were American submariners sighted on Balabac. In fact, De la Cruz had only just returned to Baliluyan only a few hours before you arrived from checking these rumors out.

"Sometime on July 3, there was an explosion and possible submarine sinking west of Balabac and several days later, submariners were spotted rafting to Comiran Island. They were captured or possibly killed."

"We don't know?"

"In his report de la Cruz said the stories differed slightly. The general consensus is there were at least six submariners when the Japanese found them, four were taken to the prison camp. The other two escaped, were shot trying to escape, or were shot after capture, depending on the person de la Cruz talked to. There were two names involved: Tucker and Martin.

"There are rumors of some more newly arrived submariners up north at Puerto Princesa. It's hard to tell because if you're captured with Filipinos, the Japanese might accuse you of being a guerilla too, not a POW, so you would be kept in the prison portion, not the camp portion of the compound, and getting information about who is in the prison portion is much harder. But there have been rumors recently of a submarine sinking July 26 near Palawan and a few survivors of that one swimming to southwest Palawan and captured before they could get to us. The name *"Robalo"* is mentioned both times."

"You have got to be kidding me."

"No. Why?"

"We ran across them during our last patrol, just as we were going home and they were starting out. Just eerie that four days later they might have…"

"We're hearing no other names. We don't know if the submarine in question was crippled in some explosion on the 3rd then sank on the 27th or if there are two submarines besides yours we're dealing with, we just don't know. But after we heard the rumors, de la Cruz, before leaving to confirm them, ordered all of his men to keep a look out for submariners on the Balabac Islands."

"Which is how you found us," I said.

"Exactly."

"I see." It was sobering to think, also frightening to think if true, how close we came to swimming to Comiran that night. More might have made it, but we all might have been captured, or maybe worse.

"One of our men is with a contingent of guerillas at Puerto Princesa now, and should be arriving back soon. Who knows? We may find more survivors of your boat."

"We can only hope, I guess."

After a moment of silence, Palacido mercifully changed subjects and said, "So you have it working again?"

"I believe so," I said hopefully.

"I don't miss the noise, but it is rather convenient, especially since it charges the batteries too."

"Well then, let's fire it up and see, shall we?" I said turning it on.

She sputtered a little at first, but soon smoothed out to a level *thrum*.

"Congratulations." Palacido said. "We've been trying to fix that wretched thing for ages."

"Well that's my chore for the day. What do you have for entertainment around here?"

We have some great magazines, Reader's Digest I believe, and only six years old," Palacido said with smirk.

"Oh joy." I drawled sarcastically.

"Hey, you have no cause to complain until you've memorized them all. Just don't forget to bathe before Mrs. Edwards sees you."

As we waited for a response to our situation, we found that we had spare time for the first time since departing Freemantle. I began to learn more about the guerillas and Coastwatchers stationed here.

The guerillas were an amazingly complex organization scattered in groups all over the Philippines, and with over one-thousand men on Palawan and Balabac alone. When Captain Mayor introduced himself as a Captain of Section D of the Sixth Military District, it also meant he commanded over eighty men and four officers, which coordinated operations all over Palawan. The guerillas acted as a first line of defense, they spied on the Japanese, provided connections to the friendly people of Palawan, and even recorded sinking Japanese ships which could eventually be accredited to a submarine or two. All this information was collected sent to Brooke's Point, where the Coastwatchers would radio the necessary information to Australia and catalogue the rest in case it was needed. Since with every sent message, the Japanese might be able to triangulate their position, using the radio was very dangerous. However, after the last attack on the point, I hoped the Japanese would know it was suicide to fight their way up here to the radio.

Henry Garretson was a guerilla as well, but usually in bed with the fevers and shivers of malaria. They had no quinine to cure it, and the Atabrine[27] they did have, couldn't relieve his symptoms. As a precaution, the Coastwatchers started us on Atabrine tablets to keep the chances we'd catch anything down. Not wanting to end up like Henry, we took it faithfully.

The six Coastwatchers stationed here primarily catalogued and transmitted the information gathered by the guerillas. In addition, they would also patrol with the guerillas, and generally coordinated all their actions with them as well. All were Americans of Filipino or Hispanic descent, and it comforted us to be around fellow countrymen.

George and Bill, whom most called "Red", were the Army boys, and had been in the camp since December of 1943. Charlie arrived at the camp with them but had been patrolling with guerillas after escaping Puerto Princesa prison. Today, like most days, they were trying to earn their keep by fishing in the local streams.

We had also heard about a mysterious Finn by the name of Kierson, but he was away on a scouting mission for the guerillas and

---

[27] Quinine can be used to treat and cure malaria. Atabrine is a synthetic version, though not as effective. Quinine is originally derived from the bark of the Peruvian Cinchona tree, and by the dawn of WWII, over 90% of the world's quinine production came from the Dutch East Indies, known today as Indonesia. When the Japanese took over that area in March 1942, the Allies supply of quinine was interrupted, and they had to rely on atabrine as much as possible and keep the quinine for desperate cases. Atabrine did not necessarily cure malaria with a single treatment and was used more often to suppress symptoms, especially in an emergency. Without atabrine, most of the Pacific campaign would have been much more difficult, if not impossible.

we had yet to meet him.

From the mountain, I could little dots of coastal kumpits and canoes, and further out to sea, the occasional massive Japanese convoy or warship. If they thought this side of Palawan was less patrolled by American submarines, they were wrong. I didn't see any attacks, but I wondered who was out there watching them.

As there was little else to do, I found a large shady tree under which I could comfortably read. The six-year-old Reader's Digests provided a surreal form of entertainment as I read about "The Value of the American Wilderness", "The Simple Lives of Farmers", and "The Public's View of Unions Now". Life seemed difficult then with the ongoing depression, but now, looked a lot simpler. Surreal or not, they were practically the only thing to read.

I was drowsing under my tree the next morning, dilapidated Reader's Digest blocking the sun from my eyes, when I thought I heard, "Hey Jacobson, you interested in a little hunting?"

I peeked out from under my magazine, and saw George standing over me, a carbine rifle in hand.

"Sounds like fun. I hunted birds as a kid, and where I'm from, the deer only slightly outnumber the hunters. Why? Offering to take me deer hunting?"

"For those piddly little things? Around here, they're the size of a poodle, and too far up the mountain. Besides, I'm craving a side of bacon."

"Pigs?" I hadn't seen any of those either.

"Boars. And it's too dangerous to go out there by alone. Red and Charlie wanted to fish today though, so do you want to go hunting?"

"Sure. Beats lying around here all day. I'm sick of reading these."

"You have no cause to complain until you've memorized them all."

"Palacido said the same thing. Is that your motto?" I joked.

"Are you going to make me play, 'Give me an article name and I'll quote you the opening sentence'?"

"You play that?"

"Don't get me started. Come on."

We trekked into the woods. The forests of Palawan are huge and primitive; trees so ancient that six men would be hard-pressed to encircle the trunks sit next to young densely-packed trees competing for space. Innumerable vines twined around the limbs and branches. The sound of birds and monkeys played to the backdrop of the constant dripping of water through the canopy.

We were soon soaked with sweat and humidity, and I wondered if it was possible to get any wetter without the help of a body of water. The foliage was waist high in most places, making it impossible to see animals of any kind. George told me we had to find a pig-trail and either stalk them or wait for them to come. I was supposed to keep my ears open, listen for the pig rooting around the trees and let him know. I carried a stout limb in my hand, hoping I really wasn't going to have to bludgeon one to death.

George had just stopped, fingering the trunk of an ancient tree with bark gnawed away when we heard the low, rhythmic grunting of a boar. We froze, then slowly and silently stood up. He was the strangest pig or boar I'd ever seen: grey, he stood on tall legs with a very long snout, flanked by an enormous mutton-chop beard.

George put his fingers to his lips, quietly raised the rifle, and took careful aim. I got ready with my makeshift cudgel, just in case. There was no way I could stop a full-grown boar like this one if he charged, I was just supposed to give us enough time to scuttle up a tree. The boar suddenly tensed, then ran screaming into the woods just as George got his shot off. "Bugger." He said, as we heard the keening pig continue to run through the woods. "We'll keep going I guess. There's got to be more pigs in this forest.

We found more boars over the course of the day, each taking turns with the carbine, but several were too far away to get a clear shot, and others escaped through the dense screen of undergrowth. We found a well-traveled animal path, and climbed up a tree to wait, though we quickly fell to talking rather than hunting.

"George, mind if I ask how you and Red and Charlie got here?"

He stretched out on the branch and leaned against the trunk. "Not much to tell really." He said. "Red and I were stationed together at Nichols Air Base near Manila, just a short ways above Cavite."

I nodded. I had heard about the Japanese bombing that base the same day they bombed Pearl Harbor.

"Red and I didn't know each other then, and the day that the Japs attacked, I just kept running around trying to preserve our planes, anything. I didn't really think. I saw the *Sea Lion* sub get blown sky-high with a direct hit, it was an absolute disaster. The entire airfield was evacuated to Mindoro a week later, while MacArthur and the rest of the men started the move to Bataan and Corregidor. So we were spared the Battle of Bataan and what happened afterwards.

"But when we heard all personnel were expected to surrender when Corregidor did[28], a lot of us took to the hills of Mindoro rather than just let ourselves be captured. About fifty of us managed to get to Panay Island hitching rides on fishing boats, trading kumpits, or anything that would float. I met Red on the fishing kumpit that took me there.

"We tried to settle in, but the Japs just kept coming, and it was getting harder to hide. Most of the natives were willing to help us, but it only took one to betray us. So we built a batch of rafts and sailed east until we found Cuyo Islands. These were so small and sparsely populated, we hoped they wouldn't bother spend manpower

---

[28] May 6, 1942

on them. It worked for about a year and half too. The only sign of the enemy was a naval officer and a civilian who were trying to "recruit" the locals. I made sure they went "missing", and apparently they weren't missed by the enemy enough to warrant looking for them immediately. Anyway, late last year, the Japanese finally came in huge numbers. Red and I and some others were lucky as we were in the hills when they landed. We had enough warning to hide in a crack in a rock while the Japs tried to find everyone. I don't know how many they got overall, I saw about thirty guys being herded into lifeboats as the sun set, including some of the natives that had been helping us. Others were just murdered.

"Afterwards, Red and I resurrected one of those rafts that had gotten us to Cuyo and we took off east again and landed in north Palawan. As you can imagine we spooked easily by this point and jumped at any shadow or crack of a twig. Then one night we stumbled, literally, into Charlie. He was on patrol with the local guerillas. After escaping the prison, he took up with the local guerillas helping other escapees and such. He won't often talk about his time in the camp, and I don't blame him. I've seen a little with my own eyes what the damn Japs do to prisoners, and regret every moment of it.

"It quickly became too dangerous in northern Palawan. They call south Palawan "Free Palawan" because there are no Jap bases and we are more or less left alone. But up north, there is a lot of Japanese pressure and influence, and the danger of betrayal got too great. So the guerillas shipped us down here to wait for pick-up last December. The Coastwatchers arriving this summer has been a great boon what with the radio and all. But I'm getting bored. All I can do is hunt for food because it's too dangerous to do anything else. My white skin gives me away, you see. Hopefully, since you're here, they'll come and get you and we can all get out of here. I might even get my chance to do something against the enemy myself before this war is over."

"Do you know what happened to Charlie?" I asked. He had been quieter, jumpier, but still had a sense of humor, and would occasionally join in on card games or conversation.

"Kind of. He doesn't talk much, which I'm sure you noticed, and I don't know if he was always quiet or what. He was in Fort Hughes when the Battle of Corregidor broke out, and one of the POW's at the surrender. He told me that those islands are pock-marked, burnt and all blown to hell now. He was taken to Bilibid Prison in Manila. It's this huge compound that housed only the worst and most dangerous prisoners before the war. Thick walls, iron bars, the whole bit. No one has ever escaped. Later, he was marched to the north of Luzon to Cabanatuan. Lastly, he was shipped to Palawan on a merchant freighter. What little I've gleaned from him about that trip makes my skin crawl. I guess there were not many lights in the hold, and there was only fresh air when they dropped food down in there. I can't imagine how terrifying...he still sometimes has nightmares about 'being buried alive' in the ship's hold. To make things worse, they're transported on regular cargo freighters, and some of those don't make it to their destinations, as you know."

"His did though, and docked at Puerto Princesa, which is virtually a ghost town these days. The natives all took to the mountains when the Japanese landed. They took over the old Constabulary, which was already tattered, and ransacked the village to repair it. It's desolate up there. The barracks are huge, U-shaped, partly transformed into a jail, and metal roofed, so it's got to be hotter than blazes under the sun.

"Charlie and the other prisoners were told they would be building a road, but they're really building a giant set of runways using nothing but broken-down hand tools. Charlie says that if you didn't work as fast as they thought you should be able to, the guards beat you with sticks as thick as your wrist. They're supposedly experts at inflicting pain without breaking bones, because a man with a broken bone can't work. It's hell up there. Those guards would beat you for anything from disrespect to stealing or just from wanting to break up the monotony.

"So Charlie and another guy, Joel Little, decided to make a run for it. The airstrip is a couple of miles from the prison camp, and the men mostly labor under the eyes of the guards, but they let one or two men at a time go into the woods to relieve themselves. So, Charlie and Joe asked permission to go, and they did. The guard never saw them again. The Filipinos in that area try to help the men as much as they can by leaving food, notes of encouragement, whispering news about the war to the men to encourage them. In Charlie's case, they joined a group of guerillas, to help the local fight. Joel decided to go with another bunch to Panay leaving Charlie here on Palawan when we bumped into him. So that's more or less what happened to him.

"But there were no more escapes from the prison. The guards were furious. They counted the men off into groups of ten: now no one even attempts to escape, because if any group is found missing a member, the rest of the group will be shot."

He shuddered. I didn't say much, just thanked God that we had thus far been spared that.

A rhythmic grunting broke into our thoughts. The large boar from the early morning was back, rooting among the forest floor plants. Blood flowed from his shoulder.

"Looks like you didn't miss him after all," I whispered to George.

"And I don't intend to again. Ribs are sounding REALLY good. Pity there's no barbeque sauce."

He raised the carbine to his eye, steadied, aimed, and the pig took off into the forest shrieking before a shot could get off.

"No wonder that old bastard is still alive. He can sense danger from a mile away." I said.

"Probably tough anyway." He de-cocked the rifle in frustration.

"Dammit. It's been so long since I've had any decent meat; hamburger, ribs, bacon and eggs. If I ever see rice again my entire life, it'll be too soon. Even over-dried, over salted jerky would be fantastic now."

"Well, I promise you, unless the cook on the incoming submarine is a total hack-job, you'll get great food on the ride home. And if he is a total hack-job, I'll cook you bacon and eggs myself."

George cracked up. "You're on Jacobson."

We did manage to shoot a pigeon-like bird on our way home, and though it was the scrawniest looking thing I'd ever seen, everyone was glad to have a bite or two of it for lunch. Any meat other than fish was a welcome change.

-12-

SHOT IN THE DARK

After lunch, the Coastwatchers with their guerilla contingents started returned to the compound. Corpus accepted their reports and talked to each one briefly, before retiring to his office. They noticed us very quickly, and as soon as official business was over, Palacido introduced everyone. The four returning Coastwathers were Sergeant Jaime "Slug" Reynoso, Sergeant Ramon "Butch" Cortez, Corporal Teodoro Rallojay, and Sergeant Ritchie Daquel.

"Well this explains what the ladies meant by, 'bring the new Americans tonight,'" Rallojay said with a grin.

"What's tonight?" Jim asked.

"The Women's Auxiliary Service is throwing a party for us and the other Americans here at the Point. Apparently, the invite is now expanded to include you all." Palacido explained.

"Does this mean we'll finally get to evacuate some of the civilians from around here?" Slug asked. "With these guys here, there might finally be enough to warrant a submarine or ship or something."

"We'll see, we've heard nothing official from Perth yet." Palacido said.

Captain spoke up, "I thought Corpus said that Perth contacted us two days ago."

"They did, but their message was not about evacuation." Palacido held up his hand to quiet the incoming flood of questions. "I'm afraid that's all I know right now. Sergeant Corpus should update you later tonight.

"Okay fellas, you're dismissed to make yourselves presentable. We'll leave at 1700."

I started to head for the Edward's house when I heard Palacido say, "Jacobson, could you wait a moment." I turned to find Palacido standing next to Reynoso, Captain and Jim.

"What's up?"

"I thought for a moment we'd all go for a walk," Reynoso said.

We hiked into the woods a ways, my curiosity piquing, but waited until Palacido called a halt and we gathered in a tight knot around him.

"I thought perhaps, since you are all submariners, I might have a word with you about some things we heard when I was up near Puerto Princesa and the prison camp.

"Does the name Kimmel mean anything to you?"

Captain looked worried. "Manning Kimmel?"

Reynoso nodded. "Yes, did you know him?"

"Manning Kimmel commands the *Robalo*. I had met him on several…" his voice trailed off and he looked sharply at Reynoso. "What do you mean 'knew'?"

Reynoso hesitated, "We couldn't get accurate enough accounts to make it official, but apparently, the POWs at the camp told some of the guerillas that a submariner named Kimmel was delivered to the camp three weeks or so ago. Last week, after a couple of American Aircraft buzzed the Puerto Princesa compound, he was…killed."

"Killed?" Captain looked from one to the other.

"With all due respect sir, I'd rather not tell you. If the reports we've heard are correct—"

"What the hell happened?" Jim interrupted.

"He along with several other men were likely pushed into a ditch and …set ablaze. At least, that's the story we're getting." He added quickly.

"God…" Captain breathed.

I gasped as my stomach leapt to my throat. *No man deserved that fate*, I thought. "What about the others?" I croaked out.

"According to one of our contacts near the camp, Dr. Mendoza, four *Robalo* crewmen were captured and declared to be guerillas by the Japanese. They managed to smuggle a note out with their names and the name of their boat. Everyone in that section was loaded on a Japanese destroyer on the fifteenth of August. No one could say for sure what the ship's name was, and no one can find out where the ship was destined.

"No other submariners have arrived since the known and suspected *Robalo* crewmen, so if more of your crew has survived, they are not there."

Before we got our hopes up, Palacido quickly added, "But you have to know, we haven't found any more Americans roaming these islands, or heard any rumors of any either. You may have been the only ones to escape your boat. I'm sorry if you were hoping for more."

It was only a slight shock to us. After all, the chance anyone made it out of the *Flier* had been very remote, and swimming to the surface with the Momsen lungs alone would have been nearly lethal.

I turned and managed to master my emotions. Subdued, Jim and Captain set off in different directions, no doubt absorbing this disturbing as well as any man could. We had heard rumors of these horrible camps but I never thought that it could be that bad. The three of us, watched their retreating backs for a moment, then Palacido and Reynoso quietly turned and retreated to the Coastwatcher house, leaving me alone.

I tried not to think that afternoon. It was difficult. Submariners are used to death. We had to be. When you heard about another submarine or two which vanished without a trace every time you came back to port, you ended up becoming somewhat fatalistic about it, but we expected to all go together, as a team, a company. Being left behind from my own boat was like being partially amputated, but if I went, I always thought it would be into the arms of the sea. I was reconciled to the possibility and at ease with that idea, but not as a human torch.

I heard voices, and saw George, Red and Charlie hiking up the path, a basket full of fish slung over George's arm.

"Hey Jacobson!" George waved. "I saw our boar again. Too bad I only had a pole this time."

I joined them, and quickly started talking fish, hunting, and anything else to take my mind off Kimmel. As the sun began to set, we started to gather to go to the party.

"They promised tuba for drinks, you're going to love it."

"What's tuba?"

"It's this great fermented drink the locals make from the sap of coconuts. It's as close to beer as you can find around here."

"Great! I haven't had a beer since my last night in Fremantle."

"Oh you poor baby, you want to know the last time I was in a bar?"

The chattering and jibing went on for several minutes. Some of the guys kept looking at their watches. "It's time to go, where are Palacido and Corpus?" Daquel asked.

On cue, Palacido walked out onto the Coastwatcher's veranda and down the ladder to the group.

"Are we ready to go?" He asked.

"Been ready," Reynoso said.

"My, my, aren't we eager? Afraid your girl forgot what you looked like while you were up north?"

"Aw, come on, cut me a break, Sarge," Reynoso grinned.

"Hey, where's Corpus?" Rallojay said.

"He said to go ahead, that he'll catch up in a few minutes." Palacido looked slightly worried when he said that.

The rest of the Coastwatchers looked slightly exasperated. "I guess we can wait for him," Reynoso offered.

"I know, I told him that, but he insisted that we go on without him."

"Well, we're still waiting on Captain and Mrs. Mayor as well, so I'll stay behind and wait. The rest of you go on ahead."

"I'll stay and keep you company," Ritchie Daquel offered.

"Okay then. Now men, I'm sure the *Flier* guys would appreciate a slower walk to the village since their feet are still healing."

"Oh good! We didn't miss the bus!" George called out, Red and Charlie in his wake.

The native village we were going to visit had been the one where the doctor and hairdresser had come from. It was north of the settlement further up the mountain, about a twenty minute walk. The guys kept going on and on about the tuba, which was apparently a village specialty.

A cool breeze was a welcome change from the day's humidity. Additionally, our feet had begun to heal, making it easier to walk, and the rich black soil cushioned our feet.

We laughed and joked and I began to relax. I was shipwrecked on a tropical island, about to go to a luau, and be served tropical drinks by the locals…any more idyllic and it would be movie.

We heard the muted crack of a gunshot and we threw ourselves to the ground on instinct.

"It came from the base!" I heard one of the watchers say. They took off back down the trail at a run, while we followed as quickly as we could on our injured feet.

Everything was in an uproar. Mrs. Edwards and Mrs. Mayor's children were huddled around their mothers, and Captain Mayor walked out from behind the Coastwatcher's house, carrying his young son who was yelling, "Why won't Sgt. Corpus get up? He's just lying there!"

My blood turned cold. Mr. Edwards, rounding the corner of the same house, saw us clumsily running forward and held up his hands to stop us. "Don't. Just keep clear right now," and in a lower voice, " Sgt. Corpus shot himself while Palacido and Daquel were greeting the Mayors. It's pretty bad."

"Is everyone else all right?"

"Physically, yes." He looked over to his wife and motioned that she should take everyone into the house. I glanced through the stilts holding up the Coastwatcher's house, and saw Corpus' form surrounded by the Coastwatchers, some standing, some kneeling. "Palacido told me to tell you that he'll come and talk to you as soon as the women and children are inside where they can't see. Excuse me, I need to tend to my family, though call if you need me."

Shortly after the women and Mr. Edwards had taken the children inside, Palacido crept around the corner. We could see him from where he stood, though he was hidden from the Edward's house. His hands were covered in blood. "We need to bury him quickly in this heat," he said with no preamble. "And obviously, there will be no party tonight. I need someone to tell the villagers why we're not coming."

"I'll go," Red said, indicating George and Charlie. "I know the way and the people."

"Thank you," Palacido said. "I need someone else to get Mr. Sutherland for the funeral service, such as we can do."

"I'll go," said Charlie.

"Daquel and I will prepare Corpus. We also need a coffin and someone to dig a grave. There's not much wood around here, so you may have to scrounge."

Soon, I was on the coffin detail, with two Coastwatchers, while the rest were digging a grave in the woods.

The lumber pile was sparse and problematic. Three years after being cut off from the rest of the world, there was not much left. We had to splice and creatively join many pieces.

We finished with about thirty minutes of light left for the funeral and burial. We carried the coffin behind the Coastwatcher's house were Corpus lay so the children wouldn't see.

He hadn't been that big in life, and he seemed even smaller in death. Despite that, he only barely fit in the coffin.

The funeral was quick, though solemn. Sutherland said a prayer over the grave, and we filled it in and covered it with stones to keep it secure.

At the end of the ceremony, Palacido picked up a rough cross made from two limbs bound together with a vine and hammered it into the soil with a shovel.

Dinner, long delayed, was quiet, and Palacido excused himself to man the radio for the night's transmissions, and to inform Brisbane of Corpus's death.

I needed some space to think, and strolled around the compound after dinner. After a few turns, I passed the radio shack, still lit by a Coleman lantern. Palacido sat in front of the quiet radio, massaging his forehead with his hands.

"How are you holding up?" I asked, stepping to the doorway.

"Hmm?" he said looking up. "Oh, I've just been thinking back over the events of today. Wondering if I could have done something different or seen this coming.

"He had been moody before, and once told us he felt useless and like extra baggage. He got really quiet again after Perth radioed two days ago, maybe that was what finally did it. But still, I tried to keep an eye on him, you know? Turned my back for just a few seconds to greet the Mayors…"

"There's nothing you could have done Palacido. You tried, he was just determined."

"I know that, but still…"

"What did Perth say that makes you think it put him over the edge?"

"Well, we radioed them about your boat going down and included the supposition that *Robalo* might have too, and they radioed back the next night. No word about whether or not they're going to extract you, but an earful for us." Palacido found the transmission on a piece of paper. "Ah, here it is. They start by essentially asking us why we didn't tell them the straits were mined and tell them about naval movements, et cetera. We've only been here two months, for all I know those Straits have been mined since the time of Noah. They didn't lay the mines on our watch though. This last bit was the killer: 'Your mission is to cover that area and advise me instantly of all important enemy dispositions and naval movements. Results thus far are disappointing and immediate improvements in your intelligence coverage and report is desired and expected.'

"I think Corpus might have taken this as blame for the loss of both boats and crews. I know he'd been depressed since he read that, and the news of both the submarines were lost in this general area came as a real blow."

"I don't think any of the Fliers blame you," I said. "At least I don't. Our orders told us to stay in deep waters to avoid any possible mines. That's just one of the chances that we take as submarines."

"Thanks," he smiled. "Poor fellow, I guess he just couldn't take it anymore, and needed out."

There was nothing to say to this, and I just stood there awkwardly for a moment. Palacido stood and stretched, saying, "Well, I'll see you and the others bright and early tomorrow. We've got planning to do."

"We do?"

"Yup. Perth just called again. They're coming to rescue you."

13

EVACUATION PLANS

"That far out? Are you sure?" Palacido, Captain Mayor, Captain Crowley, Jim and I were pouring over the Japanese maps of the area. The Coastwatchers had gotten them from someone who stole them off a Japanese supply ship that had run aground further north.

"Trust me, a fully loaded submarine needs at least sixteen feet beneath heron the surface, and we'll want to give our rescuers plenty of depth to work with. I saw how far out those reefs extend on our way up here, we'll have to go out at least five miles out."

"I'm with Captain," I said. "It'll have to be at least that far out. We're going to need a large enough boat that can get everyone out there. Is Sailor available?"

"He's off on another trade trip. It would take a while to get him back here, and it sounds like Perth wants you back as soon as possible." Mayor said. "There's a tribe a little south of here that has a large collection of boats. The chief's has an outboard motor. We might be able to purchase or borrow it for trade."

"Can we go today?"

"If we leave soon, and the chief lets us have his boat with the outboard motor, we can be back by dinner time. I'll see what monies I can scrounge up."

"We have some left from our original supplies too, I can give towards this," Palacido offered.

"Would he trade for its use? I'm sure that whoever rescues us can spare a gallon or two of diesel as a part of a trade if he'll trust we're good for it." Captain said.

Palacido and Mayor burst out laughing.

"What? What's going on?"

"I'm sorry, sir," Palacido said, tears running down his face. "I know you mean well, but if there's one thing we keep trying to get rid of around here, it's diesel. We all but bathe in it, and we can't trade the stuff away fast enough because everyone else has so much of it too."

"Where do you get it?" I asked.

"Strange thing about living around here, 50-gallon barrels of diesel fuel marked with Japanese symbols keep washing up on shore every few days." He looked very meaningfully at me.

"Ah, well, you're welcome."

The day passed slowly. I amused myself carving cribbage boards, which was rather silly because there were no cards. Jim was asleep under a tree, and George, Red and Charlie were trying for that boar again. Baumgart and the other enlisted Fliers were fishing for dinner.

Out of sheer boredom, I tried to make sandals for my feet by weaving some of the local grasses together, but no matter what I did, they rubbed on the still-healing sores.

It was funny, but I had a large family, and my siblings and I were always under each other's feet, then at college I lived with a bunch of guys at the fraternity. On the submarine, I often wished for a spare moment and space to gather my thoughts or relax. Now, with all the time and space in the world, I found myself aching to do something, anything.

I ended up doing what I usually did these days when I was forced to be still and quiet: remembering *Flier*. How before a shift one evening, Ed jokingly complained that since, once again, I was the Diving Officer while he was manning the periscopes, I was going to "duck" him again. I had been unfortunate enough to duck the periscope underwater the last several times Ed was trying to take bearings, but I told him it wouldn't happen this time.

"You're going to do it, Jake, it's inevitable."

"You willing to put some money on that inevitability?"

"Easiest money I'll ever make."

So when Ed spotted five columns of smoke that evening, I made absolutely sure the periscopes stayed steadily above water for as long as Ed wanted to take bearings. I think he took more than usual. [29]

We were southbound and this convoy was northbound, probably headed for Manila. They were coming on fast, with several escorts. Since it was so close to nightfall, we decided to wait until dark.

They passed by, letting us count the number of ships: nine freighters and a half-dozen escorts. We plotted their course for four hours. They were heading north–north west, staying almost precisely four miles from Mindoro's shore, and traveling at nine knots. On the surface, *Flier* could make more than twice that speed.

Captain decided to do an end-around attack, outrunning the convoy, then sitting and waiting for them. By the time we reached our planned position, it was only an hour before midnight. If all went as planned, the convoy would pass between us, and Mindoro's shore.

The escorts never saw us, whipping past as we sat silently, the freighters lumbering in their wake. We targeted the first two ships of the closer column, sending three torpedoes at each, we then fled south while the torpedoes were still en route. I watched from my position on the aft bridge as the first torpedo hit and exploded, shooting water and debris in a blinding flash. Seconds later, the second torpedo hit, and she started to sink by the stern.

Another flash and a geyser of water, and the smaller second ship took two hits. Both ships broke ranks and made a run for the beach.

"Sonar reports two hits on the first target, two hits on the second," Jim said.

---

[29] These events took place June 22-23, 1944 west of Mindoro Island in the Philippines

The escorts turned and roared back to their charges, passing far astern of us, dropping depth charges in their wakes, thinking we were submerged. It was almost comical.

The smaller freighter suddenly disappeared both from our radar and our sight, though in the night, it was difficult to tell if she sank or had run aground.

The big one drifted helplessly, her engines dead, slowly taking on water in her stern. The other freighters couldn't stop to help their friend with an enemy submarine somewhere about, and sped up, going around the wounded ship, leaving her behind to limp along and take her chances as well as she could.

We raced ahead north, thinking we might get another shot, and sure enough, an hour later, they were perfectly positioned again. Painted black on a moonless night, we snuck past the escorts, closed in on the convoy and lined up for a torpedo spread.

Captain and I started to give bearings on the large leading ship, while radar gave range. We had only four torpedoes left at the bow, and I watched them stream away, counting the seconds to impact by the rhythm of my chewing gum. The countdown came and went, nothing happened. "What the hell?" Crowley asked himself. "FOUR duds?" It wasn't unheard of, but highly unusual, and a disappointing situation.

"Boom… Boom" Two of our torpedoes exploded on the stern of our freighter, geysers exploding into the night sky. Seconds later, we heard the third one strike another ship in the convoy.

"What happened down there?" Captain called into the Conning Tower. "Those were supposed to hit along the length of that ship, not the stern!"

"We were giving range to the closest ship in the convoy Captain, isn't that what you wanted?" Pourciau replied through the hatch.

We looked at the convoy. The closest ship to us was actually behind the lead. "No, but at least it worked!"

"Aye sir."

"Reverse course, ready the stern tubes!"

Flier turned through the waves, allowing me to start taking readings while Captain watched the escorts, and they were closing in too fast.

"LIDDEL!" he roared through the hatch. "The escorts! What course is the widest gap between them?"

A second later he shouted, "two–zero–five degrees sir!"

"Full speed ahead on that course!"

Flier soared above the waves and charged the enemy. We flashed by so fast and so close to one it didn't have time to react or ram us. The others didn't see us speed through the night away from them. As we retreated, I watched the first ship we had hit settle beneath the waves with the gurgling bubbles swallowing her hull, the other one, though hit, looked like it could continue with the convoy.

Crowley wanted to finish off the cripple of our first attack, lagging three miles behind the main convoy, and completely dead in the water. Every time we tried cutting through or under the convoy, the escorts converged on our position. Apparently, the one escort we had practically waved at on our way out now had a fix on us. They were too far away to fire or drop depth charges, but they were determined not to let us have our quarry. On surface, *Flier* was faster than they were, and more nimble. Underwater, we had clear advantages, but together, those escorts and their Sonar kept us from the freighter. At one point, six were converging on our position, trying to catch us.

We approached from the south several times, then circled and came at her from the north, but they blocked us every maneuver or charge we tried. "Hell with this," Captain grumbled. "What worked once, might work again. Liddell, we're going to try to slip between two of them, let me know on the next pass where the largest gap is."

"Aye sir."

"Captain?" I said, looking through my night goggles. The freighter, now over five miles away, suddenly rolled over, and sank.

He stared, then said, "Never mind then." The escorts, watching their protectorate sink with probable dismay, apparently decided we weren't worth chasing with the convoy increasingly far ahead and who knows how many other submarines in the area. They fled the scene, and we decided that the convoy was too far and too fast to catch before we ran into another sub's patrol territory.

The convoy was likely headed to Manila. "Raise Commander Krapf of the *Jack*," Captain said. "They're behind us, near Manila, and might welcome the exercise."

We later heard that the *Jack* took out two more of that convoy. Of the nine freighters that we spotted, only four arrived…

BLAM!

The explosion blasted me awake, and I was on my feet before I really realized what was going on.

"What was that?" I heard someone yell.

"It sounded like gunfire!" another shouted back.

"Have the Japanese landed?"

Palacido and several people were heading to a small hilltop clearing further up the mountain which served as a lookout station. I ran with them, by the time I scrambled to the top on my healing feet, there was nothing to see: no Japanese ships, no landing craft, not even a fishing boat.

"See anything?" Palacido asked everyone who had a set of binoculars on them.

"No sir," several men chorused.

That was a relief. To be safe, Palacido sent a few men to scout down to the beach to check for the source of the explosion.

They returned with no answers, but Captain Crowley had joined them on the way back, excited about his trade with the neighboring tribe. He and Mayor had purchased a small sailing kumpit and towed it back with the chief's own powered kumpit.

"And all for a little bit of cash and the promise of a barrel of lubricating oil from the rescuing ship," he said.

That evening we sent the plans for the proposed evacuation to Perth. Also that night came orders from Palacido's headquarters in Brisbane asking him to formally assume command of the Coastwatchers.

The next day was a flurry of preparations. Just in case Perth did approve of our plans, we were going to try and evacuate the civilians around the base as well. Henry Garreston was going to need a cart to get to the beach since he was too sick to walk. The Edwards and Sutherlands were deciding whether to risk the dangerous ride to Allied land, or stay deep in the jungles of Palawan. Pamphlets were starting to trickle in showing the names of the Sutherland and Edwards family members, with rewards for their capture, and it only took one desperate person to betray their whereabouts.

In the afternoon, the word suddenly came that a submarine would be standing by at our coordinates on August 30th to pick us up. That left us only thirty hours before evacuation.

Runners informed the Sutherlands that they had to dispose of all their personal belongings in 12 hours and be ready to head for the beach after lunch. Mr. Edwards arranged for a carabao cart to transport the few of us whose feet were still a touch tender and Garretson. Mr. and Mrs. Edwards decided not to leave, despite the fact that two of their daughters were already attending college in the States.

"My wife is a native to this area," he said, as a way of explanation, "and it's my home now too. If something does happen, we can hide with her people, and we speak the language so we have a good chance at disappearing if worst comes to worst. Besides, we're needed here."

Late that night, as I walked past the radio hut, I thought I heard Captain...singing. I stopped, but there was no doubt about it, he was singing "Sweet Adeline".

Quietly I crept up to the shack, and peeked through the window, trying to keep out of sight. Palacido was smothering a laugh as Crowley trilled "You're the flower of my heart, Sweeeet Aaaa—deee—liiine!" Whoever was on the other end of the radio was singing along to the tenor part, and both were surprisingly good.

"Thanks John." The radioed voice said, "I just needed to make sure. It sounded too incredible to believe."

"I understand, Cy. I'd want to make sure myself before I put my..." Captain suddenly stopped, then swallowed hard, "before I put my crew in danger."

There was pause on the other end, then, "We're all set for tomorrow?"

"Affirmative. We'll hang three lights from the Point lighthouse when it's all clear and we're on our way." I saw Palacido signal Captain about something "A question from the men here. Some nearby civilians have requested evacuation too. Would you mind?"

"How many?"

"Six to eight people."

"You know the risks John. I haven't been cleared for a turnaround. A submarine in a war zone is not the place for civilians."

This must be our rescuing captain, I thought. His orders were to pick us up, then continue on his patrol with us aboard.

"Understood. But they've been looking for a way out since they were trapped here with the invasion."

"Women?"

"And children too." Crowley said.

There was a pause. "I could confine them to Officer's Country I suppose. And I'll have to inform COMSUBSOWESPAC. But it shouldn't be a problem if they stay put."

"Thank you."

"Until then." The line went dead.

"You know Jacobson, you may as well stop skulking in the shadows and come in here." Captain called out.

I walked in the room, trying not to look sheepish. "Sorry sir, I just followed the sweet sound of your voice." I grinned while Palacido fell over laughing.

"Very funny." He said with a crooked half-smile. He turned to Palacido, who was gasping for breath. "Do we have everything?"

"I think so," Palacido gasped, wiping his eyes, "I can't think of anything else that we need for evacuation. If we leave here no later than noon tomorrow for the beach, we should have plenty of time. Now, if you'll excuse me." He gasped, and left the room wiping his eyes.

Captain quickly brought me up to speed. If the coast was clear tomorrow, one of the guerillas was going to hang three lanterns in a vertical row from the concrete lighthouse on the bay. Once the submarine saw that, she would surface, and we would motor out to her, the kumpit returning with the lubricating oil the chief had demanded in payment. If something went wrong, we were to try again on the 31st.

"Sir, one more question,"

"Yes, Jacobson?"

"Why the concert?"

He smiled. "We're being picked up by the *Redfin*. Captain Austin and I were in the Men's Quartet at the Naval Academy together. Guess he wanted to check my actual identity."

14

ENEMY SURPRISE

The sound of paper rustling woke me the next morning. A tall, sparsely built man who looked like real Robinson Caruso sat at Mrs. Edward's table and carefully poured a pile of black powder from a drawstring bag onto a sheet of newspaper.

"No offense, Kierson," Captain was saying, "But you're nuts."

The stranger laughed. "Maybe a little, but how else are we supposed to get ammunition around here?"

"Hello." I said.

"Good morning Mr. Jacobson," Mr. Edwards said. "Meet Vens Kierson, world traveler, native Finn, and creator of ammunition from Japanese Mines among other things."

"Wow!" I exclaimed.

"Don't yell, you'll make me jump," Kierson half-joked. A few guerillas had seated themselves at the table and were carefully packing the powder into old ammunition shells then topping them off with small round pebbles.

"Sometimes Japanese mines come loose from their mooring chains and float on the surface." Kierson explained. "Some will come to rest on the beaches around here. They're supposed to deactivate if they come within a few feet of the surface, but that's not always the case, so dismantling them for the powder charge is still dangerous. But with ammunition so scarce around here, this is how we keep supplying our arms." His calm and educated experience contrasted with his frontiersman appearance. I watched him in fascination wishing I had met him earlier.

After a large goodbye breakfast from Mrs. Edwards, we began to gather in the clearing. Mr. Sutherland and his family soon arrived.

"May I present my wife Maise, my son, Alastair, and my little daughter Heather," he Sutherland said. "We'll be coming with you. I'll be sad to leave, but I'd rather have the children safe."

Alastair stared at all of us in awe for a bit before blurting, "Are we really going on a submarine?"

"That we are, son," Captain said.

Henry Garretson slowly climbed down from the house, and got in the cart without help. George, Red and Charlie were ready to go, and Palacido was checking his watch when I heard, "There is still room?"

"Going Kierson?" Palacido said with a tinge of regret.

"Yeah, you don't need me anymore, and the guerillas have been telling me I need to go ever since I arrived last night. I think they fear for my safety."

"I can understand that. I'll sure miss you though."

"I'll miss all of you too, but it's time for the next adventure."

"So with the Fliers, Sutherlands, George, Red, Charlie, Garretson, and Kierson now, that brings the total to seventeen people." Palacido concluded.

I whistled in amazement. Seventeen extra people on a submarine with no extra room on a good day would be tight, very tight.

In the past seven days, my feet had healed quite well, and I was able to walk most of the way to the beach, following the carabao cart. I fell in next to Kierson, and soon learned how he came to be at such a remote place as Brooke's Point.

He had immigrated from Finland with his family to the Spokane, Washington area when he was a teenager. After a year of schooling, he had dropped out to be a lumberjack for Boeing. When Boeing started building frames out of metal instead of wood, he became a diver and worked in Alaska for fishermen and salvage companies. He earned enough money salvaging that he left to travel around the world, and continued his salvage work in Hong Kong, th

Philippines, and China for over twenty years. He was working for the Chinese government when the First Battle of Shanghai broke out in 1932. When that happened, he fought with the Chinese, unsuccessfully trying to drive off the Japanese army.

"Of course, back then," he told us, "we knew that they were hankering for an empire in China, we just didn't know it would go that far. After that incident and I had an opportunity to strike out for the Philippines and work in the mining industry, which was great until the Japanese came here too. I took to the hills this time, and with no way to leave, I joined the guerillas." He gestured to Garretson, "Henry and I met while we were salvaging the *SS Panay*[30]. She was bringing us supplies when the Japanese hit her with a torpedo. Thankfully she hit the floor standing straight up in shallow water, so we were able to retrieve rifles, gas masks, and ammo which made up most of the cargo.

"Then we came here hoping to collect supplies for the guerillas on the Visayas, but ended up staying, partially of Henry's malaria, and partially because the guerillas here were faced with severe shortages in food and ammunition. I had learned a few tricks in the Visayas that I could put to use here."

"Converting Japanese sea mines into bullets."

"Among other things. I salvaged grounded ships for cargo, created a new currency for this area out of Japanese Charts. Since I'm irly fluent in the local languages now, I trade with a lot of the ple around the island for food and supplies. It's a lot easier than ing on the immediate locals, especially when last year's harvest poor."

es," Palacido said, who had been listening in on the

---

k of *SS Panay* is today a popular tourist dive site near Sipalay City on idental. Located in 135 feet of water, divers on the *Panay* can still see d boxes of ammunition on the wreck right were Kierson and their teams left them.

conversation. "What Kierson won't tell you either, is that when he arrived on Palawan, the guerilla force was unorganized and nearly disbanded. He helped re-organize the group into what you've seen. We're going to miss you terribly."

"Well, I have taught all of you everything I know. You'll make it.

"So, I've been on the western coast of Palawan for nearly a month now. Imagine my surprise at finding an American sailor on the beach and the guerillas telling me that I was going to be evacuated by submarine in less than twelve hours. I wasn't all that interested in leaving, but they are insisting I have to go. Still, it'll be nice to be back in civilization again, I have been curious about Australia, and could go back to America, so either way, I am ready for whatever is next."

"I'm sure a good shave would be welcome too." I said, jokingly.

He scratched his beard. "The warm water is what I'm looking forward to. You'd be amazed what you can do with a bolo knife though. It's very effective." I had no problem whatsoever imagining this man shaving his face with one of those machetes from the Bugsuk Battalion. None at all.

It took us a few hours to slowly work our way down the mountain side. Garretson groaned quietly with every bump in the road, and the children, bored with the cart, ran squealing through the trees, called back frequently by the Sutherlands.

My feet were holding up well, scar tissue looked almost like the coral itself had grown to the bottoms of my foot, but I wasn't too worried. We were finally going home, and if all went well, I would be able to get a message to my mother before she heard anything about the *Flier's* fate.

Howell sprinted up the path, red-faced, sweaty and panting, with other guerillas at his heels. "Captain…" He bent over, gripped h knees and pulled in deep lungful's of air. "Captain Mayor s me…to look for you. A Jap ship has pulled in and anchored miles off the point."

Palacido looked up sharply at the other guerillas. "It is true," one said. "It arrived over two hours ago. They weighed anchor, but have made no attempts to come on shore via lifeboat or any other method, and if we cannot tell if they are armed."

"The rest of the convoy?" he asked.

"There does not appear to be any convoy at all. None of our scouts have reported seeing any ships for the past twelve hours. It would seem that this one is alone and without help for at least ten miles on either side."

"Is she in distress?" A torpedoed ship might beach herself, rather than sink, which would explain her odd behavior.

"No damage. She looks brand new."

"She's just…sitting there?"

He nodded. "We are continuing to watch her, and keeping out of sight, but we cannot hang the all clear in the lighthouse now. It is very strange behavior."

"What could she be waiting for?" I wondered aloud.

The guerilla looked somber. "For all we know they are waiting for your submarine to show herself before blowing us all to hell."

Palacido ran ahead with the guerillas, while those of us from the *Flier* tried to hustle everyone along as quickly as possible. However, we should have learned on the way up, there is no way to hustle a bao. Even with nothing to wallow in, the stubborn brute still his sweet time.

tain Mayor met us with concern in his eyes. "I've got men it out, and we've dragged the kumpits under cover, so if we y to get you to the rendezvous while she's still here, we can m somewhere else. Please make your way to my house eck this situation out."

your submarine is wise enough to stay out of sight."

Mayor said.

"They've probably already seen it," Jim said confidently. "Pity we can't raise them yet, someone might be able to tell us if that thing came down on its own, or if it's a trap and a convoy is waiting around the corner."

"If there is a convoy, I doubt she'll surface or stick around." I said. I didn't say anything, but privately I thought things didn't look good for our evacuation tonight.

The party organized at the house to wait and watch. We didn't know what to do. Captain and Jim, after talking with Howell for some time about what happened, decided to go and look at the ship themselves, with the help of a guide. The rest of us were ordered to stay put. I chafed at the order a bit: but as the senior officer left behind, the welfare of the party was now my responsibility. Not that anyone would wander off or cause trouble, our main concern was keeping everyone quiet and non-panicky.

Captain and Jim returned within an hour, and with a gesture, told me to meet them outside. "She's still sitting there," Jim told me quietly. "The rendezvous point is some distance off-shore so our sub could still get us, if we can launch and sneak around her in the dark."

"With her sitting there though, I don't know if it's worth the risk," Captain said. "*Redfin* has orders to try again tomorrow night if something prevents rescue, though they were probably thinking more along the lines of rough seas."

"That Maru could move in a few hours," I said.

"Or it might not," Jim interjected. "If she thinks this is a good place to stop and fix something internal like their engines, then they may be here for quite some time. And that's assuming she isn't here specifically to catch the lot of us."

"It might be worth it to go back into the mountains tonight," Captain said, "in case this ship is holding an invasion force for a night raid and hope she gets herself underway. If it was just us, that would be one thing, but with the civilians, especially Mrs. Sutherland and the children, I don't want to place them in any more danger than I have to."

"What if we were to cast off further down the beach?" I asked. "We might not be precisely where the rendezvous is supposed to take place, but we'd be in the area. Even though we won't be able to put the all-clear lanterns in the Point Light, and I'll bet *Redfin* is watching this situation very closely if she's anywhere around. If we used the transmitter to try and contact her, we might be able to complete this tonight. If the civilians are willing to take the risk, I don't think we should just hope that the Maru will move in time. If she doesn't, we're right back here in twenty-four hours, but without a back-up date."

"Jacobson's got a point sir," Jim said. "The kumpits are small, and close to the water, and despite the nearly full moon tonight, they'll be difficult to see from more than a mile away or so. If, instead of using oars or sails, we tow the small kumpit behind the large motored one, we'll cut down our silhouette, and if we launch far down the beach and give the Maru a wide berth, we'll be nearly invisible. We might find the sub. If we don't, there's still tomorrow."

"Very true," Captain said. "He seemed the think carefully, looking up at the sky.

"Are we still going to go for it, sir?" I asked. It sounded like he meant to, but with all the caveats and conditions…

"We don't have to make any firm plans right now. I'll talk to Kierson, Garretson and the Sutherlands. As civilians, they have the right to know all the risks of trying this, and see if they want to continue. Not to mention, we may still get lucky. That ship might move before sunset."

To a person, all the civilians in the rescue party agreed to risk pickup if necessary that night despite the extra danger. With an invasion looming, this may be their one and only chance to escape.

The Booke's Point light. Photo courtesy of the family of Ens. Al "Jake" Jacobson

Mrs. Mayor made dinner for us in grand fashion, while her daughter, who was around six, played with the other children. The Mayors had decided to stay. They had been born here and intended to defend their home, and they knew other places to hide in the mountains besides the settlement.

The mountain covered the forest in shadow, as the sun sank into the west, and the ship never moved. The eeriest thing about her was the lack of men on the decks. If it hadn't been for the fact the guerillas and Howell watched her come in and anchor, I would have thought she had run aground and had been abandoned.

Late in the afternoon, we decided to try and contact the *Redfin*. We couldn't use lighthouse to help her find us, so we had to hope she was looking for us on a radio frequency.

"Here goes nothing," Howell said, fiddling with the radio.

He started to call the *Redfin*, using the assigned code names, but no answer came back. Every few minutes, Howell called, as we hid in the trees and watched the sky flame red in the hidden sunset, then begin to darken. If we could contact her now, we would at least know she was waiting for us if we decided to risk the boats.

One hour passed, then two. She wasn't replying but it was early yet, she might be on an unusual frequency, or not risking an answer this close to an enemy ship.

"It's time." Jim said, watching the waves. "We'll need at least an hour to get out to the rendezvous point. If we're going to do this tonight, it needs to be now."

The Fliers grabbed and hauled the kumpits to the waves, making sure the towing cable was securely fastened to the small kumpit in the rear.

The Sutherlands hugged and bade the Edwards, Mayors, and the guerillas good-bye. Kierson and Garretson roughly shook hands with everyone. George, Red and Charlie talked to some of the guerillas in a low voice. For us, who had spent little time here, this was a chance to go home. For the rest, they were leaving home, possibly never to return.

The Fliers all settled in the motorized kumpit with Palacido, while Butch sat in the towed kumpit with the civilians, and both boats were equipped with oars in case the motor died. Howell and Miller hefted the radio into the front kumpit, along with a flashlight. Another, less reliable radio was left behind with the beach party, so they could keep in touch with the boats.

Jim, Baumgart, Russo and I gripped the sides of the beached kumpit and shoved off into the water, leaping onboard as soon as the water splashed around my knees. Butch, Kierson, and Mr. Sutherland did the same for the one behind. I looked back at the beach. With the enemy so close, no signal fire had been lit, but in the dim light of the rising moon, I took a last look at the guerillas, the Mayors, and the Edwards family waving from the beach. They were soon lost to sight.

Palacido started the motor, and followed the edge of the island south for three or four miles, putting distance between us and the ship before turning for the rendezvous point.

The wind whisked by our faces as we moved slowly around the large ship, and we strained our eyes searching for the sailors that should be on deck and on watch. After the last time the Japanese attempted to invade this area, one would think these sailors would be on extra watch duty in case the guerillas stormed and killed them too. But there was no one, no lights, no movement, nothing. And that scared us worse than seeing hoards of the enemy might have. She might be harmless, she may be unarmed, but she certainly had a radio and could call for backup.

The hour passed slowly. We felt nervous and jumpy, watching for any activity, straining our ears for any click of a gun or clacking of raising anchors. Howell discovered quickly that the radio on the beach broke, severing our link to the guerillas. We were on our own and were going to have to find *Redfin* without help, if she even showed up. Anything could have happened since we last spoke: the ship might be the last of a convoy that had been attacked, *Redfin* could be on the ocean floor…I forced that thought from my mind roughly. The most likely answer was that *Redfin* would not reveal herself with the enemy so close. Or she may miss us in the dark.

Howell began to call out quietly for the *Redfin*. He used the voice, and then the CW Keying[31], since he was unsure after the failure of the radio on the beach if the voice transmission was working at all.

The rendezvous time of 2000 hours came and went. There was no sound besides the waves and breeze and no new shadow on the moonlit water to announce *Redfin*. Howell called again, and again, and we each took turns cranking the radio generator lever keeping the power to the set.

Two hours passed. Howell's voice started to rasp, but there was no response. The waves lapped the sides of the kumpit, and the moon rose higher in the sky. What happened?

"*…not hear…difficulties…W keying better…*"

"They're there!" Howell whispered excitedly. I looked around at the surrounding ocean, but there was nothing there. The Japanese ship was now a tiny speck against Palawan's mountains, so that couldn't be keeping her away.

"I'm switching to CW keying, sir," Howell announced, "I think that's what they were requesting. Perhaps sending a light signal would help them find us if this doesn't work."

"I'll do it, sir," Russo volunteered, grabbing the flashlight and signaling over the side, first to the east, then to the north, then to the south, then back east. Wherever *Redfin* was, she would see us.

But after the first rush of success, there was nothing again. We knew she was out there, and she had trouble hearing us, but what was

---

[31] CW (Cable and Wireless) Keying is similar to a telegraph, using Clicks on a radio frequency to spell out a message.

taking so long?

The civilians in the other boat shifted restlessly, I could hear Mrs. Sutherland shushing her small daughter from crying. We took turns cranking the generator that supplied the radio with energy, and Russo kept at it with the flashlight, though at a much slower pace.

Midnight came. The moon had long ago passed its apex and was sinking in the west, throwing us into its light. I began to wonder how long we would stay out here before giving up for the night and trying again tomorrow.

"Suddenly, the radio started to click frantically. Howell frowned in concentration, then gave a quiet yell of triumph. "Russo! Stop signaling! They see us, and they're on the way!" It was hard not to yell in victory.

It was 0043 hours, August 31. We had been signaling for nearly three hours.

The first thing I saw was the moonlight glittering off her wake. *Redfin*, painted black, faded into the night sky, but the silvery arrow of the wake steadily moved closer. The rumble of the engines grew to a growl. She bore down onto us, and for a moment, I had a glimpse of the frightening aspect our victims might sometimes see, but *Redfin* turned to our port side.

"Captain Austin!" Crowley called out, but the four engines downed out his hails. "Captain Austin!" He yelled, heedless of the enemy now nearly three miles behind. *Redfin's* engines stopped, then reversed, arresting her forward momentum and tossing us around in the backwash.

"Crowley!" I heard from the figure on the bridge, "You're a sight for sore eyes! Take her down to the water!"

There was a loud hiss of air releasing from the ballast tanks, as we all screamed and shouted with excitement and joy. I threw a mooring line to one of the submariners flooding onto the deck and he tied us to one of *Redfin's* cleats. We were so eager to get aboard that when a hand was held out to me, I didn't hesitate or ask permission to come aboard. I just grabbed it, and vaulted onto the deck.

Captain Austin jumped down from the bridge. He was tall, slightly balding, but walked with the confidence of a leader. He held his hand out to Crowley, who grasped it, shook it, then hugged one another. "Boy, am I ever glad to see you too, Cy!" Crowley said.

I helped haul the second kumpit in and give a hand to the civilians and children on board. Alastair's eyes were as big as saucers. "Is this a real submarine?" He asked in awe.

"It sure is, little man," the sailors laughed. "And we've got your own room ready for you downstairs."

"Evening Captain Austin," Palacido bounded onto the deck. "Been a while, hasn't it?"

"Sergeant Carlos Palacido as I live and breathe. How on earth did you get here? I recall dropping you off about a hundred miles south."

"It was too hot back on Ramos. It's nice to know the ol' *Redfin* is holding together well. She looks just as pretty now as she did then."

"Wait a minute." I looked at Palacido. "*Redfin* was your disembarking submarine?"

"Sure was. May of this year. Never thought I'd see you again with all the hundreds of boats in the ocean."

"Small world I guess. We've got your lube oil ready, anything else you need?"

"Everything. I know you're still on patrol, but whatever you can spare, food arms, ammunition, clothes, anything would be very appreciated."

"You're in luck. We received orders two hours ago to run straight for Darwin the moment we're clear. Navy doesn't want to risk the civilians. So I think we can load you up nicely, we'll just re-load in Darwin."

He gave a couple of quick orders and the civilians were hustled

USS Redfin, taken around 1944. Official Navy Photograph

up to the bridge and loaded into the boat. Moments after they disappeared, more sailors began flooding out bearing cases and cans of fruit, vegetables, bags of flour, yeast, and ground coffee. Butch and Palacido began to laugh as we bucket brigaded and packed the two kumpits. Four rifles, two .30 caliber machine guns, 10 Colt pistols, 3 carbine rifles, and nearly 25,000 rounds of ammunition of different calibers. Then the men of the Redfin started to dig deep bringing out clothes, shoes, including a brand new pair of size nine and a half shoes for Mr. Edwards, cigarettes, playing cards, toilet paper, pencils, writing paper, three bags of medical supplies including the crucial atabrine and even the scarce quinine to combat malaria, and items still kept coming. Tears and laughter were rolling off the two Coastwatchers, as they packed the kumpits higher and higher, and they settled lower and lower into the water. By the time the crew of the Redfin had given most of their spare clothes, radio tubes, soap, and typewriter ribbons, the kumpits edges were only two inches higher than the water surrounding it. "It's Christmas in August!" Butch crowed. "I can't wait to see their faces when we get back to shore."

"Sir?" One of the lookouts up in the rings said, "That ship has not moved, and I still have yet to see any sign of moment whatsoever."

"That is so strange. Is she one of yours?"

"One of ours? No, she's one of theirs." Crowley said.

"She's flying no marking of any kind we could see, and I had to consider that you might be on that ship."

"She's a small Maru," Crowley confirmed. "No one can see what's she's doing, even up close. It's more than a little suspicious."

"We won't be able to move as fast on our return journey either." Palacido said. "I don't understand it, if they were ever going to attack now would be the time."

"She's definitely not abandoned, either." Austin said, "We watched her come down from the north and anchor there." He paused for a moment studying the silent vessel. "You know, I'm sure she's chock full of good equipment you could use. And my men could always use some gunnery practice."

Palacido grinned. "Sir?"

"Just don't forget to capture any crewmembers that make it to shore, you wouldn't want them running loose in your territory."

"Yes, sir!" Palacido gave a smart salute. "And thank you."

A sailor was hauling one last container to the deck. "The battery acid you wanted sir." He said, and handed it to Butch who loaded it onto the second kumpit.

"Coleman?" Palacido peered at him in the darkness. "Is that you?"

"Palacido! Well how are you?"

"We're doing well. Still have that signed silver certificate I gave you, or did you spend it already?" Palacido said as he hefted the acid down to the kumpit.

"Nope, still have it, safe and sound."

Captain Austin stepped in. "Thank you Coleman, I need you to inform the Sutherland family and any of the other civilians in Officer's Country that we're going to firing the cannon over their berths, so don't be frightened." Austin turned to the bridge while Coleman said a quick "Aye Sir!" and wished Palacido and Butch luck before swinging up to the bridge and plunging back down the hatch. "Assemble the Gunnery Crew!" Austin said to his XO who had remained on the bridge, and moment later, several men in helmets and life jackets swarmed down the bridge, to the large deck gun on *Redfin's* foredeck. I suddenly felt homesick.

"You'd best get clear Palacido, and good luck to you." Austin said. "I'll wait until you're well out of the way, but you'd best move as fast as you can."

"Thank you sir." He said. I was one of the few people left on the bridge. Most of my crewmembers had already taken their leave and gone below. I shook Palacido's hand before he jumped into the kumpit, and threw him the mooring lines attached to REDFIN. The outboard motor sounded quieter now, and they ponderously plowed out into the darkness.

The moon had set behind the island, and the Maru was all but impossible to see as she blended in with the dark shadow of the mountain ridge of Palawan. The gunnery crew's pointer and trainer, unable to see their target well, were cranking the muzzle to match the bearing the lookouts overheard called down. A second crew was loading the 20 mm on the bridge firing deck with the repeating rounds, and aiming carefully.

As I climbed up to the bridge, it all felt sadly familiar. *Redfin* was a close sister to *Flier*, even though there were subtle differences. It was surreal in a way to be aboard another submarine, so like her and yet, not nearly the same enough. A hand grasped my shoulder. It was Captain Austin, "Your name sailor?" he said.

"Ensign Alvin Jacobson, sir."

"Thank you. Please join your crewmates down below Ensign." It wasn't spoken in anger, but it was nonetheless a command, and until we reached Darwin, this was my new commanding officer. I swung down into the Conning Tower, met by the smells of sweat and oil that brought back memories. Men were peering into the Radar screens, calculating on the map tables, another standing at the wheel waiting for a direction to move. "Ahead, one-quarter speed, battery power." Austin called down the bridge hatch, the orders rapidly repeated all over the boat. Within seconds, *Redfin* gripped the water, and silently began to creep up on our target.

I slid down into the Control Room, gleaming with polished brass and steel. It was all there: The helm station, trim station, everything. I knew most of us were probably in the Officer's Country until this was over and we could be debriefed by Captain Austin, and stepped through the bulkhead.

The Sutherlands had been placed together in the COB's room, the only cabin with four beds. I saw the sailor called Coleman in there with them, patiently answering Alastair's many questions, while reminding the family that the gun would be right over their heads.

George, Red and Charlie had been billeted in the XO's room, with three bunks, while Kierson and Henry Garretson were in the cabin I had had on the *Flier*. All these people, as non-quals, were going to be restricted to their cabins for the next few days, except for supervised visits to the bathroom. Their food would be delivered to them, all in an effort to make sure they were out from underfoot in case of an emergency. Even with the orders to report directly to Darwin, we were still a week out and deep in enemy territory.

I found my crewmates in the Officer's Wardroom, just as the *Redfin* thundered and shook. "*Boom! Boom! Thunk! Thunk! Thunk!*" The four-inch and 40 mm were firing so quickly that it was difficult to get to my seat in the Mess. I could hear George and the other guys yelling in triumph and giving high-fives, while the children, who I expected to be frightened despite Coleman's assurances, were laughing. Alastair was even yelling "Get 'em! Kill 'em!"

Redfin surged forward, rocking violently under the kickback of her guns. For ten minutes she kept up the barrage, knocking dust from the cork-covered walls and rattling the clocks. We held on, braced against the wall and the strut under the table as she shook and roared, then suddenly, all was quiet. She slowed, stopped, and I heard men in the forward torpedo room call out, "Ready torpedo tubes one, two and three!" There was a scurry up front as beds were folded and stowed, the tubes checked and pressurized and the back-up torpedoes slid out of their storage racks into position to take their place in the tubes the moment its current occupant was fired. The men waited, quiet, for the orders on range and bearing that were due to be radioed in moments.

"Stand down." Austin's voice came over the boat's intercom. Moments later, as the torpedo room was being put right, the engines roared, and *Redfin* turned smoothly out to sea.

15

REDFIN

Redfin's stewards, Henry Hoyt and Otis Morgan, brought us food and drink, and it was wonderful to eat good-old American sub food again. I told them quickly about George's hankering for bacon and eggs, and they laughed, saying that they would fix that craving right now if the civilians were willing to stay up for it. After the excitement of the night, there was going to be no sleeping for hours, so an early breakfast of bacon, sausage, eggs, toast, juice and coffee was fixed, and the smell was incredible as it wafted down the passage. George even defied orders and snuck down the three feet of passageway to the Wardroom to thank me, it was everything he had missed.

Captain Austin and some of his officers came to see us about an hour after the firing ceased. Captain Crowley thanked them again for rescuing us, and introduced us all in turn.

"It was only what you would have done if the circumstances were changed, John," Austin said. "And now, allow me to introduce my XO, Commander Charles Miller, the COB William O'Hara, more commonly known as "Jeep", and Lt. Mitchell, Lt. Reinhardt, Ens. Helz, Lt. Taylor, and oh yes, I'm sure you'll get to know this one quite well, our Doc, Bernie Ross."

Ross stuck his head in for a second and waved. "If you guys are good for a while, I'll check in on the civilians."

We were, and Ross left.

"Well, I can see that Otis and Henry put you right at home. I'm glad."

"Did Perth tell you anything about what happened to us?"
"A bit, I'll wager you're the reason the Balabac Straits are now closed until further notice. That was the reason why we had to travel all the way around the northern tip of Palawan to get here. I think you are

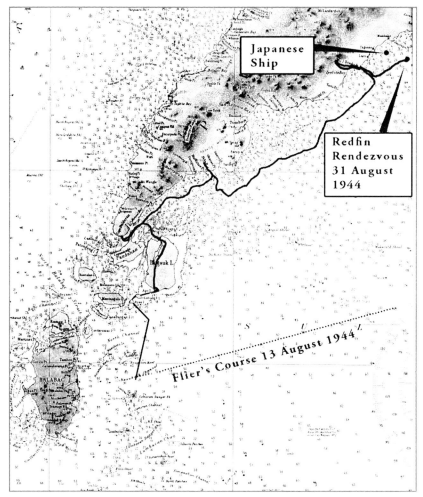

The full journey of the Flier Survivors from 13 August to 31 August. The survivors covered more than 125 miles.

the first submariners to come back home."

Crowley looked down at the table. I knew he was thinking of the men under his command who were never going to come home. Since he had survived, there would likely be another investigation on his return to determine if he had screwed up and was responsible for the deaths of his men, but I knew there was no way he could be held responsible for that mine or whatever had taken us down. Still, knowing you were not responsible didn't stop you from constantly going back over the infinite "What ifs" that inevitably rose from the depths of memories.

"Were you able to sink her?" I asked Captain Austin, who was looking as though he wished he hadn't said anything.

"No," he said, smoothly transitioning to the topic I laid on the table. "She was manned though, all right. Within moments of our first salvo, she had hauled anchor and fled to the south. She must be really shallow-bottomed though, she stayed in the shoals where the water can't be more than a few feet deep. I couldn't get any closer, and we only managed to hit her once or twice at that range. The first flash actually blinded most of my gunners, and they had to work from shouted commands from the lookouts, so their aim wasn't as good as it usually is. I had hoped she'd head for deeper water and I could fire a torpedo at her but she never strayed from the shore and shallows. Pity, I really wanted to take her down for those guerillas."

"Yes, well, I was worried that you wouldn't appear at all with that thing there." Crowley muttered.

"I almost didn't. Seems recently, my job has been a multi-million dollar ferry. I pick you up this patrol, dropped those Coastwatchers and all their gear off last patrol, and the rendezvous on my second patrol was a total disaster. I was really suspicious about this pick-up because of that."

"What happened?" Howell asked.

"I was assigned to pick up about six Australian agents at the tail end of my first patrol on *Redfin*, near the Sibutu Passage. I looked, saw the security signal, responded, and received acknowledgement of my signal from the beach. They couldn't get their hands on a boat, so I sent Ensign Helz with a small landing party to shore in a rubber boat. I saw him signal through the trees again and again, receiving varying replies, which made me suspicious. But Helz decided to make a cautious landing, asking another seaman, Carinder, to cover him with a rifle. No sooner do they step away from their raft than an enemy soldier runs out of the woods and tried to run Carinder through with his bayonet, then more and more Japs start to fire from the woods while my men are held down behind only a rubber raft. Helz and the Carinder managed to get back, and they launched back into the water, bullets whizzing all around them. I was too far away to do much, and the changing tide was trying to sweep them back to shore. It took nearly seven hours to recover them, none the worse for wear, but all the time I knew that our position could have been reported from the first hour we had been here. We saw neither hide nor hair of the purported Australians, and it may have been a trap."

"No wonder you were suspicious. It gets more dangerous every year out here." Captain said.

"I was surprised at how well you remembered 'Adeline' I must say,"

"We sang it to the point that it would run through my head for days. I couldn't forget it if I wanted to." Captain smiled "I felt rather foolish singing, especially with Jacobson here listening in," the enlisted men started to snort into their napkins, doing a lousy job of smothering a laugh, "but it was worth it if it got you out here."

"I'm glad,"

"Captain Crowley, can you tell me, is it true, the rumors about the *Robalo*?" Cmdr. Miller asked.

"Depends on what you heard."

"That she's gone too with all hands."

"Close enough to the truth. She's gone."

Miller's face fell, as did most of the officer's. "Is something wrong?" Jim asked.

"One of our guys, Kimball Graham, was transferred to the

Robalo. We were hoping it wasn't true."

"I'm sorry." There was nothing else that could be said.

"Come on guys," Austin said gently, "we need to get back on station and let these guys find a place to rest. With the civilians taking over Officer's Country, you'll have to hot-bunk[32] it wherever you can on the way home." He addressed us on that last sentence. "I know that you're all qualified, but we have a rhythm here that works well, so I won't need your services unless it's a battle situation. Please try to stay out of our way, but enjoy the Mess Hall, the movies, anything we can offer, and any bunk that's open. Officers," he said addressing Jim, Captain and me, "You are more than welcome to join us when we partake of meals, though it may be a little crowded. After Doc Ross checks you out, feel free to make yourselves comfortable wherever you can. Is there anything else I can do?"

We had no requests, so Austin retired to his cabin to sleep off the night's work. *Redfin's* Doc was very unhappy at the state of our feet. Mine were starting to heal over all right, though they were still raw and tender in some places. Some of the guy's feet were red, raw, and scabbed over with pus more than blood, but after a thorough antiseptic wash and bandaging, which stung horribly, Doc assured us all they would heal well with no more than scars to remind us of the last two and a half weeks. He also prescribed quinine, just in case we had been infected with Malaria.

"Captain Crowley?" the Cmdr. Miller, who was on duty, stuck his head in, "It's coming on dawn and we're passing the southern end of Palawan. Just thought you'd like to know if you wanted to go on the bridge."

We trooped up to the bridge, a last good-bye to our loyal boat

---

[32] Hot-bunking: A common practice in modern nuclear submarines, though not on WWII boats, hot-bunking is where two or more people share a bunk, and sleep on alternate schedules. Therefore, one guy gets up, and the other goes to bed while the bunk is still "hot".

Seven of the eight Flier survivors on the deck of the Redfin. Back row left to right: Lt. Jim Liddell, Cmdr. John Crowley, Ens. Al Jacobson. Front row left to right: QM3c James Russo, MoMM3c Wesley Miller, MoMM3c Earl Baumgart, CRT Gibson Howell. Not pictured: TCR2c Don Tremaine (ill with malaria) Photos courtesy of the family of Lt. James Liddell.

and friends. Due to the danger, *Redfin* was miles away from the site we had been at, and Palawan was smoky mass on the horizon, the smaller islands invisible. We all stood in silence until Palawan faded out of respect for the fallen.

The trip home was uneventful. *Redfin* stayed on the surface as often and as long as she could, only diving to avoid a patrol plane or convoy. The civilians were thrilled with the motion of the boat, tossing in the waves, perfectly still underwater, and the peculiar groans and rushing noises when she dove and surfaced.

The crew adopted the children, making them toys from various items around the sub, even a pair of sandals for each of them, woven out of *Redfin's* stock of leather. Maise Sutherland, embarrassed to go home shoeless because her carefully saved last pair (she'd worn through all the others) were too small for her swollen feet, was delighted to find a pair of silk stockings in her cabin one night, donated by a *Redfin* sailor who had been intending to send them to a girl back home, where silk was scarce. Mrs. Sutherland had never had a pair before.

Tremaine came down with Malaria three days after coming on board, and had a rough time of it, but Doc Ross soon got him on the mend. Even Garretson was feeling a bit better.

I spent my time playing cards, visiting with our friends, or sleeping wherever I could find an open bunk, especially in the Forward Torpedo Room, where it was coolest. I didn't write to my family. Whatever I sent would be censored, and perhaps forbidden. It would be weeks before they began to worry though, and by then I would know what I could say and not say.

After crossing the Sibutu passage and returning to the open ocean, Captain Austin allowed the evacuees and crew some time on the deck to get fresh air. The sun felt good on my face again.

I was dressed in gifted clothes, like the rest of the Fliers, and had even been able to beg a shower the night before. The fresh breeze

The Brooke's Point evacuees. Standing, left to right: Liddell, Crowley, Baumgart, Howell, Miller, Harry Garretson, Russo, Maise Sutherland, Heather Sutherland (held by her mother), Alastair Sutherland (boy), Sandy Sutherland, Vans Kierson. Kneeling left to right: Jacobson, George Marquez, Bill "Red" Wigfield, Charlie Watkins. Not Pictured: Donald Tremaine. (According to some sources, "Harry Garretson" in this photo is Don Tremaine, and Garretson is not pictured.) Photo courtesy of the family of Lt. James Liddell

blowing across my face felt heavenly. Alastair and Heather Sutherland, cooped up so long in the cabin, raced squealing around the deck frightening their mother because submarines don't have railings.

One of the crewmen of the *Redfin* had a camera, and took a picture of Captain Crowley and Captain Austin together on the Aft Bridge, which lead to more photos to commemorate our rescue. Tremaine was too ill to come on deck, but Garretson stood for the Brooke's Point evacuees photos. We looked respectable and healthy, the sunburns were healing, and we slowly began regaining the weight we had lost aided by excellent kitchen staff of *Redfin*.

"We're only a few days out now." Captain Austin told Captain Crowley. "I'll get to stay long enough to replenish my stores, then back out to sea."

"We owe our lives to you, Cy."

"Just what you'd do for me had the tables been turned and you know it. It's nothing."

Australia came into view the morning of the 5th of September, and *Redfin* pulled into Darwin on the early morning of the 6th. Our showing up there was a surprise and none of the usual crowds that greeted a returning submarine showed, nor did *Redfin* fly her celebratory brag rags, flags or broom that she would have at the close of a patrol. We were met at the dock by a several Marines, and a convoy of cars. We separated from the Sutherlands, Kierson, Garretson, George, Red and Charlie as they were driven into town somewhere. I never saw them again.

We loaded into a pair of jeeps and were driven to the base at Darwin where the hospital corpsman checked us over thoroughly. They pronounced us all temporarily unfit for duty and needing R & R until our feet healed and all suspicion of malaria had passed.

Rumors of *Robalo*'s fate buzzed around town. We didn't say anything though. There was enough time for the truth to come out, after their families had been informed of their fates.

Captain, Jim and I went out to the docks late in the evening to see *Redfin* off. Captain Austin was checking off the last of his stores, checking systems checks, and greeting his crew as they straggled in, dusty and sweaty from an afternoon baseball game.

"Permission to come aboard," Captain called across to Austin, who smiled at us, "Permission granted," he called back. We stepped across, pausing on the deck to salute the flag that waved proudly at the stern of *Redfin*.

"I wanted to thank you again for saving us."

"I told you it was nothing. That's what we do in the Silent Service. Come to see us off?"

"We can't stay that long. Admiral Christie has chartered a plane to Perth for us, and it's leaving soon. Still, " Captain held out his hand to Austin, "Happy Hunting. I hope to see you again."

"God willing. Good luck, John." He shook hand with each of us in turn, and we disembarked. *Redfin's* engines roared beneath her, as if offering her own good-bye before she disappeared into unknown regions of the Pacific.

Al Jacobson at work on USS Ling in 1945. Photo Courtesy of family of Alvin Jacobson.

-*Epilogue*-

"…a pair for two and a run of three for five means that I have one-hundred-twenty-one points, and I win again!" Mary said gleefully.

"I knew I never should have taught you this game," Muriel Jacobson said wryly. "You sure you're not a cribbage shark or something?"

"Guess you're just a good teacher," Mary grinned and shuffled the deck. "Another hand?"

"What time is it?" Muriel asked, looking around for the clock in her friend's den.

"Looks like about 4:25, or thereabouts," Mary pointed to the clock hanging over the radio.

"I think I'm good for one more hand then. Mom will want me home to help make dinner for Papa. It doesn't take long now that it's just the three of us. It seems so strange, with Edna Mary and Marilyn back at college, and David now in the Army Air Force. We were all at the lake just a while ago."

"Oh, so he got in?"

"Sure did, and Mom's more worried than ever."

"Well, I hope they all come home soon."

"Me too."

Mary dealt the cards again, and the 4:25 newscast began on the radio. Both girls ignored the news and concentrated on the game, until…

"We've just received news that the *USS Flier* is overdue and presumed lost at sea with all hands," the announcer read methodically.

Muriel froze, her eyes widened and she started to shake like a leaf.

"Muriel, are you going to play a card or what?" Mary said

playfully, looking up. Muriel's face was now white.

"Muriel?" Mary ran around the table, "What happened? Are you okay?" She touched her friend's shoulder in concern.

Muriel uttered a single, strangled gasp, fled the table and crashed through the back door, leaving her friend behind.

She dashed through the backyards of her neighbors, tears falling down her cheeks. The families of sailors were not encouraged to talk about which ships their family members were on, so Mary hadn't known that Al was on the *Flier*, and that Al was…was…Muriel couldn't yet bring herself to think it.

She pounded through the back door of her house, and started screaming, "Mom! MOM!" Her mom ran out to the back hall to catch her nearly-hysterical daughter.

"What is it? What happened?"

"It was on the radio, Mom, they said Al's submarine went down with all hands!" she cried.

"Muriel, Muriel it's okay, it's okay," her mom gripped her shoulders hard, "Look at me, Muriel. It's okay—"

"How can it be okay? Al's…"

"He's alive, Muriel. I got the letter yesterday!"

It took a moment to register. "You got a letter yesterday? Did…did Al get reassigned and we didn't know?"

"Come over here and sit," her mom said, leading Muriel to a rocking chair in the sunroom. She pulled a letter from her apron pocket. "I only found out yesterday and I'm sorry I didn't tell you, but your father and I were given strict instructions not to say anything to anyone until it was announced on the radio. I didn't think the notice was going to be today though."

Muriel took the proffered letter with shaking hands and read aloud, "My dear Mr. and Mrs. Jacobson, Your son, Ensign Alvin Emmanuel Jacobson, Jr. United States Naval Reserve, who was aboard a ship the loss of which will be announced in the near future, is safe and well." She started to cry in relief and for a moment, the two of them sat holding each other. Eventually, Muriel was able to continue.

"'The circumstances of his rescue are such that information concerning it should not reach the enemy, and it is requested that you do not divulge any reports that may come to you concerning his experiences, or disclose the name of the ship in which he served. The Navy department shares in your pleasure over the safety of your son. It is hoped that he will communicate with you in the near future. Sincerely yours, L. E. Denfield.'

"What happened?" she asked her mom.

"I don't know. I haven't heard from Al yet. Now I had better call your sisters at school. I don't want another case of hysterics if they hear about this like you did. If you need time to recover, I can handle dinner myself."

"I'll be okay, just give me a few minutes, I think," Muriel smiled weakly. The last half-hour had been hard, but she was determined to be strong

"All right," her mother turned to go, then turned back and said, "I love you."

"I love you too, Mom."

Muriel took several deep breaths and felt much calmer. She'd go back over to Mary's after dinner and try to explain if she could.

The tree outside the sunroom swayed in the breeze and Muriel started to laugh remembering the stories about Al and that tree. He had climbed when he was around ten years old to peek in at Mom in the sunroom, and fell and broke his collarbone. Papa then forbade him to climb it again, but soon after his collarbone healed, Al placed a refrigerator box under the tree, climbed the box and fell again, re-breaking his collarbone. He argued that he shouldn't get in trouble because technically, he had obeyed because he wasn't climbing the tree.

Perhaps it was that stubbornness, determination and creative recklessness that had gotten him through, and perhaps one day he would tell her what had happened, if allowed to.

Suddenly Muriel decided her mom was right, she could live with the mystery for now, just knowing that Al was all right somewhere. As she went into the house to help her mom with dinner, Muriel said a quick prayer for her brothers, wherever they were, and for those families of the *Flier* that might not be receiving the letter they had gotten.

"Gentlemen! The war is OVER!!! Japan has surrendered!" Commander Molumphy's voice roared over the intercom.

I yelled as loudly as the rest of the men on the *Ling*, my new submarine. We had cleared Panama Canal just a day prior, on our way to help with the invasion of Japan. The Sub Force was short on experienced officers, so after I was cleared, I elected to return to sub duty because I wanted to see this war to its end, and now it was finally over.

"To celebrate, we are going to fire every last shell on this blessed boat at that little scrap of rock off our portside!" Molumphy continued. "Gunnery Crews, report to your stations!"

It took us a couple of hours to fire every shell out of the *Ling's* guns, but a day later, the reason was obvious: we docked at a Panamanian port and loaded the ammunition lockers with as much alcohol and liquor as would fit, and had express orders to report directly to New London as fast as possible.

The past year since the *Flier* incident, much had happened. After the *Redfin* left Darwin, we were loaded on a plane and flown to Perth to collect our pay, find clothes that fit, and order new uniforms.

Baumgart had friends in Perth and went to stay with them. Captain Crowley spent most of his time with Admiral Christie going over the details of the incident. The Navy flew the rest of us to a remote gold-mining town called Kalgoorlie. Admiral Christie thought that this would be the best way to prevent our story from spreading to the other submariners.

Though we were told that the mine was running at capacity, the placed seemed deserted when landed. We soon learned that it was horse race week and the miners had unionized so they could spend time at the races. Between races the town livened up though.

In the peace, I finally allowed myself to remember my friends: Ed, Reynolds, Pope, Hudson, Clyde, Doc, Elton, Dag…there were far too many who hadn't made it. Why had I?

More news kept trickling in. Now the *Harder* was missing. The invincible Sam Dealey might have gone the way of "Mush" Morton and the *Wahoo*. Because of our adventure, the Navy refused to accept the loss for nearly six months, and stretched its intelligence networks to the breaking point looking for any trace of Dealey and his men. In the end, the Navy had to accept the inevitable.

After a couple of weeks, the Navy brought us back to Perth for the official investigation into the *Flier's* demise. It was held at the same berth that *Flier* had tied up to, but the old *Orion* was gone, replaced by her sister, the *Eurayle*.

This time, not only was Captain being investigated for his possible part in *Flier's* demise, but also Admiral Christie, who commanded the Perth-based submarines and drafted the orders to go through the straits. Because of what we had learned about the *Robalo* while we were in Bugsuk, her fate was tied into this investigation. All of us except Captain, who was an interested party inside the courtroom, sat outside during the two days of the inquiry. They talked to me for all of ten minutes in total. All they wanted to know was my name, rank, and where I had been the night *Flier* went down, what I thought had sunk the *Flier,* whether I had properly adjusted my eyesight before lookout duty, but nothing really detailed. No one cross-examined me, or indeed, any of the other survivors, though they talked with Liddell and Howell longer than the rest of us.

In the end, the loss of both boats was ascribed to the risks of war. We had operated as safely as we could with the best intelligence available, but sometimes that simply wasn't enough.

The ban on Balabac Strait was never lifted for the remainder of the war.

Every *Flier* crewman on the second patrol, living and dead, was awarded the Purple Heart, and Captain was awarded the Legion of Merit for leading the escape. Liddell, Howell and Russo received commendations as well.

After the investigation, I was sent home to Michigan to be with my family for an extended leave. They Navy, knowing the story of our escape would encourage the public, but not wanting us to reveal the Coastwatchers, encouraged us to talk about everything up until the guerillas found us. My family kept a scrapbook of those articles. Some of them made up some interesting stories about how we must have gotten back. Sadly, at first some newspapers reported that most, if not all the *Flier* crew survived, falsely raising the hopes of their families.

My mother insisted that talking about everything that happened to me would help me work through it, and as she was an excellent short-hand secretary, she also wrote down my adventures. I didn't tell her specific names or places where we went, but talking about it did help.

Coming back from leave I soon learned that I was the only member of the *Flier* to report to the *Ling*. I worked with her during her shakedown trials in the Atlantic and did a little bit of U-Boat hunting.

After the war, I returned home to Grand Haven, Michigan. Some called me a hero, but I could never think of myself that way. How heroic is it to survive?

My brothers survived the war too. Charles and I were assigned to Boston for a few weeks before our discharge, and did we ever have fun painting the town red.[33]

Charles had been in the midst of the battle for Leyte Gulf. At one point, he had to leave his station to deal with an emergency, and an enemy shell blew it apart seconds after he left. David became a bombardier, and was part of the firebombing of Dresden. My mother, convinced that forcing me to work my way through my memories had helped me, sat with them and made them talk through their experiences too. Her advice proved to be ahead of its time as talking about wartime experiences is now a treatment for Post-Traumatic Stress Disorder.

I returned to the University of Michigan that fall and finished my degree in one year. I hadn't studious before the war, but now college seemed simple compared to what I had been through. After college I worked for a company in Chicago before returning to my father's brass casting business. He had me start on the foundry floor and work my way up the ranks like anyone else.

I finally met the "gorgeous girl" Ed promised me at my sister Muriel's wedding, nearly a decade after *Flier*. I guess you can't rush perfection. Mary was kind enough to marry me in 1955, and we soon had three beautiful children and a nice house near my family. From the outside, it appeared as though I'd left my WWII memories behind me.

But the *Flier* never really left me. Sometimes the aftereffects were

---

[33] True story. Due to a lack of parking, Boston started to paint its "no parking" curbs yellow. Al and Charles painted the curbs near their place red. When the city re-painted those curbs yellow, Al and Charles re-re-painted them blue. It got enough attention to show up in the Boston paper, though no one knew who was responsible. Al kept a copy of the article in his scrapbooks.

strange. While I had no problem with eating rice, the thought of coconut made me sick. I refused to go anywhere without a knife. It was the last thing out of my pocket at night, and first thing I grabbed in the morning, even before my wallet.

Sometimes, Mary would wake me in the middle of the night and told me I was muttering, "Keep swimming, just keep swimming," in my sleep, but I wouldn't tell her why.

My feet never healed and remained deeply scarred.

For years after the war ended, various family members of my lost shipmates would write me heart wrenching letters. They seemed to ask, 'Why you and not my husband, or son, or brother? Why couldn't our loved one escape too?' I wrote back to them, giving what comfort I could, and prayed the letters would help bring peace.

Decades later, after most of the WWII records of the Submarine Force had been declassified, I received an invitation to speak at a Lion's Club meeting. Mary, who now knew about what I had been through, convinced me that others needed to hear stories from actual WWII veterans, and that my children especially needed to hear my story, to keep the memory of *Flier* alive. I had never been so nervous, telling that story with my son in the audience.

I had been warned that the Lion's Club meetings ended at 1:30 sharp, not a moment later, but the day I told my story, I hadn't finished by the closing bell. No one moved a muscle, and stayed, skipping work and errands, until the end of the story.

The men of the *Flier* didn't see each other again until 1994, the 50th anniversary of the *Flier*'s destruction. Five of us, Crowley, Liddell, Miller, Russo, and I were able to go to Annapolis, the home of Crowley, to visit together for the first and, as it turned out, the last time. We caught up with everyone else's life. Captain Crowley and Jim had both been assigned to be CO and XO the brand-new *USS Irex*, which apparently made some of her crew very nervous. The *Irex* was in the Canal only a day behind the *Ling* when Japan's surrender

The Flier Survivors at the 1994 reunion: From left to right: Al Jacobson, James Liddell, John Crowley, Wes Miller, and James Russo. Earl Baumgart, Gibson Howell, and Donald Tremaine were not able to attend. Photo courtesy of the family of Al "Jake" Jacobson

was announced.

We wondered what happened to the Coastwatchers, if they got out, but no one knew.

We poured over charts of the area, and decided that though Captain Crowley had originally stated that we landed on Mantangule Island (and so the record reads to this day) we really had landed on the much smaller Byan Island.

A year later, most of the records of the *Flier* became declassified, and, since I was now retired from my company, I was free to do something I had wanted to do since 1944, search for the *Flier* and bring closure to the families left behind.

I did find the niece of Palacido, who told me all the Coastwatchers who were left after Corpus' suicide survived and made it back home. Palacido was alive and well and a baker in Laguna Beach California. She sent me a copy of the report he had submitted to the military about his time on Palawan. It was a very interesting look at what happened to them after we left. They sheltered escapees from Puerto Princesa, moved closer to the former prison camp after the massacre, and Reynoso married his native girl. All five were awarded the Bronze Star for their efforts in the war.

The death of Cmdr. Crowley in 1997 spurred me to overhaul my memoirs and go back to the Philippines with my now grown son, Steve. We left from Grand Haven and landed in Manila. There, we were greeted by Dr. Nellie Abueg, President of the Palawan Historical Society and her husband Congressman Alfredo Abueg, who helped us make arrangements. Many changes had happened in the fifty plus years since I had been on Palawan. It is still one of the most remote, pristine, and beautiful islands of the Philippines, but modern development had still radically changed the jungle I had known. I visited the memorial erected at Plaza Cuartel, where the Japanese massacred more than one-hundred and fifty prisoners, and said a silent prayer for those who died there. It was the mercy of God alone that kept us and the other *Flier*'s from this fate. I prayed for the *Robalo* sailors, including Kimmel if he had been here, and tried to find more about what had happened to them while I was in Puerto Princesa.

Brooke's Point, a three-hour drive south on good roads, was vastly different. The only houses there in 1944 were the Mayor's house on the beach and the Mayor's and Edwards houses inland. Today, it is a town of 40,000 people. Huge freighters dock where the Maru anchored in 1944. The mayor or Brooke's Point was the granddaughter of Mr. Edwards, who survived the war.

Rio Tuba, was a further two hours on a not-so-good gravel road. In 1944 there were only two houses here, but now it is another major port shipping nickel from massive mines nearby. They even have a full-time Coast Guard station and large department store.

We chartered a boat there and went back through my memories.

Al at Brooke's Point in 1998. It had developed from a small, war torn village to a thriving community of 40,000 people. Photo courtesy of the family of Al "Jake" Jacobson

We passed Byan Island, and I recognized the beach where we landed that afternoon in 1944. It looked so familiar I almost expected to see the seashells I laid out fifty years ago. Where we cast off in our raft from Byan there is now a ship builder who builds 50–60 foot yachts and a housing development for employees. They have a deep well to get their water.

We landed on Bugsuk and found the abandoned house is now the village of Sebring. The house was gone, but the cistern is still there, though the water is now safe. The Mayor family returned after the war and their descendants built a beautiful home about 100 yards away from the old house site, where Steve and I were welcomed for the night.

The most emotional and difficult time though, was when we chartered a ship to take us to the spot where the *Flier* sank. When we arrived at the coordinates that Captain Crowley and Jim figured *Flier* sank, the surroundings didn't look right. We traveled south until the silhouettes matched what I remembered in those last moments fifty-four years before.

Once again, I could see the land on three sides of us, Comiran Island off the port bow, Balabac dead ahead, Palawan a faint shadow to the north. Bayan was hidden by the exposed tops of Roughton and Natsubata Reefs, proving we had been pushed around them by the currents, and didn't swim in a straight line.

Some people told me that we should have swum to Comiran Island to preserve more of our shipmates, but the rumored fate of the *Robalo* crew and the POWs at Puerto Princesa convinced me that we made the right choice and God was watching out for us that night.

The captain of the chartered ship told us that native fishermen and divers have seen *Flier* on the few days a year when the ocean is crystal clear. She apparently sits straight up on the ocean floor, her bow buried deeply in the bottom. No one approaches her, for she is very deep, nor could anyone tell me if the aft hatch was open and others might have escaped.

I stood there on the bow of that ship with my son and wrote down the GPS coordinates of where I thought I had been the night *Flier* went down, about a mile from the accepted coordinates. Perhaps someday, I would be able to come back with the equipment to find her, but for now, it was enough to know she was left in peace.

Alvin "Jake" Jacobson died on October 16, 2008, after years of declining health, before he was able to find the *Flier* himself.

In April of 2009, his son Steve and grandson Nelson Jr., along with experienced divers Mike and Warren Fletcher, and YAP Films, a documentary company, went to Balabac Straits looking for *Flier*.

They anchored at the coordinates Al wrote down on the chart, and when the Fletchers followed the line down they found their weighted bags had landed on the *Flier* herself.

She sits upright listing slightly to the starboard, in 330 feet of water, surrounded by a beautiful bed of white sand and rock. After six decades underwater, she is encrusted with corals and is home to dozens of species of fish. The Fletchers called her one of the most beautiful wrecks they had ever seen.

She had been hit on the starboard side, in the Control Room area, almost directly beneath where Al sat that night. The fact that he was sitting at the deck gun below the bridge wall might have spared him injury or death. Her bow shows some damage, perhaps from when she hit bottom going at full speed.

The aft escape hatch Al always wondered about is closed. The forward escape hatch, however, is open.

But there were no other recorded survivors of USS *Flier*.

The Navy, using the footage and photographs brought back from those dives, compared them to the last known configuration and photographs of the *Flier*. On 1 February, 2010, they officially announced that the wreck in Balabac Straits could only be USS *Flier*.

Like all sunken warships, the *Flier* is considered a war grave by international law, and is not to be disturbed. The men of the *Flier* will be left in peace.

-APPENDIX -

THE LOOSE ENDS

FM SONAR

The loss of *Robalo* and *Flier*, spurred the development of the FM SoNAR device used specifically to detect mines in enough time to change course. The chilling gong that sounded when it found a mine was nicknamed "Hell's Bells", and was a submariner's worst nightmare. However, it did save many submarines towards the end of the war.

JAPANESE MINES

After the war, the Navy learned that the Japanese had invented a new type of sea mine. The old mines American intelligence knew about could only be laid in waters a few hundred feet deep, so submarines were always ordered to stay in water at least five hundred feet deep when possible.

Naval Intelligence had always suspected that Balabac Straits had been mined. An examination of Japanese records after the war proved that Balabac was indeed mined at least twice, once using the old mines in 1941, and again in 1943 by the *Tsugaru Maru* in 1943. *Tsugaru* laid the new Type 93 Model 1 Deep Sea Contact Mine, which could be laid in water nearly 3,500 feet deep. However, there is no way to know which type of mine *Flier* struck that fateful evening. The *Tsugaru* did not escape punishment. She was sunk by *Flier's* sister *USS Darter* on 29 June, 1944. Darter herself would end up resting near *Flier* and *Robalo*. She grounded on a shoal west of Palawan on 24 October

1944. Her crew was saved by the submarine *Dace*.

THE FATE OF THE ROBALO

The story of what happened to the *Robalo* and her crew has never been fully settled.

In the transcripts of the investigation into the loss of USS *Flier* and USS *Robalo*, Captain Crowley stated that de la Cruz told him the *Robalo* sank 40 miles west of Balabac on 3 July, with at least four people washing up on Comiran Island. Two were captured and at least two others escaped, were shot while escaping, or shot after being captured. The names of the survivors were Ensign Tucker and Martin. De la Cruz also said he was able to discover *Robalo's* last port of call was Darwin in late June. These details convinced command that this story was plausible, since those names and facts could not have been known by either Crowley or de la Cruz through normal means.

Ens. Tucker and Wallace Martin, along with two other men, Floyd Laughlin and Mason Poston, who were captured in an unrecorded location, were transported to Puerto Princesa and imprisoned together as rouge guerillas rather than POWs. According to Filipino Guerillas in northern Palawan, on 2 August, they dropped a note out their window, which was picked up by an American POW and made its way to the guerilla forces. The note contained at least these men's names as well as the name of the *Robalo*.

According to intelligence from the people of the island, the prisoners were loaded on a ship on or around August 15 and never heard from again. Al reports in his memoirs that the prisoners were placed aboard the *Takao Maru* and were signed for by the ship's captain Aida Sakutaro, with the intended destination of Manila. He does not identify where he obtained the information, but it is the author's opinion that he likely obtained it during his trip to the Philippines later in his life. Al Jacobson was a careful researcher all his life, especially as concerns this story. Inquiries have been made in Palawan regarding this record, and at the time of publication, were still awaiting verification.

Eventually the US Navy concluded that the *Robalo* may have sunk on 27 July just two miles west of Palawan Island, with Tucker, Martin, Laughlin, and Poston landing together on Palawan Island, not Comiran. The original suspected cause, forward battery explosion, was revised to a mine strike.

During the war, Admiral Christie told the Kimmel family that Manning Kimmel had gone down with his sub, to spare them the story that Al Jacobson heard, which had also reached Christie's ears. If Kimmel really had been taken prisoner, whether he died in August or not wouldn't have mattered, for the entire camp was slaughtered on December 10, 1944. Apparently afraid the invasion of the Philippines was coming to them, and what would happen if they were found with so many Prisoners of War, the Japanese guards herded all the POWs of Puerto Princesa into air raid shelters, dumped aviation fuel over them, and set them on fire, shooting and torturing those who managed to break out of the shelters. Only eleven men escaped, six of whom were delivered to Palacido and the Coastwatchers at Brook's Point for pickup[34]. When the Americans liberated Palawan in March of '45, they found three large mounds of partial remains which were exhumed and sent to St. Louis Missouri, where most are buried together in a mass grave.[35] (A few who could be positively

[34] For more information on this horrible tragedy, read Last Man Out: Glenn McDole USMC Survivor of the Palawan Massacre in WWII by Bob Wilbanks
[35] The site of the Massacre is Plaza Cuartel Park in Puerto Princesa and contains a monument to those who died.

identified were buried according to their families wishes) The number and identities of some the men who died that horrific day are still debated. What is known is that no *Robalo* sailor was ever returned to the US after the war.

USS REDFIN

The *Redfin* completed her fourth patrol and three more after, commanded by Austin and then Charles Miller, who was promoted after Austin went stateside. *Redfin* finished the war being credited for six ships sunk and a total of 23,724 tons of shipping destroyed. She was decommissioned in 1946, then re-commissioned in 1953 as a radar picket submarine and served through the Korean and part of the Vietnam wars. She was later sold for scrap metal, the fate of a number of gallant submarines.

USS FLIER COMMENDATIONS

The *Flier* was awarded one battle star for her successful patrol, and during the war, was given credit for the four ships her crew claimed. However, after the war, the Japanese claimed they had no records of any ships being at the convoy points near Mindoro nor near Cape Bolinas on the dates *Flier* named. The only ship they were given credit for sinking was the ship on the very first attack. Their victim's name was *Hakusan Maru*, a 10,380 ton ship that had been built as a merchant vessel and converted into a troop ship. When *Flier* sank her, she also took out 2,000 Japanese troops likely headed to the Battle of Mariana. As Jacobson would later say, he felt sorry for the men, but it would take a good sized Marine unit to take out those soldiers if they had gotten where they were going. *Hakusan Maru* also appears on the rolls of the Japanese "Hell Ships" fleet; those that were used to transport POW's, like Charlie Watkins. Thankfully, there was no evidence that she carried Allied POWs on the day she sank.

WORLD WAR II SUBMARINE STATS

In total, fifty-two submarines were destroyed during WWII with a loss of over 3,700 men. Submarines had the highest casualty rate of any active branch of military service during WWII: 22%. Of those fifty-two subs, four grounded with no casualties, one was scuttled following the Japanese attack on Manila, and thirty-eight sank with their entire crews. Eight submarines, including *Flier*, had some survivors, totaling 199 men. 191 men were captured by the Japanese, some dying at their prisoner of war camps. Only those of men from the *Flier* were able to elude the Japanese and return home to serve again.

THE REST OF THE EVACUEES AND COASTWATCHERS

Following the war, George Marquez retired to California, where he kept in touch with Larry Coleman of the *Redfin*. Charlie Watkins returned to Miami by the end of 1944, but his trail went cold there.

Larry Coleman also found Palacido in Laguna Beach, California, and returned the Silver Certificate with the signatures of all the Coastwatchers to him in 1995. Palacido never married and ran a popular bakery until his death in 2000.

The Sutherlands, after medical exams and interviews with MacArthur's team about the Philippines for the upcoming invasion, tried to return to Scotland. Due to the war and travel restrictions, they made it as far as South Africa, where they had another son in 1946. After a brief visit to Scotland, they returned to Brooke's Point in 1947 and resumed missionary work until 1951. The Sutherlands traveled the US for fundraising for Brooke's Point, until Sandy

Sutherland was diagnosed with cancer. He died in 1976 and was buried, as he requested, in the Brooke's Point cemetery on the shore of Sulu Sea. Masie Sutherland and the children continued to serve in Palawan for years, though most of the children, including Heather and Alastair, later moved to the USA.

This author was unable to discover the fates of the other Brooke's Point refugees or Coastwatchers.

AUTHOR'S NOTE:

This book has been an interesting journey. I first learned of Mr. Jacobson while I was transcribing board meetings at the Great Lakes Naval Memorial and Museum of Muskegon, Michigan. Mr. Jacobson was one of the nominees to fill two vacant places on the Board of Directors, and the man who nominated him quickly told the *Flier's* story. As the curator and exhibit designer of the museum, I remember thinking "I have got to interview him, this story is amazing!"

It would be another six months before I met him, but in the meantime, I was given the memoirs he had written in 1944 by the museum director. After his trip to the Philippines in 1997, Al had re-typed the 1944 memoirs, re-inserting the names and locations, and adding information that had come to light afterwards. In many ways, it was a bare bones account, but full of little gleams of adventure beyond anything I had read before, in the amazing voice of a man who had lived the impossible.

Like most Americans born two generations removed from WWII, my education about it was somewhat limited, and mostly concentrated on the European Theater, pausing just long enough to mention Pearl Harbor and the atomic bomb.

My grandfather had served under General Patton in North Africa, Italy and Germany, but refused to talk about it, so WWII was a bit taboo for me. Though I had very little interest in WWII until I landed my job at the museum, I quickly grew to admire and respect these men who not only pulled some truly outrageous stunts during WWII, most of them returned to rebuild America during a time of unprecedented prosperity.

When I finally met him in his office, Mr. Jacobson told me that he had been contacted my several authors in the past few decades since the story had been de-classified, but nothing had ever been published beyond some small articles or short accounts within larger books on the Pacific front of WWII. He was now the only survivor left, and wanted the men lost aboard the *Flier* to be remembered long after he was gone. He agreed to work with me, and over the next two years, answered many questions, was interviewed multiple times, donated artifacts that he had, wrote letters, anything I needed.

In the meantime, the museum had launched a large capital campaign to build a climate-controlled facility to house its numerous artifacts, and the story of the *Flier* was planned to be a large part of that. So now the book, which had taken the form of a historical novel, and an exhibit to go with it, landed on my plate.

A lot of this book's design was taken directly from Mr. Jacobson's written memoirs, supplemented with our interviews. While I've read every account from every member of the *Flier* I can get my hands on, when two accounts differed, I often fell back to Mr. Jacobson's memories. Other research helped flesh out the environment Al and his crewmates passed through, from the Filipino guerillas to the Coastwatchers, to contemporary accounts of intelligence (which often differ from what is accepted now as established fact, as in the case of the *Robalo*), to general descriptions of submarine life.

All I can say is that to this day, I'm still in awe of him, what he survived in 1944, and what he contributed to his family, business, and community when he returned.

These men, some of whom have since passed into "Eternal Patrol", protected this country while they should have been in school, college, starting families, or careers. They are the Greatest Generation because they did what it took to protect their country regardless of personal inconvenience or loss. Some sacrificed their youth, some their health, some their sanity, while several hundred thousand sacrificed their lives as well. These submariners have not forgotten their crewmates, nor has any veteran I've ever met forgotten those who they knew that didn't come home. Even more amazing, many of these men went on to re-establish a kind of "normal" when they returned home.

There are only seven WWII era submarines left in the United States, all of them museums all. These seven boats stand as a memory of the fifty-two submarines which were lost, the nearly 200 more that served, and the men who served on them.

When this book was researched and the bulk of it written, Al was the only man alive from the *Flier's* doomed second patrol, all others having passed on between 1997 and 2005. Al died October 16, 2008, before this book was published. His two great desires were to see this story told to the public, and to find the *Flier's* resting place. I have tried to present this story to the best of my ability, and his family fulfilled the other dream. My only regret is Al never saw either, and his family has said that they wish he had been there on that boat when *Flier* revealed herself for the first time in 66 years.

I have lived with this tale for nearly five years now, and I know I'll miss it. Yet, it is only one of thousands of stories about a time where "courage was commonplace, and self-sacrifice the norm."

SUBMARINES AND WWII PACIFIC WARFARE

From the beginning of the U.S. Naval Submarine Force in 1900 to the immense nuclear vessels that prowl our oceans today, the submarine holds a unique place in the Navy, and indeed, in the human imagination.

Man has long wanted to dive beneath the waves, and submarine plans can be found as far back as the Renaissance. The first "submarine" was Cornelius Drebbel's design that demonstrated in the Thames River in 1620, but it wasn't until the mid-19th century that technology had developed sufficiently enough for people to have a "true" submarine. The *CSS Hunley* became the first submarine to sink a ship in battle in 1864 during the American Civil War.

It wasn't until John P. Holland invented the "Holland" boats that a submarine, as a naval vessel, became cemented in the minds of people all over the world. Holland figured out that each submarine needed two engines: a diesel/gas engine for running on the surface, and an electric engine for running underwater. The diesel engine would also charge the batteries for the electric one, and the boat's capabilities were only limited to the amount of fuel carried on board. Holland sold his boats to anyone who was willing to purchase or commission one, and is the father of the American, English, Russian, Japanese, and Dutch Submarine Forces.

In America, submarines, while considered useful, were a bit of a curious misfit until WWII. They were assigned to guard harbors and patrol shorelines watching for enemy vessels. The attacks of the German Wolf Packs during WWI proved that submarines, if designed right, had more versatility. These new post-WWI American boats, patterned after the captured German U-Boats, were called "Fleet Boats" and were designed to travel with convoys to provide protection. However, with the destruction of the American Fleet at Pearl Harbor on December 7, 1941, submarines, none of which had been attacked, were left as the largest line of defense between the Imperial Japanese Navy and the western coast of America.

This was the golden hour of the submarine. There were only twenty-one submarines in the Pacific on December 7, 1941, one of which would be destroyed during the attack on Manila Bay December 8, 1941. By the end of the war, over three-hundred twenty-seven submarines had served and fifty-two paid the ultimate price, along with their crews. These boats and their crews compromised only 1.6% of the total Navy, yet they caused over 60% of Pacific wartime enemy losses: over six million pounds of ships, submarines, planes and one train[36] were destroyed by these boats and their crews. The losses in the submarine service were equally devastating. One in five men who signed up for the service never came home.

Foot for foot, the submarine is the most complex weapon in the naval arsenal, then and now. As a *Gato-class* submarine, *Flier* sported ten torpedo tubes (six in the bow, four in the stern) and twenty-four torpedoes. These could be fired when the submarine was surfaced or submerged. In addition, on her decks, *Flier* carried three guns intended for last-defense warfare, since she would have to be surfaced and exposed to use them. These guns, a large 3-inch .50 caliber deck gun (later replaced by an even larger 4-in .50 caliber), and a 20 mm and 40 mm anti-aircraft guns.

The deck on which the smaller two guns were located was called the bridge, and that was where the officers would stand watch while the

---

[36] The crew from the USS BARB "sank the train" on July 23, 1945.

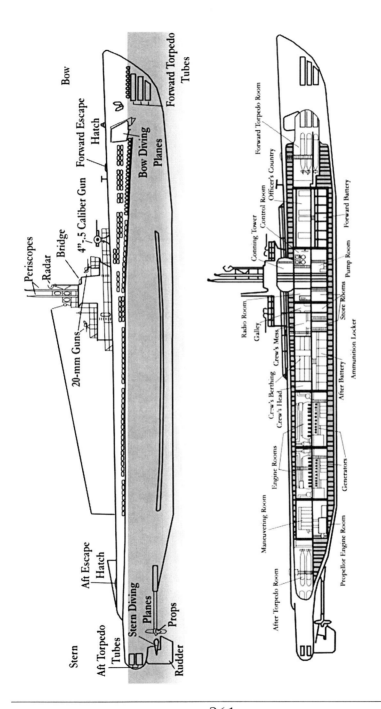

Bow

Forward Torpedo Tubes

Forward Escape Hatch

Bow Diving Planes

4".5 Caliber Gun

Periscopes

Radar

Bridge

20-mm Guns

Stern

Aft Escape Hatch

Stern Diving Planes

Props

Aft Torpedo Tubes

Rudder

Forward Torpedo Room

Officer's Country

Forward Battery

Conning Tower

Control Room

Pump Room

Store Rooms

Radio Room

Galley

Crew's Mess

After Battery

Ammunition Locker

Crew's Berthing

Crew's Head

Engine Rooms

Generators

Maneuvering Room

Propellor Engine Room

After Torpedo Room

submarine was surfaced. Above the bridge on *FLIER*, there was yet another tiny deck with just enough space for the four lookouts to stand, called the "Lookout Platform".

She controlled her depth using two pairs of diving planes, one near the bow, and one near the stern.

She also had two propellers, more commonly called "Props" or "Screws". These could be used together or use opposing forces to swiftly maneuver the submarine. For a hard turn for example, one prop would pull full speed forward, while its twin would pull backward. On the surface, these five-foot bronze props could propel the submarine to speeds of 20 knots, while underwater, the limit was around eight.

Inside, the submarine was relatively simple. Photographs of construction show the interior of a WWII submarine was essentially a long tube, divided into eight rooms, each room having an upper and lower level. Over the third section, the Control Room, there was a smaller tube sitting on top, which contained the Conning Tower.

The eight rooms were, in order: Forward Torpedo Room, Forward Battery also known as Officer's Country, Control Room, After Battery, which contained the Galley, Crew's Mess, Crew's Berthing, and Crew's Head (Bathroom), followed by the Forward Engine Room, After Engine Room, Maneuvering Room, and finally, the After Torpedo Room. The Conning Tower, as before mentioned, was located above the Control Room, and accessed by a steel ladder.

FORWARD TORPEDO ROOM

This Room was the largest and most heavily armored room in the submarine. It contained six torpedo tubes and sixteen torpedoes. It also housed sixteen men, most of whom were torpedomen. Each

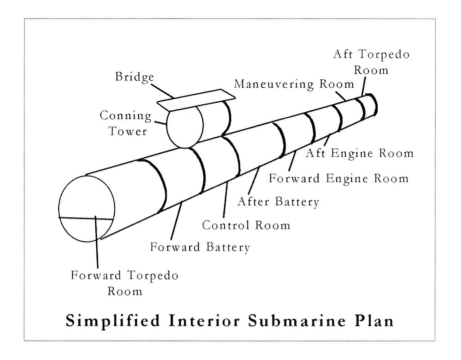

Simplified Interior Submarine Plan

man was given a bunk and a small (about one foot cubed) locker in which to keep his personal items. Due to the space constraints on a submarine, each man was limited to one change of clothes, and one set of shoes, along with anything else he could pack in his locker. To save space, most men stowed their clothes under their mattress. There was no real second level in this room, just enough storage space for two spare torpedoes. The forward torpedo tube also contained the main escape hatch. This hatch was designed to be used by the men to escape if the submarine sank in around two hundred feet of water, or to link with a submarine rescue chamber for a deeper (two hundred to five or six hundred feet) rescue. If the submarine sank in over five hundred feet of water, the inner hull would likely rupture due to the water pressure at those depths.

FORWARD BATTERY A.K.A. OFFICER'S COUNTRY

The next room, through which one would have to step through a tiny water-tight door to access, was the Forward Battery. The first of two battery arrays sat under the floor giving the room its name. These wet cell batteries provided the submarine with anywhere from four to forty-eight hours of energy, depending on how much the submarine was using. They had to be cleaned every day with pure distilled water, and any amount of salt in the mix had the potential to cause a massive Chlorine Gas explosion which could destroy a sub.

The main level was Officer's Country. In addition to housing the officer's bunks, there as a pantry where food was kept warm for the officers, the Wardroom where the officer's ate, relaxed, and also discussed business, and lastly the Yeoman's office. The yeoman kept all the records of the submarine for the voyage. Five cabins housed a total of eight officers and four of the most senior enlisted men.

CONTROL ROOM

The Control Room was, with the Conning Tower, the heart of the submarine. The Control Room contained the air systems for blowing and flooding the ballast tanks, the helm, the planes wheels which controlled the diving planes, and the electrical panels for the boat. In the center of the room sat a gyroscope compass which always pointed true north and also served as a map table. At the far stern-end of this room there was the Radio Shack where two men would monitor incoming and occasionally, outgoing messages. Beneath this room was the Pump Room which pumped water into the ballast tanks, but also could pump out the occupied areas of the submarine if necessary.

CONNING TOWER

The Conning Tower was where the real action took place. The

periscope viewing stations were up there, as well as the Radar stations, and the Torpedo Data Computer, which helped compute the torpedoes trajectory based on the submarine's course and speed as well as the target's distance, course, and speed. The first of two firing buttons were also located here (the second buttons were located in the their respective torpedo rooms) There was a ladder going from the Conning Tower to the bridge overhead, and while on patrol, this was the only easily accessible exit, the others were either bolted shut or were difficult to access without attaching their ladders.

Gato and Balao class submarines contained two periscopes. The forward and larger periscope was the "Target Acquisition Periscope." It had a larger field of view, including an angled lens to view the sky for air patrols, and was able to magnify for greater detail. It was, however, so large in circumference that it made a large wake in the water. So the second periscope, the "Attack" Periscope was added. It had no ability other than simple viewing, but it was slender and nearly impossible to see in the waves.

Like her sisters, *Flier* had two types of Radar, both of which were used primarily to scout for airplanes. Submarines did not fight airplanes unless they were unable to dive. An airplane was nearly impossible to shoot down, while a submarine was an easy target for any plane loaded with bombs.

AFTER BATTERY

This room was one of the more complicated in terms of the amount of things packed in there. On the main level, a four-foot wide, seven-foot deep steel-clad room was the Galley, where Breakfast, Snack, Lunch, Snack, Dinner, and Snack was made for all seventy-two crew members daily, along with gallons of coffee. Of the seventy-two crew members, usually five were assigned to the cooking duties.

Submarines got the best food in the Navy, and actually better than the entire American Armed Forces. While most WWII vets groan at the mere thought of canned or freeze-dried food, submariners had fresh meat, cheeses, and anything they could desire. Recipes from a published WWII Submarine recipe book include items like Teriyaki Steak, Shrimp Creole, BBQ Ribs, and French Silk Cheesecake. Not surprisingly, some men signed up just for the food.

Next to the Galley was the Crew's Mess, where four four-foot long tables were expected to seat twenty-six men at a time. It took three whole seatings for each of the three major meals (the snacks were simply left out for those who wanted or needed it). This room, between meals, was the main area the men could go to relax, write home, play cards, or do anything else. In an effort to improve morale, the Navy also gave them the makings of their own movie theater, a tradition that has since continued. While in dock, the main access to the sub was also in this room. Called the After Battery Hatch, it was bolted shut during patrol and often filled with potatoes before leaving, giving it the unofficial moniker "Potato Hatch".

Beyond this room was the Crew's Berthing, where thirty-six to forty-two beds were stationed. Also in this room was Hogan's Alley, a little area where the Pharmacist's Mate, was stationed. Submarines were so dangerous and medical personnel so valuable that doctors and nurses were not permitted to serve in the submarine force. The Pharmacist's Mate was expected to keep the crew comfortable and alive until the submarine could rendezvous with a friendly ship somewhere if greater help was required. Despite these restrictions, records exist of at least three successful appendectomies and other minor surgeries.

Finally, there was the small and cramped Crew's Head. Two toilets, two showers, and two sinks for sixty-eight enlisted personnel.

Beneath the Galley and Crew's Mess there were three storerooms for food, and one for the surface gun's Ammunitions. Under the Berthing and Head was the second battery array.

ENGINE ROOMS

There were two engine rooms, identical mirror images of each other. *Flier* and other Groton-built boats were usually equipped with four General Motors V 16 engines. Each engine was 1600 horsepower; two in the Forward Engine Room and two in the After Engine Room. They were split into two rooms separated by the water-tight door instead of one, just in case one room flooded or became inoperable. Each engine was connected to an electrical generator directly beneath it. The generators not only charged the batteries, but also provided power the submarine while it ran on the surface. There was one hatch to the deck in the after torpedo room, but this was also bolted shut before leaving on patrol.

MANEUVERING ROOM

This room was the most critical room in terms of the submarine functioning. All of the electrical systems originated from this room, and since all the systems fed off the batteries, anything that damaged this room had the potential to paralyze the submarine. The center of the room was occupied by a large cage which contained all the live wires and switches. This left less than two feet of width in the passage along the port side of this cage for the men to work around. Beneath this room were the main motors that ran the props.

AFT TORPEDO ROOM

This room was nearly identical to the forward with a few exceptions. Twelve to thirteen men bunked in this room. There was a secondary escape hatch in this room which could be used only if the submarine sank in less than two hundred feet of water, and there was no provision to link with an exterior rescue vehicle if the submarine sank into deeper waters.

USS Flier on 20 April, 1944 outside Mare Island, following her refit.(Official US Navy Photo)

TABLE OF FIGURES

BIBLIOGRAPHY

Allied Warships. *USS Flier (SS-250) Submarine of the Gato Class.* n.d. http://uboat.net/allies/warships/ship/2996.html (accessed August 31, 2006).

Alls, James. *Behind the Badge.* n.d. www.behindthebadge.net/bloodstripes/memory/mem_s.htm l (accessed August 31, 2006).

Amunrund, Peter. ""Men Against the Sea: The Loss of the USS FLIER SS-250." *US Submarine Veterans of WWII.* n.d. ussubvetsofworldwarii.org/FLIER.html (accessed June 14, 2006).

Arellano, Renato, and Josie Arellano. "Christmas Letter 2000-2001." December 2000: 1.

Associated Press Writer. "Japs Losing Two Palau Isles, Yanks Raid S. Philippines." *News Clipping from Scrapbook of Lt. James Liddell* , 1944.

Austin, Marshall H. *Report of Fourth War Patrol of USS REDFIN SS-272.* Naval War Patrol Report, United State Navy, 1944.

Austin, Marshall H. *Report of Third War Patrol of USS REDFIN SS-272.* Naval War Patrol Report, United States Navy, 1944.

Austin, Marshall H. *Serial 0011, 4 September 1944: Special Mission 23-31.* US Navy, 1944.

Bartholomew, Bart. "The Fremantle Submarine Base." *Homepage of Paul W. Wittmer.* n.d. http://www.subvetpaul.com/TheFremantle.htm (accessed June 14, 2006).

Baumgart, Earl, and Edwin Keifer. ""The Motor Mac's Tale"." *Submarine Journal,* Spring 1998: 105-111.

Bos, Abigail. "Grand Haven Man Comes Back from Lost Sub." *Grand Rapids Herald,* News Clipping from Scrapbook of Alvin Jacobson, Jr. n.d.

Buffalo Courior Express. "Eight Survive Explosion; Sinking of US Submarine." December 8, 1944.

Burns, Lieutenant Colonol R.C., USMC. "Palawan Rescsue." *U.S. Naval Institute Proceedings,* June 1950.

Calvert, James F. *Silent Running: My Years on a WWII Attack Submarine.* Wiley; New Ed edition , 1997.

Cedar Rapids Gazette. "Eight Survivors of Lost Sub Saved by Guerillas." December 1944.

"Chart of North Balabac Strait and Vicinity." no. 14,326. Deptartment of Navy Hydrographic Office, April 1959.

Chicago Daily Tribune. "US Submarines Sunk 2 Jap Destroyers and 27 Cargo Ships." September 19, 1944.

Coastline News. "Obituary of Carlos S. Palacido." December 8, 2000.

Cole, William. "U.S. Submarine, Sunk in 1944, Found." *Honolulu Advertiser.* February 2, 2010. http://www.honoluluadvertiser.com/article/20100202/NEWS08/2020319/U.S.+submarine++sunk+in+1944++found (accessed February 2, 2010).

Coleman, Larry. *1944 Ltr.* E-mail to Rebekah Hughes. February 27, 2007.

Coleman, Larry. *Coastwatchers.* E-mail to Rebekah Hughes. February 20, 2008.

Coleman, Larry. *Flier Survivor.* E-mail to Rebekah Hughes. February 25, 2007.

—. "Alastair's Prayer." *Looking Aft,* September 2001: 1-5.

Coleman, Larry. *Redfin Patrol Reports.* E-mail to Rebekah Hughes. November 19, 2008.

Coleman, Larry. *Serial 0011.* E-mail to Rebekah Hughes. February 27, 2007.

Coleman, Larry. *The Peso.* E-mail to Rebekah Hughes. February 26, 2007.

Commander Submarine Force. "Press Release of Confirmed Discovery of USS Flier SS-250." Pearl Harbor, Hawai'i: Commander Submarine Force, February 1, 2010.

Commander Submarine Force, U.S. Pacific Fleet. *USS FLIER (SS 250) August 13, 1944 78 Men Lost.* n.d. www.csp.navy.mil/ww2boats/flier.htm (accessed May 1 , 2006).

Coye, Cmdr. John. *Report of Tenth War Patrol of USS Silversides SS-236.* United States Navy, 1944.

Crowely, John D. "Second Letter to John J. Casey concerning Lt. John Edward Casey." New London, Connecticut: United States Navy, December 19, 1944.

Crowley, John D. "Letter to Mr. John F. Casey Concerning Fate of Lt. John Edward Casey." Washington D.C.: United States Navy, October 28, 1944.

—. "Letter to Mrs. Mary Frances Casey Concerning the Fate of Lt. John Edward Casey." 1944, Washington D.C.: United States Navy, October 28, 1944.

Crowley, John D. *Narrative: of the Second War Patrol of U.S.S. Flier (All Times HOW and Approximate).* United States Navy, 1944.

Crowley, John D. *Report of First War Patrol of U.S.S. Flier SS-250.* Naval War Patrol Report, United States Navy, 1944.

—. "Speech About USS Flier." From Records of Lt. James Liddell , n.d. 16.

Cundall, Peter, Bob Hackett, and Sander Kingsepp. *IJN Minelayer Tsugaru: Tabular Record of Movement.* 2007. http://www.combinedfleet.com/tsugaru_t.htm (accessed 6 15, 2007).

Dana, Sylvia. "Remembrance of local legend Alvin Jacobson." *Grand Haven Tribune*, October 17, 2008.

Dealey, Sam. *Report of Fifth War Patrol of USS Harder SS-257.* Naval War Patrol Report, United States Navy, 1944.

Denfeld, L.E. "Letter to Mr. and Mrs. A.E. Jacobson concerning Alvin E. Jacobson, Jr." Washington D.C.: United States Navy Department Bureau of Personnel, September 14, 1944.

Department of the Navy--Naval Historical Center. *USS Flier (SS-250), 1943, 1944.* n.d. www.history.navy.mil/photos/sh-usn/usnsh-f/ss250.htm (accessed May 1, 2006).

Detroit Free Press. "8 of 17 in Sub Survive Sinking." December 3, 1944.

"Escaped Gob Outwits Japs for Two Years." *News Clipping from Scrapbook of Lt. James Liddell.* December 1944.

Eternal Patrol. *On Eternal Patrol-USS FLIER (SS-250).* n.d. www.oneternalpatrol.com/uss-flier-250.htm (accessed May 17, 2006).

A.E. Jacobson Jr.: 75th Birthday Celebration. Directed by Jacobson Family. 1997.

Fisher, Ray. "Letter to the Editor of Muskegon Chronicle." *Muskegon Chronicle*, December 7, 1944.

Dive Detectives: Submarine Graveyard. Documentary Film. Directed by Jeff Vanderwal. Produced by Eliott Halpern. Performed by Michael Fletcher and Warren Fletcher. 2010.

Forrestal, James. "Letter to Mrs. Mary Frances Casey changing his status to KIA." Washington D.C.: United States Navy, February 5, 1946.

Gilpatrick, Kristin. *The Hero Next Door Returns: More Stories from Wisconsin's WWII Veterans.* Middleton: Badger Books LLC, 2001.

Grand Haven Tribune. "A. Jacobson Jr. Survives Loss of Submarine." September 20, 1944.

Grand Haven Tribune. "A.E. Jacobson Jr. to be Commissioned Ensign." October 21, 1943.

Grand Haven Tribune. "Ensign Escapes Death in Sinking Sub." 1944: News Clipping from Scrapbook of Alvin Jacobson Jr.

Grand Haven Tribune. "Ensign Jacobson Swam 18 Hours." December 2, 1944.

Grand Haven Tribune. "Happy Reunion in Jacobson Family." October 26, 1944.

Grand Haven Tribune. "Sub Still Best Offensive Weapon, Says Jacobson." 1979: News Clipping from Scrapbook of Alvin Jacobson Jr.

Grand Haven Tribunes. "Ensign Jacobson Arrives Home." November 6, 1944.

Grand Rapids Press. "Grand Haven Man Escapes as Sub Sinks." December 2, 1944.

Guttery, Randy. 1996. http://www.tendertale.com/ (accessed September 11, 2006).

Guttery, Randy, interview by Rebekah J. Hughes. *Questions About Tender USS ORION* (September 8, 2006).

Guttery, Randy, interview by Rebekah J. Hughes. *Thansk you for your reply--need a tiny bit of clarification* (September 11, 2006).

Haywood, J. "Businessman Alvin Jacobson Jr. dies at age 86." *Grand Haven Tribune*, October 17, 2008.

Henley, Walter EM2 (ss). "The Letdown: The Near Sinking of the USS IREX." *Irex Sea Storied.* n.d. http://www.hartford-hwp.com/Irex/docs/doc09.html (accessed August 31, 2006).

Hinman, Charles. *On Eternal Patrol: USS Flier.* n.d. http://www.oneternalpatrol.com/uss-flier-250.htm (accessed May 17, 2006).

—. *On Eternal Patrol: USS Robalo.* n.d. http://www.oneternalpatrol.com/uss-robalo-273.htm (accessed May 17, 2006).

—. *USS Flier.* Janurary 27, 2010. http://www.ussflier.com (accessed January 30, 2010).

HMAS Mildura Association. "HMAS MILDURA--The Other Milduras 1941-1965." *HMAS Mildura J207.* July 8, 2006.

http://home.vicnet.net.au/~mildura/the_ship2.htm
(accessed August 1, 2006).

Holmes, Harry. *The Last Patrol.* Annapolis: US Naval Institute Press,
2001.

Howell, Arthur Gibson. "Letter to Mrs. Mary Frances Casey about
Lt. John Edward Casey." 1944, Connecticut: Personal Letter,
December 10, 1944.

Hoyt. *The Destroyer Killer.* New York: Pocket Books, 1989.

Jackson, Kent. "Discovery of Late Brother's Sunken WWII Sub
Soothes City Woman." *Standardspeaker.com.* February 12, 2010.
http://standardspeaker.com/news/discovery-of-late-brother-
s-sunken-wwii-sub-soothes-city-woman-1.613586 (accessed
February 16, 2010).

Jacobson, Alvin E., interview by Rebekah Hughes. (November 24,
2007).

Jacobson, Alvin E. Jr. *Survivor's Story.* Grand Haven: Self, 1997; 2002.

Jacobson, Alvin E. Jr., and Edna Jacobson. "Report of Flier Incident
August 1944." Unpublished, October 1944.

Jacobson, Alvin E. Jr.,. "Cirriculum Vitae of Alvin E. Jacobson Jr."
Self, n.d.

—. "Letter from Al Jacobson to Muriel Jacobson." July 2, 1944.

—. "Survivor's Story." *Submarine Journal,* Spring 1998: 1-101.

Jacobson, Alvin E., interview by Rebekah J. Hughes. *Mr.* (August 28,
2006).

Jacobson, Alvin Emmanuel. *A Survivor's Story: Submarine USS Flier lost
August 13, 1944.* Self, 1944.

Jacobson, Nelson, interview by Rebekah Hughes and Justin Hughes.
(March 12, 2010).

Jacobson, Nelson, interview by Rebekah Hughes. (May 21, 2010).

Jacobson, Nelson, interview by Rebekah Hughes and Justin Hughes.
(March 12, 2010).

Johnson, David. "Wreckage of WWII Sub Found." *Odessa American Online.* April 2, 2010. http://www.oaoa.com/news/knees-45317-german-world.html (accessed April 3, 2010).

Jones, Dave. *Capt. David Hayward McClintock.* 11 1, 2007. http://www.findagrave.com/cgi-bin/fg.cgi?page=gr&GSln=McClintock&GScid=1341&GRid=22596682& (accessed 10 26, 2009).

Jr., Clay Blair. *Silent Victory.* Emreyville: J.B. Lippencott Company, 1975.

Judd, Terry. "Family of USS Flier Explosion Thrilled about Submarine's Discovery." *Muskegon Chronicle.* Muskegon, February 9, 2010.

Keifer, Edwin. ""Tale of the Chief Radio Technician"." *Submarine Journal*, Spring 1998: 114-118.

—. ""The Captain's Tale"." *Submarine Journal*, Spring 1998: 102-104.

Keilen, Brian. "Sunken Sub ID'd as One Al Jacobson Served On." *Grand Haven Tribune.* February 3, 2010. http://www.grandhaventribune.com/paid/301379707894166.bsp (accessed February 3, 2010).

Kit J. Pourciau of the USS Flier. November 3, 2009. http://www.footnote.com/spotlight/13447/kit_j_pourciau_of_uss_flier_ss250/\ (accessed November 15, 2009).

Lavelle, James M. *USS Gunnel 5th War Patrol.* n.d. http://www.jmlavelle.com/gunnel/patrol5.htm (accessed September 15, 2006).

Lavelle, James. *USS Gunnel 6th Patrol.* n.d. http://www.jmlavelle.com/gunnel/patrol6.htm (accessed April 24, 2007).

Leffler, Jessica. *WWII Sub Found;Grand Haven Family Elated.* News Broadcast. WOOD TV-8. Grand Rapids, Michigan, Febrary 2, 2010.

Leone, Diana. "Northwest Islands Trip Yields Preservation Data." *Honolulu Star Bulletin*, June 8, 2005.

Liddell, Kirk, interview by Rebekah Hughes and Justin Hughes. (May 15, 2010).

Lupo, L. "Alvin Jacobson, JSJ Corp. founder, died at 86." *Muskegon Chronicle*, October 17, 2008.

Mansfiled, John G. Jr. *Cruisers for Breakfast: The War Patrols of the USS Darter and the USS Dace.* Media Center Publishing, 1997.

March of Time Radio Spot. *"Chief Howell Spot".* 1944. Radio Program.

March, Jack. "3rd War Patrol." *Official Website of the USS REDFIN.* n.d. http://www.ussredfin.com/ss-272/warpatrol3/warpatrol3.htm (accessed September 15, 2006).

—. *USS FLIER (SS-250).* n.d. www.ussredfin.com/ss-272/ussflier/uss_flier.htm (accessed August 31, 2006).

March, Jack. *USS REDFIN.* E-mail to Rebekah Hughes. September 29, 2008.

—. "USS REDFIN's 2nd Patorl." *Official Website of USS REDFIN (SS 273).* n.d. http://www.ussredfin.com/ss-272/warpatrol2/warpatrol2.htm (accessed September 15, 2006).

—. "USS REDFIN's Fourth Patrol." *Official USS REDFIN website.* n.d. http://www.ussredfin.com/ss-272/warpatrol4/warpatro43.ht (accessed September 15, 2006).

McGee, Eugene D. "To Sink and Swim: The USS FLIER." *Submarine Journal*, October 1996: 94-98.

McMahon, Charles. "Closure at Long Last: Kittery Woman Learns Fate of Brother's Sub, Sunk 65 Years Ago in World War II." *Foster's Daily Democrat.* February 3, 2010. http://www.fosters.com/apps/pbcs.dll/article?AID=/20100203/GJNEWS_01/702039947 (accessed February 3, 2010).

Mendenhall, Corwin. *Submarine Diary: The Silent Stalking of Japan.* Annapolis: US Naval Institute Press, 1995.

Military Times Hall of Valor. 2009. http://militarytimes.com/citations-medals-awards/recipient.php?recipientid=20668 (accessed October 26, 2009).

Miller, Vernon J. "Letter to Capt. John D. Crowley, USN (Ret.) from Vernon J. Miller." Arbutus, Maryland, September 3, 1985. 1.

Milton, Keith M. *Subs Against the Rising Sun: U.S. Submarines in the Pacific.* Las Cruces: Yucca Tree Press, 2000.

Morison, Smuel Eliot. *History of United States Sumbarine Operations in WWII.* Little, Brown & Co., 1949.

MTCM(SS)(Ret.), Royal Weaver. "USS FLIER (SS-250)." *Geocities Pentagon Base.* n.d. www.geocities.com/Pentagon/Base/7660/lost_boats/pages/FLIER.htm?200614 (accessed June 14, 2006).

Muskegon Chronicle. "Ensign Jacobson and Band Had Harrowing Experience." December 4, 1944.

New London Day. "Awards Ceremony at Sub Base Discloses Story of Heroism in Loss of Submarine Flier." January 4, 1946.

New London Day. "Crew Member of Submarine Flier Now Listed as Dead; Story of Sinking Told." April 16, 1946.

New York Times. "Submarines Sink 29 More Vessels." September 20, 1944.

News Clipping from Milwaukee Paper in Scrapbook of Alvin Jacobson Jr. "Survivor Here from Sunken Submarine Suffered Too Much, Too Little Water." December 1944.

News Clipping from Scrapbook of Lt. James Liddell. "Sub Blown Up, 8 Escape Japs." December 2, 1944.

Online Obituary for David Capt. David H. McClintock. n.d. http://www.memorialobituaries.com/memorials/memorials.cgi?action=Obit&memid=49861&clientid=canale (accessed 10 21, 2009).

Palacido, Sgt. Carlos S. *Mission Report of Sgt. Carlos S. Palacido.* US Army Summary Report, 978th Signal Service Company, United States Army, United States Army, 1945, 21.

Patton, Meagan. "Sunken Sub that Claimed Ottowan's Life now Headed for TV." *The Ottawa Herald.* Ottawa, Febrary 23, 2010.

Pearson, Jake. "Familes Learn War Heroes Fate: WWII Sailors Killed On Sub Recently Discovered in South China Sea." *New York Daily News.* New York, New York, June 22, 2010.

Poel, Clarence. "Local Veteran Retraced Survival Route ." *Grand Haven Tribune*, News Clipping from Scrapbook of Alvin Jacobson Jr. 1998.

Record of Proceedings of an Investigation... [into the] Circumstances Connected with the Loss of the USS Robalo and USS Flier. (United States Naval Court, September 14, 1944).

"Recorder, Febrary 6, 1946 F1/c Victor J. Murawski." *The Judge Report.* February 6, 1946. http://rgoing.livejournal.com/383031.html (accessed February 3, 2010).

Riddle, Phil. "Sailor with Local Ties Recovered in WWII Submarine." *The Weatherford Democrat.* Weatherford, March 28, 2010.

Schwertfeger, Charles "Red". ""God's Patrol" ." September 2001.

Schwertfeger, Charles, interview by Rebekah Hughes and Justin Hughes. (October 11, 2008).

Sharp, Cmdr. George A. *U.S.S. Florikan (ASR-9) Report: Towing U.S.S. Flier.* United States Navy, 1944.

Starmap for Balabac Straits, August 13, 1944 at 10:15 p.m. n.d. http://starmap.causeway.co.uk/starmap.sky?place=Balabac&lat=8+5+North&long=117+1+West&date=1944%2F8%2F13&time=10%3A15+pm&dst=0&step=0&unit=Dys&img=SVG&action=Calculate+...&show=S&show=P&show=C&show=N&show=B (accessed November 10, 2006).

Stum, David. "Sub Sank, Liddell Swam for Help." *Intelligencier Journal*, June 11, 1987.

Sturma, Michael. *The USS Flier: Death and Survival on a World War II Submairne.* Lexington: University of Kentucky Pess, 2008.

Tactical and Technical Trends. "Atrabine for Malaria form Tactical and Technical Trends." *Lone Sentry.* June 3, 1943. http://www.lonesentry.com/articles/ttt09/atabrine.html (accessed April 30, 2010).

"Tells How Joliet Girl's Husband Swam 18 Hours in Sea After Loss of Sub." *News Clipping from Scrapbook of Lt. James Liddell.* December 1944.

The Evening Bulletin. "Capt. Rauch Now Listed As Dead." February 22, 1946: 1.

The Herald Examiner. "Philippine Patriots Save 8 Yanks After Sub Blas." December 2, 1944: Found in Scrapbook of Alvin E. Jacobson, Jr.

Tremaine, Don. ""Tale of the Firecontrolman 3"." *Submarine Journal*, Spring 1998: 112-113.

Tuohy, William. *The Bravest Man: Richard O'Kane and the Amazing Submarine Adventures of the USS Tang.* New York: Presidio Press, 2006.

United States Army. *Report of the History of the 978th Signal Service Company.* Army Summary Reports, United States Army, 1945, 18.

United States Navy. *Deck Log of USS Flier SS-250 October 1943-June 1944.* United States Navy, 1944.

—. "Departure List: Results of U.S. Submarine War Patrols listed Chronologically by date Underway for Patrol Based on Task Force Commanders Assessments ." United States Navy, Oct 22, 1945.

United States Navy Historical Center. "Pearl Harbor Submarine Base: 1918-1945." *Naval Historical Center.* May 15, 2001.

http://www.history.navy.mil/faqs/faq66-5a.htm (accessed
September 15, 2006).

—. *Ship Lookup: USS FLIER.* n.d.
www.nwc.navy.mil/usnhdb/ShipLookup.asp?ShipID=USSS0
0250 (accessed August 31, 2006).

United States Navy. *N.D. Communique No. 540 September 6, 1944.*
September 6, 1944. www.ibiblio.org/pha/comms/1944-09
(accessed September 6, 2006).

—. *N.D. Communique No. 545, September 19, 1944.* September 19,
1944. www.ibiblio.org/pha/comms/1944-09 (accessed
September 6, 2006).

—. *N.D. Communique No. 565, January 2, 1945.* January 2, 1945.
www.ibilio.org/pha/comms/1945-01 (accessed September 6,
2006).

—. "Operation Order No. 100-44." Perth, West. Australia: United
States Navy, July 31, 1944.

—. "Press Release announcing awarding of Silver Star to Lt. John
Edward Casey." Norfolk, VA: United States Navy, April 9,
1945.

—. *Submarine Lost in Pacific During Training Exercises.* July 11, 1944.
www.ibiblio.org/pha/comms/1944-07 (accessed September
6, 2006).

—. "USS ROBALO (SS 273) July 26, 1944--81 Men Lost."
Commander Submarine Force, U.S. Pacific Fleet. n.d.
www.csp.navy.mil/ww2boats/robalo.htm (accessed June 14,
2006).

USS Flier SS-250. "Sailing List of USS Flier SS-250." Fremantle,
Western Australia, August 2, 1944. 5.

Walters, Bill. "USS Flier Dedication." *The Cabot Chronicle,* May 31,
2008.

What's On Vancouver. *Dive Detectives.* Vancouver, March 26, 2010.

Wilbanks, Bob and McDole, Glenn. *Last Man Out: Glenn McDole USMC, survivor of the Palawan Massacre.* Jefferson: McFarland & Company Inc., 2004.

Wittmer, Paul. ""Flier (SS-250)"." *Sub Vet Paul.* n.d. www.subvetpaul.com/LostBoats/Flier.htm (accessed June 14, 2006).

Wolfe, Bill. "Do you remember this USS REDFIN?" *USS Redfin SS/ASR/AGSS-272 Links.* n.d. http://www.geocities.com/Pentagon/Base/7660/RemThisR edfin.html (accessed December 14, 2006).

Wolfe, Bill, and John D. Crowley. ""Loss of the USS FLIER"." *Plolaris*, June 1981.

YAP Films. *Toronto-based Television Production Company YAP Films Discovers Missing WWII Submarine.* Toronto, March 30, 2010.

Yount, Dan. "Cincinnatti Family: Discovery of WWII Submarine Wreckage Where Cousin Died Brings Closure." *The Cincinnatti Herald.* Cincinnatti, April 24, 2010.

USS Flier, April 1944

NEVER FORGOTTEN

9 780984 612406